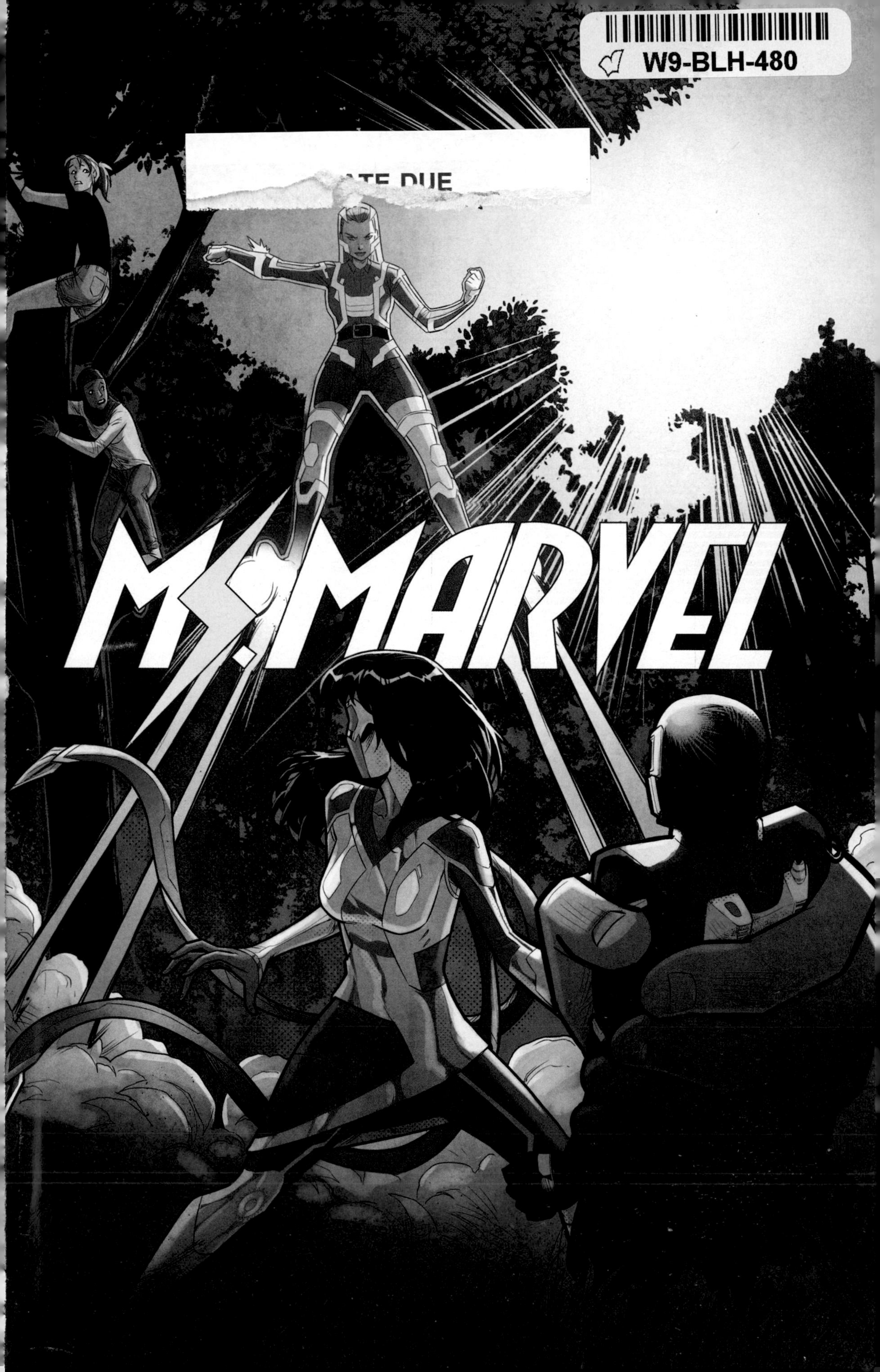
MS. MARVEL

WHEN KAMALA WAS BROUGHT TO THE DISTANT PLANET OF SAFFA, SHE LEARNED THAT ITS PEOPLE BELIEVED HER TO BE THEIR DESTINED ONE, PROPHESIED TO SAVE THEM FROM THE RETURN OF THE BEAST LEGIONS.

WHEN THE BEAST LEGIONS ATTACKED, KAMALA DISCOVERED THAT A KREE SOLDIER IN A SPECIAL NANOTECH SUIT WAS THE ORIGINAL "DESTINED ONE," AND BY DONNING THAT SUIT, KAMALA WAS ABLE TO DRIVE AWAY SAFFA'S ATTACKERS!

BACK AT HOME, KAMALA FOUND THAT HER NEW SUIT CAN ASSIST HER IN HER FIGHT TO PROTECT JERSEY CITY! BUT THERE'S ANOTHER FIGHT THAT HAS HER FEELING HELPLESS: HER FATHER'S INCURABLE DISEASE...

COLLECTION EDITOR JENNIFER GRÜNWALD
ASSISTANT MANAGING EDITOR LISA MONTALBANO
VP PRODUCTION & SPECIAL PROJECTS JEFF YOUNGQUIST

SVP PRINT, SALES & MARKETING DAVID GABRIEL

MAIA LOY ASSISTANT MANAGING EDITOR
MARK D. BEAZLEY EDITOR, SPECIAL PROJECTS
SALENA MAHINA & JAY BOWEN BOOK DESIGNERS

C.B. CEBULSKI EDITOR IN CHIEF

MS. MARVEL BY SALADIN AHMED VOL. 2: STORMRANGER. Contains material originally published in magazine form as MAGNIFICENT MS. MARVEL (2019) #7-12. First printing 2020. ISBN 978-1-302-91830-9. Published by MARVEL WORLDWIDE, INC., a subsidiary of MARVEL ENTERTAINMENT, LLC. OFFICE OF PUBLICATION: 1290 Avenue of the Americas, New York, NY 10104. © 2020 MARVEL No similarity between any of the names, characters, persons, and/or institutions in this magazine with those of any living or dead person or institution is intended, and any such similarity which may exist is purely coincidental. Printed in Canada. KEVIN FEIGE, Chief Creative Officer; DAN BUCKLEY, President, Marvel Entertainment; JOHN NEE, Publisher; JOE QUESADA, EVP & Creative Director; TOM BREVOORT, SVP of Publishing; DAVID BOGART, Associate Publisher & SVP of Talent Affairs; Publishing & Partnership; DAVID GABRIEL, VP of Print & Digital Publishing; JEFF YOUNGQUIST, VP of Production & Special Projects; DAN CARR, Executive Director of Publishing Technology; ALEX MORALES, Director of Publishing Operations; DAN EDINGTON, Managing Editor; SUSAN CRESPI, Production Manager; STAN LEE, Chairman Emeritus. For information regarding advertising in Marvel Comics or on Marvel.com, please contact Vit DeBellis, Custom Solutions & Integrated Advertising Manager, at vdebellis@marvel.com. For Marvel subscription inquiries, please call 888-511-5480. Manufactured between 2/7/2020 and 3/10/2020 by SOLISCO PRINTERS, SCOTT, QC, CANADA.

10 9 8 7 6 5 4 3 2 1

WHEN A STRANGE TERRIGEN MIST DESCENDED UPON JERSEY CITY,
KAMALA KHAN WAS IMBUED WITH POLYMORPH POWERS. USING HER NEW
ABILITIES TO FIGHT EVIL AND PROTECT JERSEY CITY, SHE BECAME…

MS. MARVEL
Stormranger

ISSUES #7-8

ARTIST	**JOEY VAZQUEZ**
	WITH **ALEX ARIZMENDI** (#8)
COLOR ARTIST	**IAN HERRING**

ISSUES #9-12

PENCILER	**MINKYU JUNG**
INKER	**JUAN VLASCO**
COLOR ARTIST	**IAN HERRING**

LETTERER	**VC'S JOE CARAMAGNA**
COVER ART	**EDUARD PETROVICH**

ASSISTANT EDITOR	SHANNON ANDREWS BALLESTEROS
EDITOR	ALANNA SMITH
CONSULTING EDITOR	SANA AMANAT

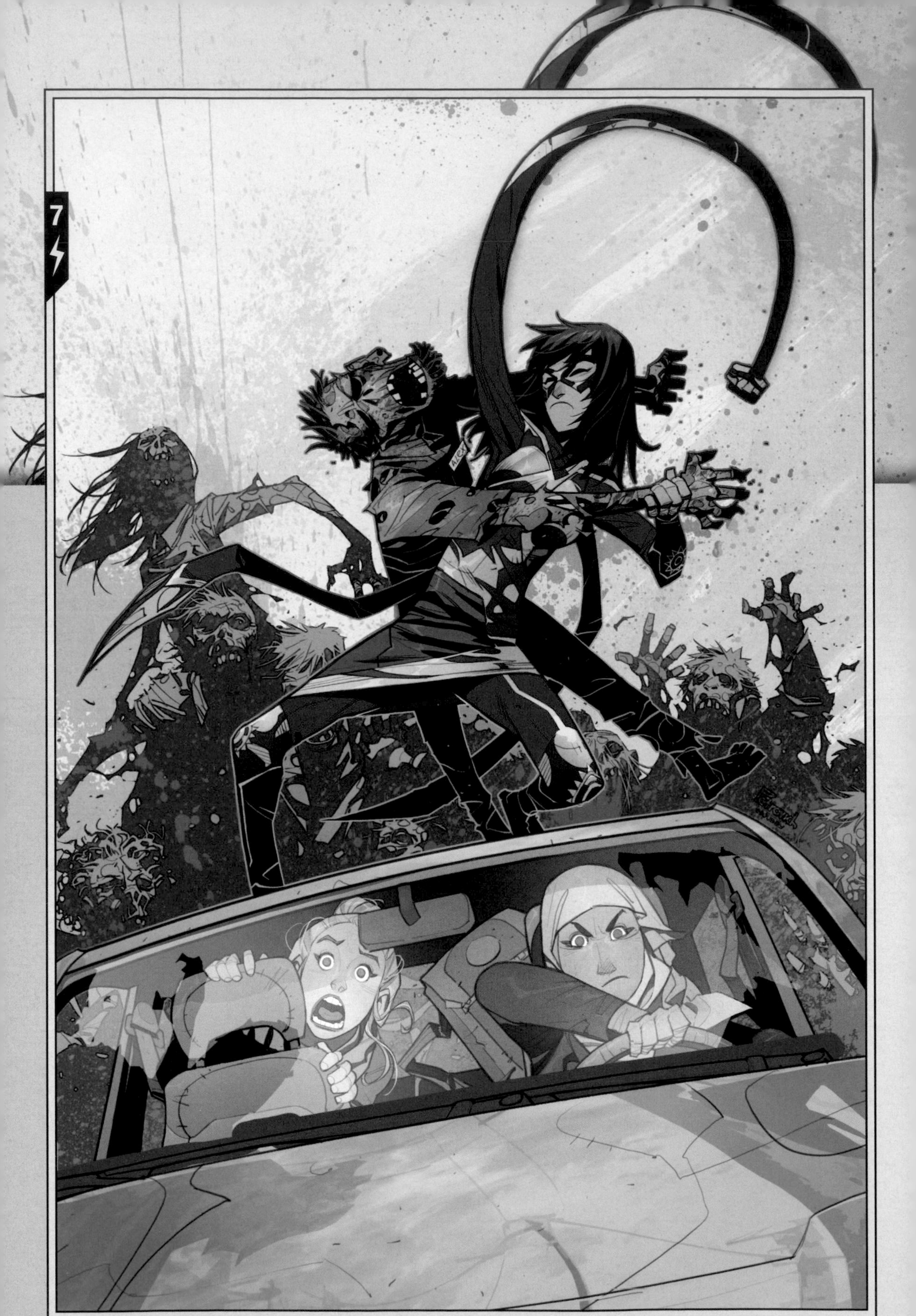
7

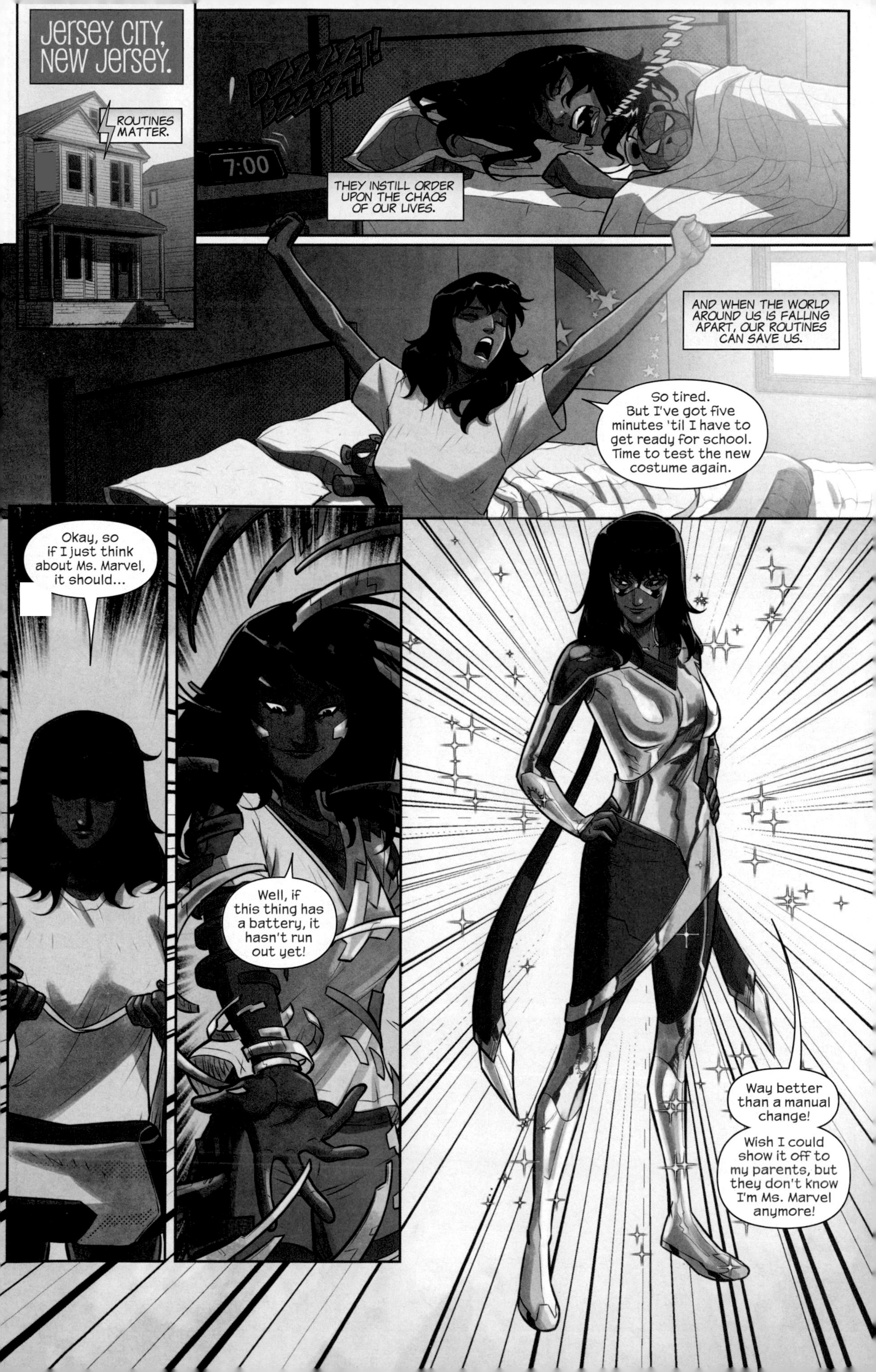
JERSEY CITY, NEW JERSEY.
ROUTINES MATTER.
7:00
THEY INSTILL ORDER UPON THE CHAOS OF OUR LIVES.
AND WHEN THE WORLD AROUND US IS FALLING APART, OUR ROUTINES CAN SAVE US.
So tired. But I've got five minutes 'til I have to get ready for school. Time to test the new costume again.
Okay, so if I just think about Ms. Marvel, it should...
Well, if this thing has a battery, it hasn't run out yet!
Way better than a manual change!
Wish I could show it off to my parents, but they don't know I'm Ms. Marvel anymore!

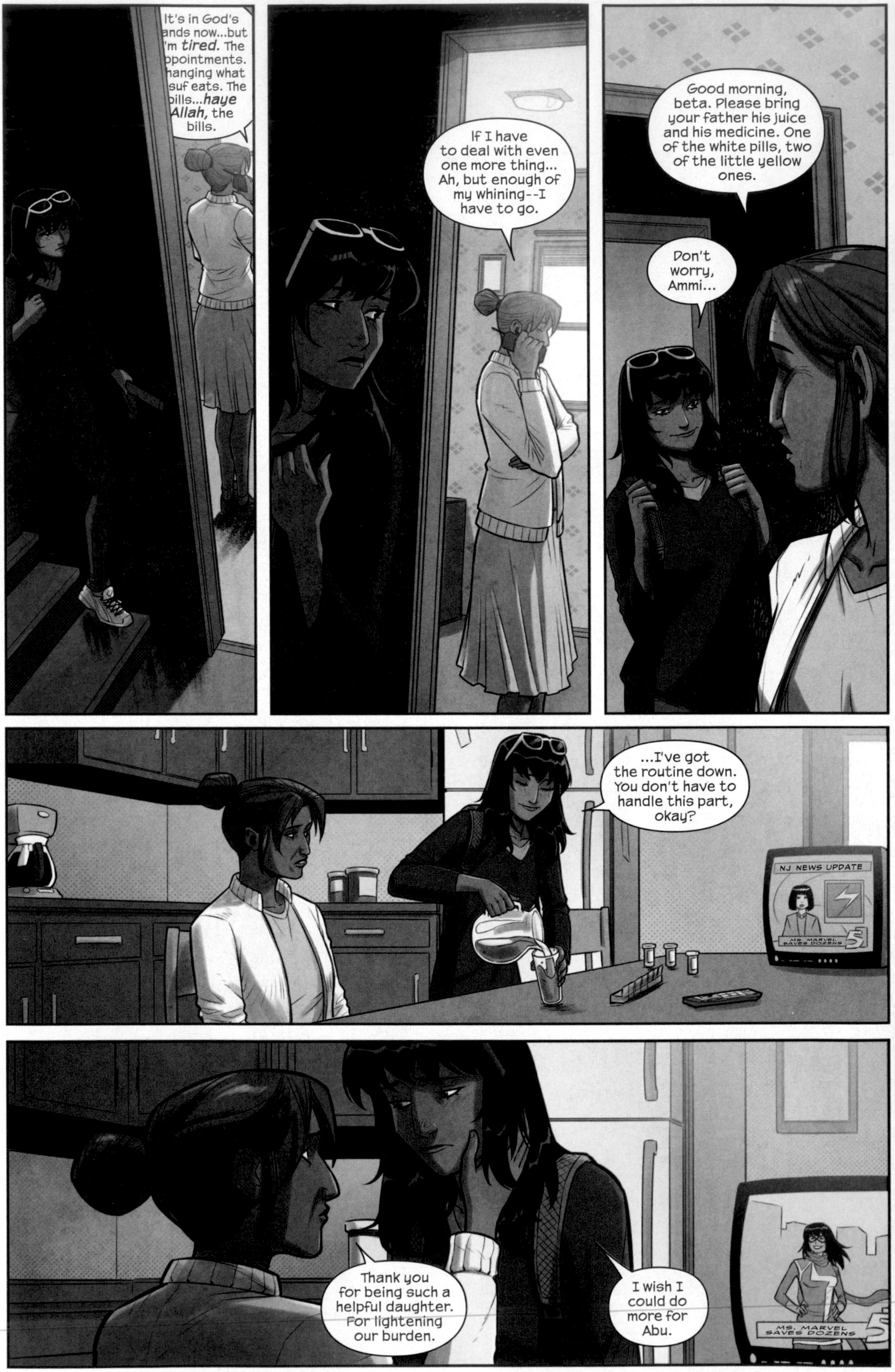
It's in God's hands now...but I'm tired. The appointments. Changing what Yusuf eats. The pills...haye Allah, the bills.
If I have to deal with even one more thing... Ah, but enough of my whining--I have to go.
Good morning, beta. Please bring your father his juice and his medicine. One of the white pills, two of the little yellow ones.
Don't worry, Ammi...
...I've got the routine down. You don't have to handle this part, okay?
NJ NEWS UPDATE
MS. MARVEL SAVES DOZENS
Thank you for being such a helpful daughter. For lightening our burden.
I wish I could do more for Abu.
MS. MARVEL SAVES DOZENS

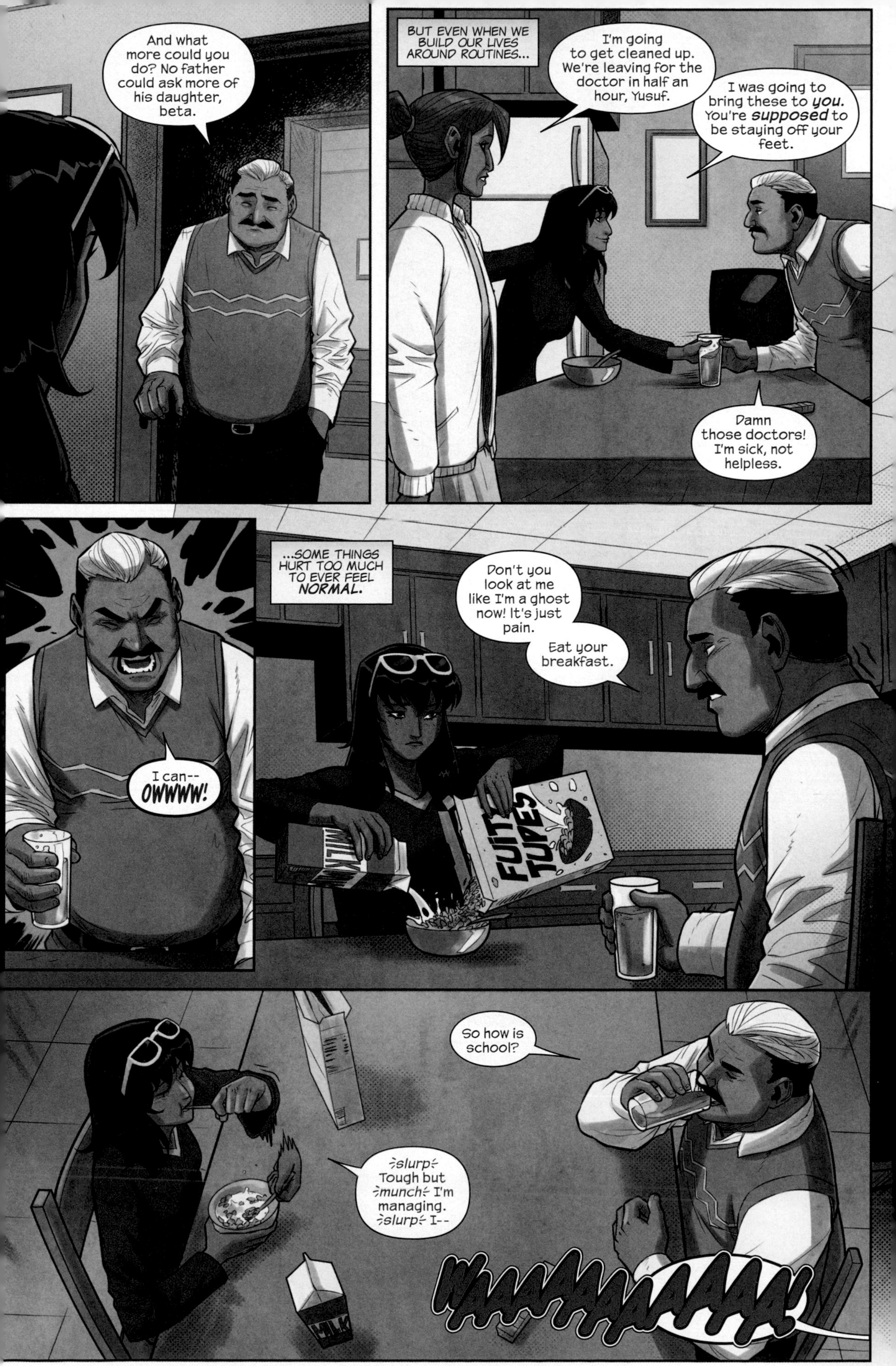
And what more could you do? No father could ask more of his daughter, beta.
BUT EVEN WHEN WE BUILD OUR LIVES AROUND ROUTINES...
I'm going to get cleaned up. We're leaving for the doctor in half an hour, Yusuf.
I was going to bring these to *you.* You're *supposed* to be staying off your feet.
Damn those doctors! I'm sick, not helpless.
I can-- **OWWWW!**
...SOME THINGS HURT TOO MUCH TO EVER FEEL ***NORMAL.***
Don't you look at me like I'm a ghost now! It's just pain.
Eat your breakfast.
FUITY TUPES
MILK
So how is school?
slurp Tough but *munch* I'm managing. *slurp* I--
WAAAAAAAAAA!

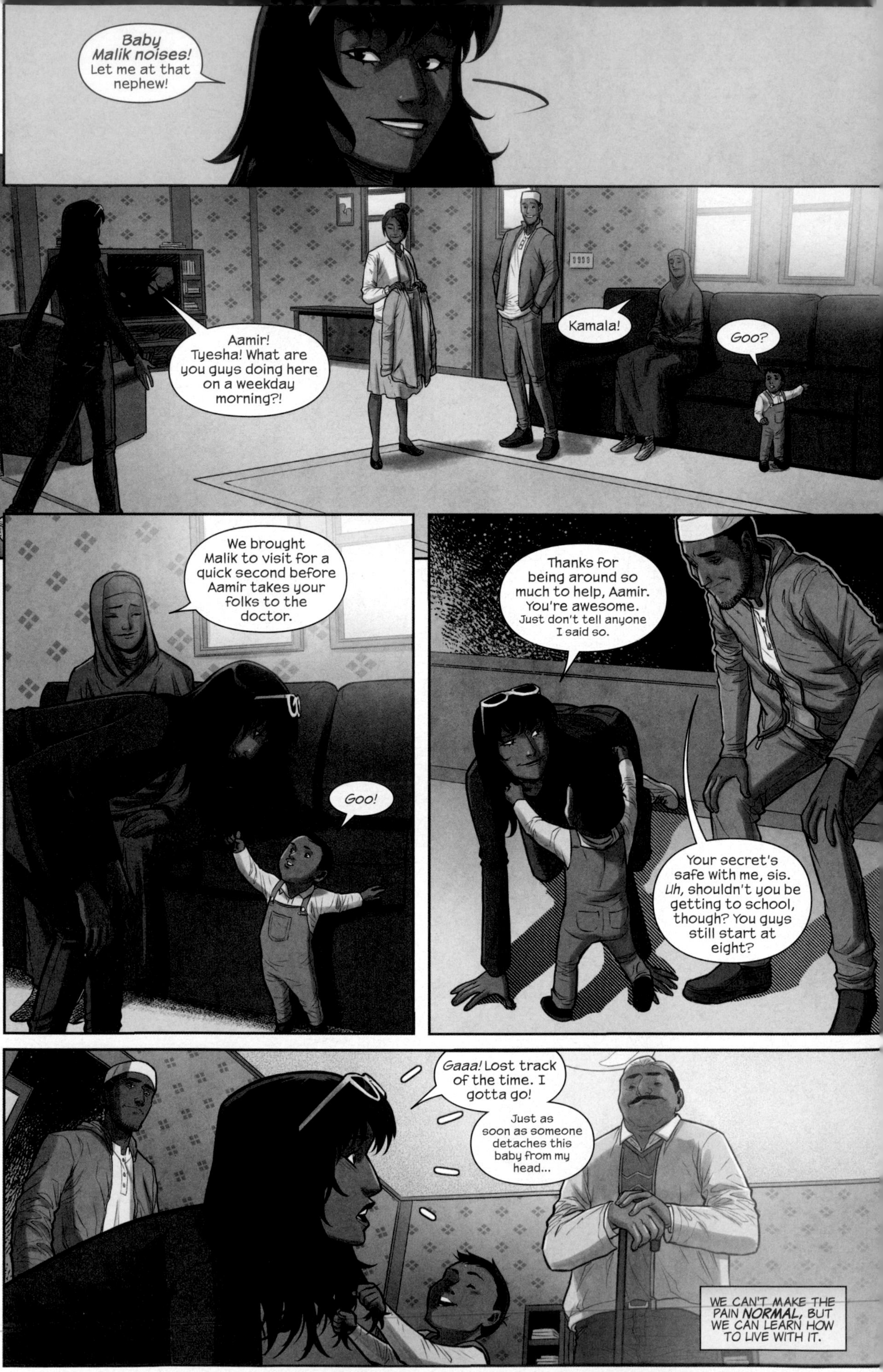
Baby Malik noises! Let me at that nephew!
Aamir! Tyesha! What are you guys doing here on a weekday morning?!
Kamala!
Goo?
We brought Malik to visit for a quick second before Aamir takes your folks to the doctor.
Goo!
Thanks for being around so much to help, Aamir. You're awesome. Just don't tell anyone I said so.
Your secret's safe with me, sis. Uh, shouldn't you be getting to school, though? You guys still start at eight?
Gaaa! Lost track of the time. I gotta go!
Just as soon as someone detaches this baby from my head...
WE CAN'T MAKE THE PAIN NORMAL, BUT WE CAN LEARN HOW TO LIVE WITH IT.

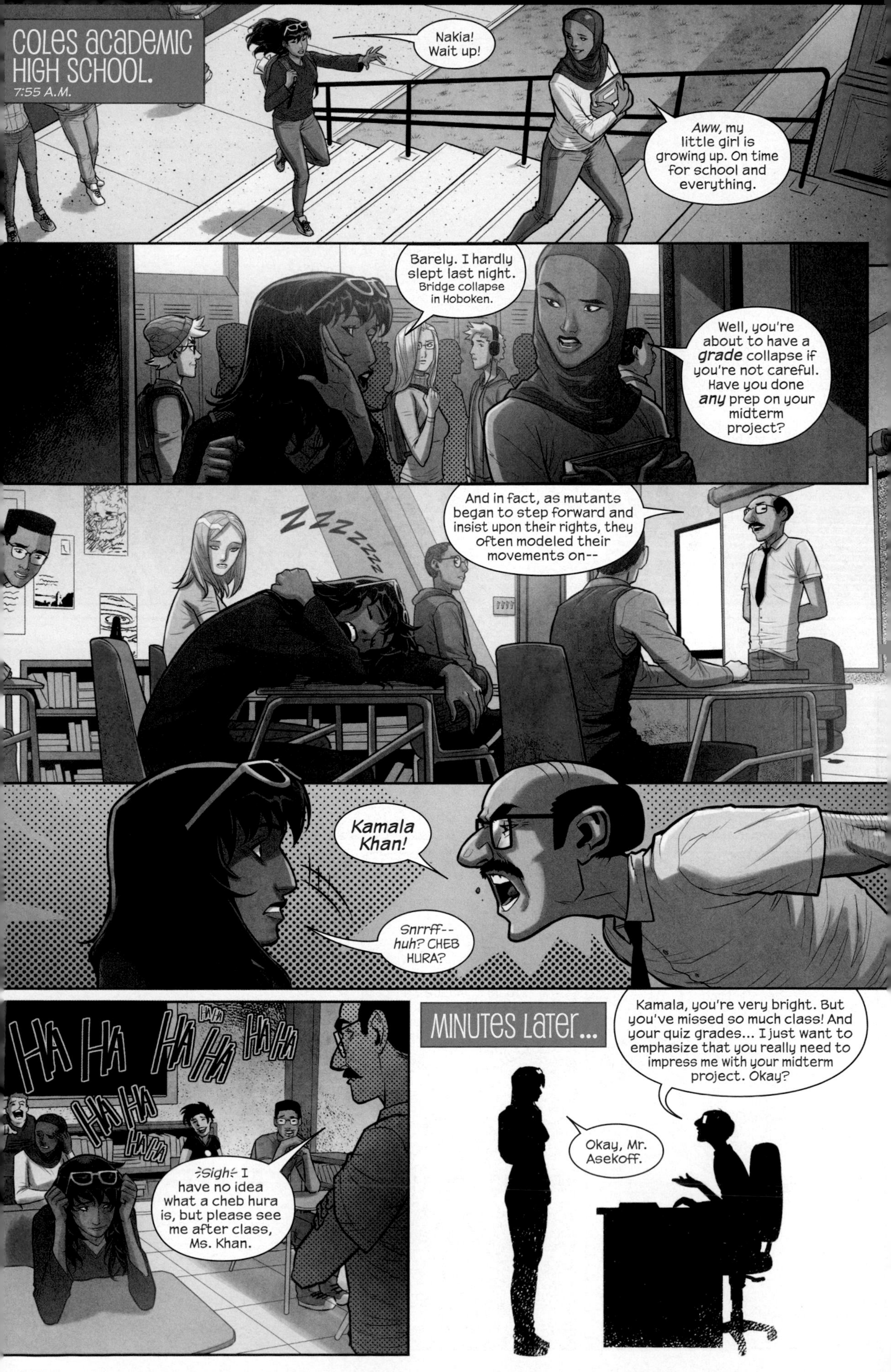
COLES ACADEMIC HIGH SCHOOL.
7:55 A.M.
Nakia! Wait up!
Aww, my little girl is growing up. On time for school and everything.
Barely. I hardly slept last night. Bridge collapse in Hoboken.
Well, you're about to have a grade collapse if you're not careful. Have you done any prep on your midterm project?
ZZZZZZZZ
And in fact, as mutants began to step forward and insist upon their rights, they often modeled their movements on--
Kamala Khan!
Snrrff-- huh? CHEB HURA?
HA HA HA HA HA HA HA HA HA HA HA
Sigh I have no idea what a cheb hura is, but please see me after class, Ms. Khan.
MINUTES LATER...
Kamala, you're very bright. But you've missed so much class! And your quiz grades... I just want to emphasize that you really need to impress me with your midterm project. Okay?
Okay, Mr. Asekoff.

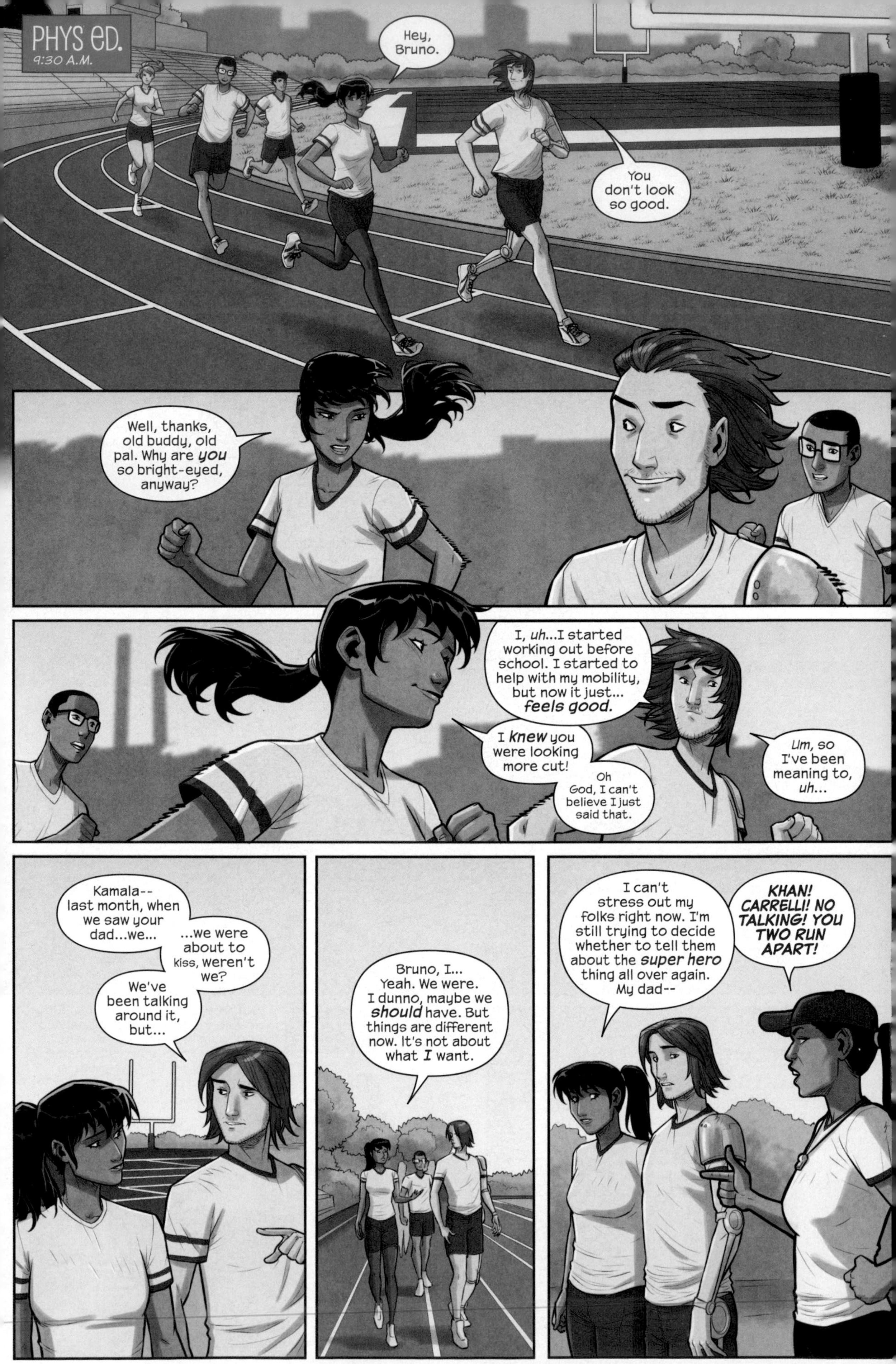
PHYS ED.
9:30 A.M.
Hey, Bruno.
You don't look so good.
Well, thanks, old buddy, old pal. Why are *you* so bright-eyed, anyway?
I, *uh*...I started working out before school. I started to help with my mobility, but now it just... *feels good.*
I *knew* you were looking more cut!
Oh God, I can't believe I just said that.
Um, so I've been meaning to, *uh*...
Kamala--last month, when we saw your dad...we...
...we were about to kiss, weren't we?
We've been talking around it, but...
Bruno, I... Yeah. We were. I dunno, maybe we *should* have. But things are different now. It's not about what *I* want.
I can't stress out my folks right now. I'm still trying to decide whether to tell them about the *super hero* thing all over again. My dad--
KHAN! CARRELLI! NO TALKING! YOU TWO RUN APART!

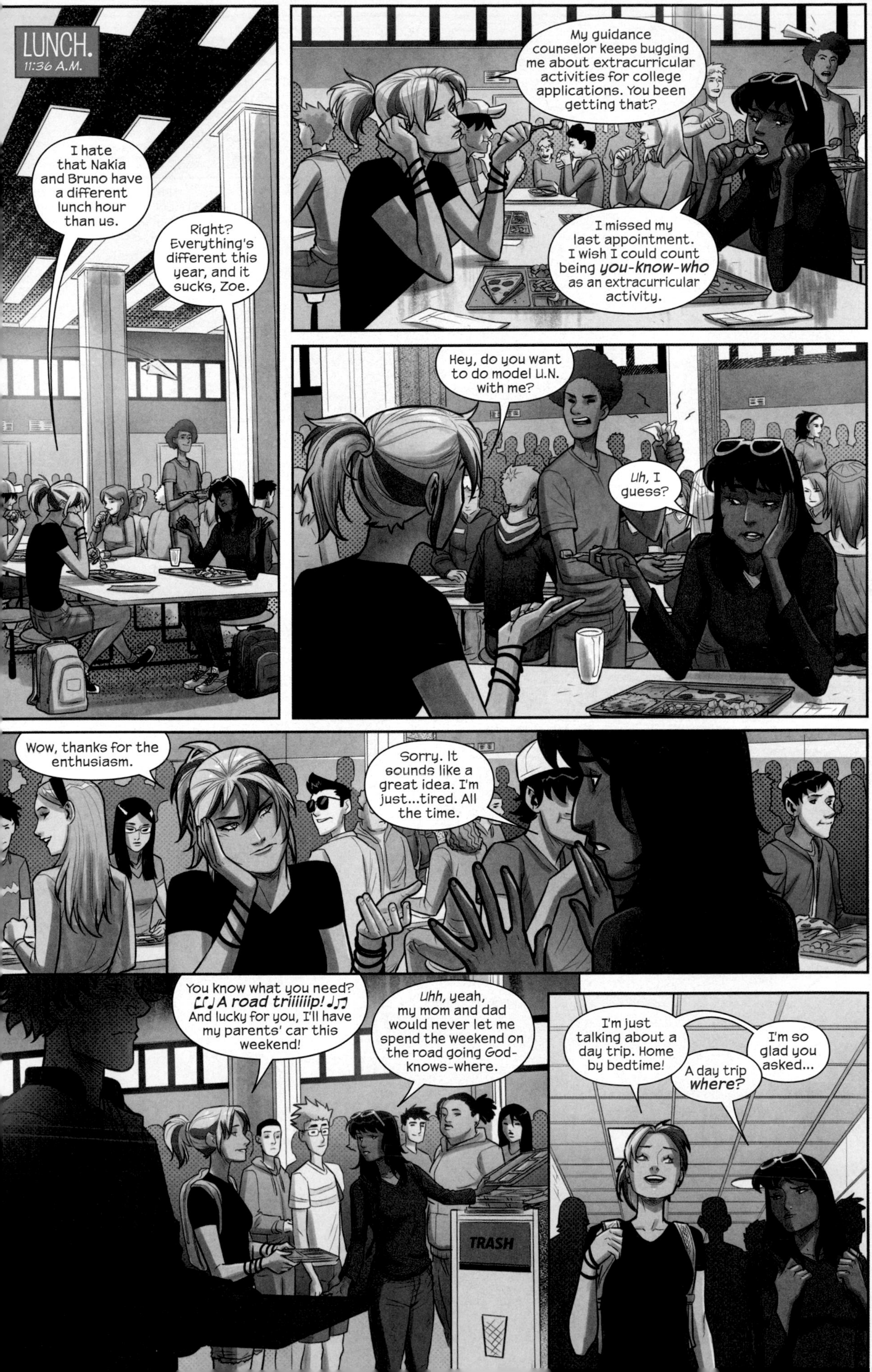
LUNCH.
11:36 A.M.
I hate that Nakia and Bruno have a different lunch hour than us.
Right? Everything's different this year, and it sucks, Zoe.
My guidance counselor keeps bugging me about extracurricular activities for college applications. You been getting that?
I missed my last appointment. I wish I could count being *you-know-who* as an extracurricular activity.
Hey, do you want to do model U.N. with me?
Uh, I guess?
Wow, thanks for the enthusiasm.
Sorry. It sounds like a great idea. I'm just...tired. All the time.
You know what you need? ♫ *A road triiiiip!* ♫ And lucky for you, I'll have my parents' car this weekend!
Uhh, yeah, my mom and dad would never let me spend the weekend on the road going God-knows-where.
TRASH
I'm just talking about a day trip. Home by bedtime!
A day trip *where?*
I'm so glad you asked...

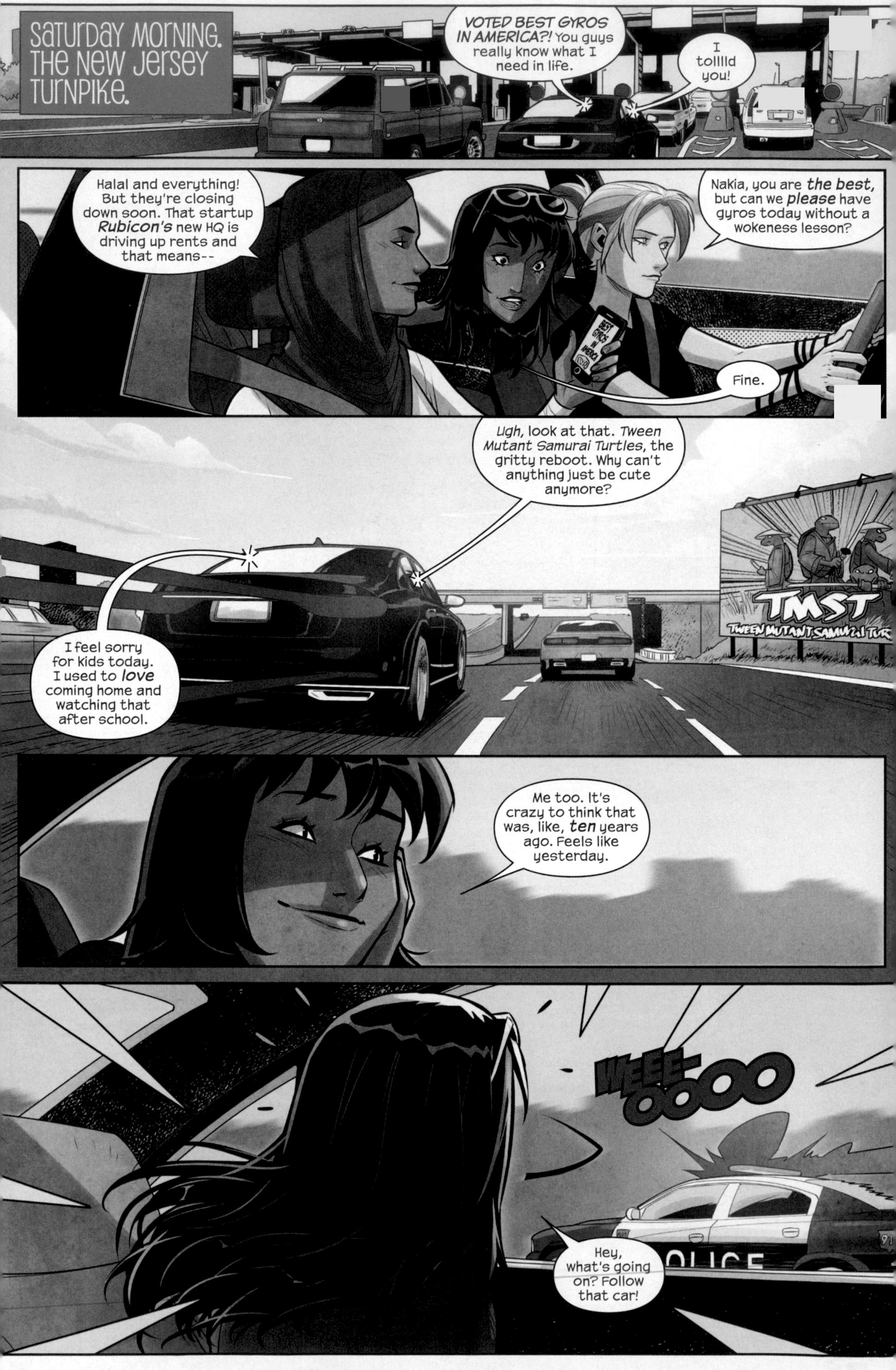

Saturday Morning. The New Jersey Turnpike.
VOTED BEST GYROS IN AMERICA?! You guys really know what I need in life.
I tollld you!
Halal and everything! But they're closing down soon. That startup Rubicon's new HQ is driving up rents and that means--
Nakia, you are the best, but can we please have gyros today without a wokeness lesson?
BEST GYROS IN AMERICA
Fine.
Ugh, look at that. Tween Mutant Samurai Turtles, the gritty reboot. Why can't anything just be cute anymore?
TMST
TWEEN MUTANT SAMURAI TUR
I feel sorry for kids today. I used to love coming home and watching that after school.
Me too. It's crazy to think that was, like, ten years ago. Feels like yesterday.
WEEE-OOOO
Hey, what's going on? Follow that car!

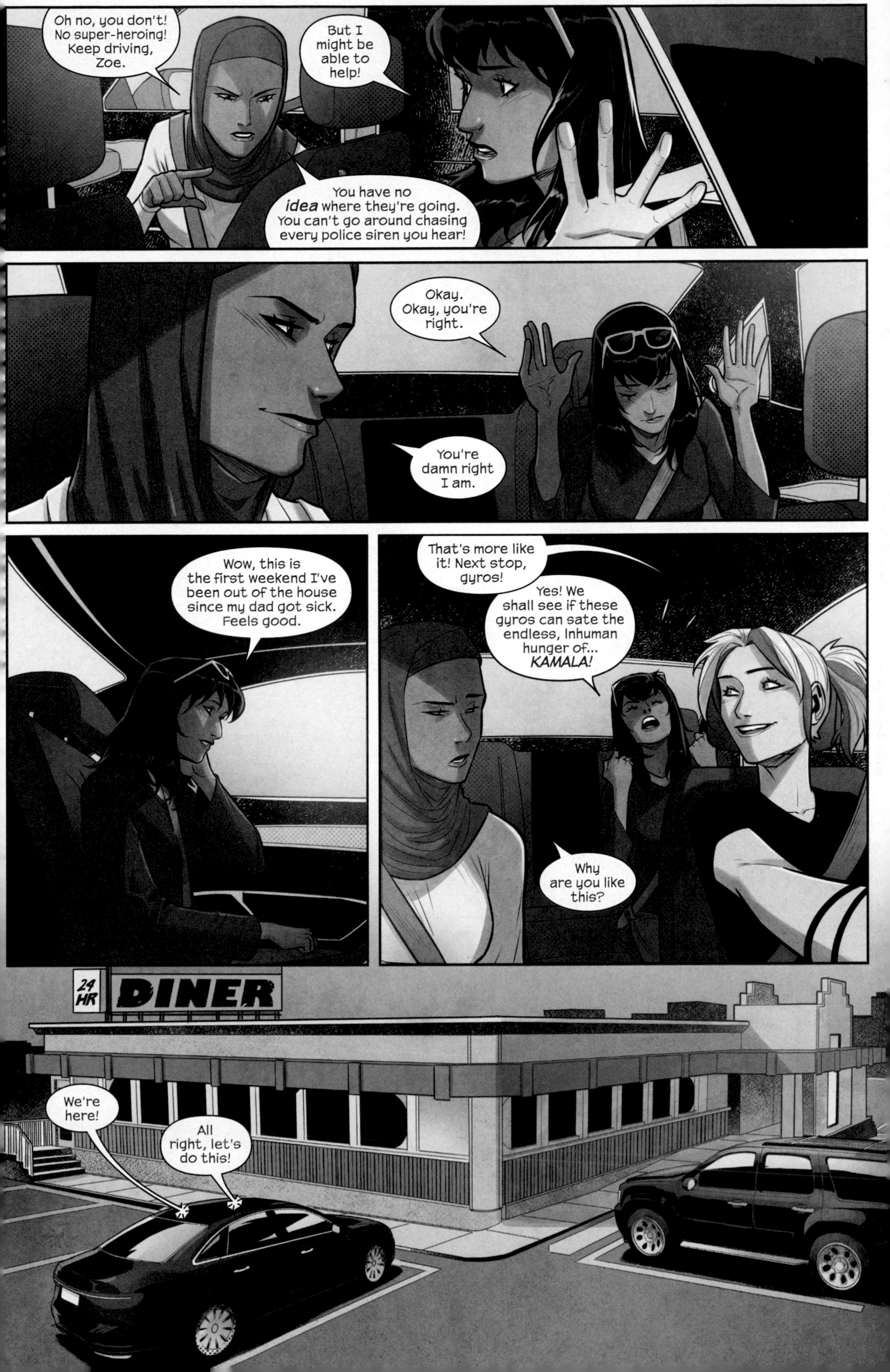

Oh no, you don't! No super-heroing! Keep driving, Zoe.
But I might be able to help!
You have no *idea* where they're going. You can't go around chasing every police siren you hear!
Okay. Okay, you're right.
You're damn right I am.
Wow, this is the first weekend I've been out of the house since my dad got sick. Feels good.
That's more like it! Next stop, gyros!
Yes! We shall see if these gyros can sate the endless, Inhuman hunger of... KAMALA!
Why are you like this?
24 HR
DINER
We're here!
All right, let's do this!

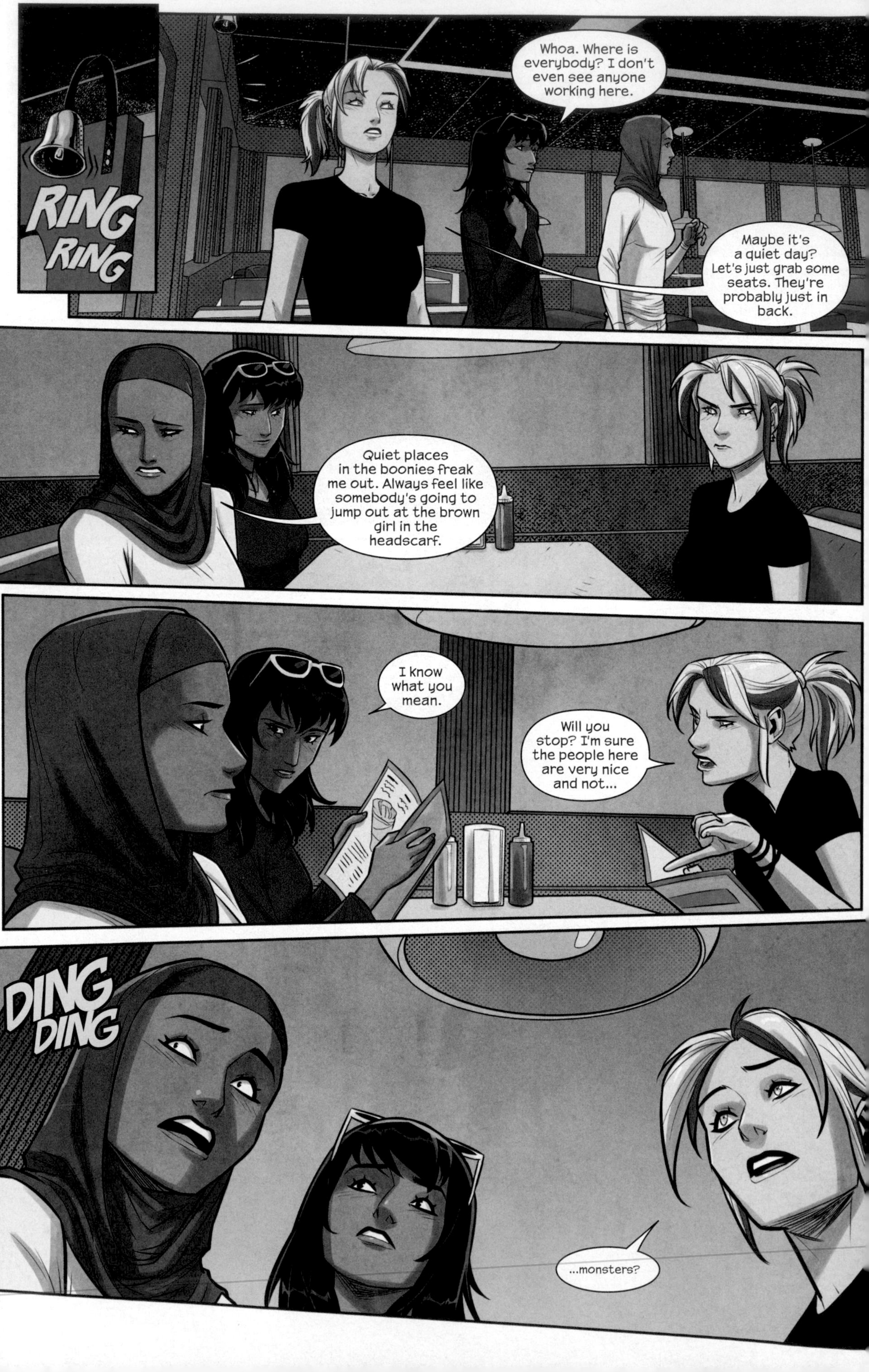
RING RING
Whoa. Where is everybody? I don't even see anyone working here.
Maybe it's a quiet day? Let's just grab some seats. They're probably just in back.
Quiet places in the boonies freak me out. Always feel like somebody's going to jump out at the brown girl in the headscarf.
I know what you mean.
Will you stop? I'm sure the people here are very nice and not...
DING DING
...monsters?

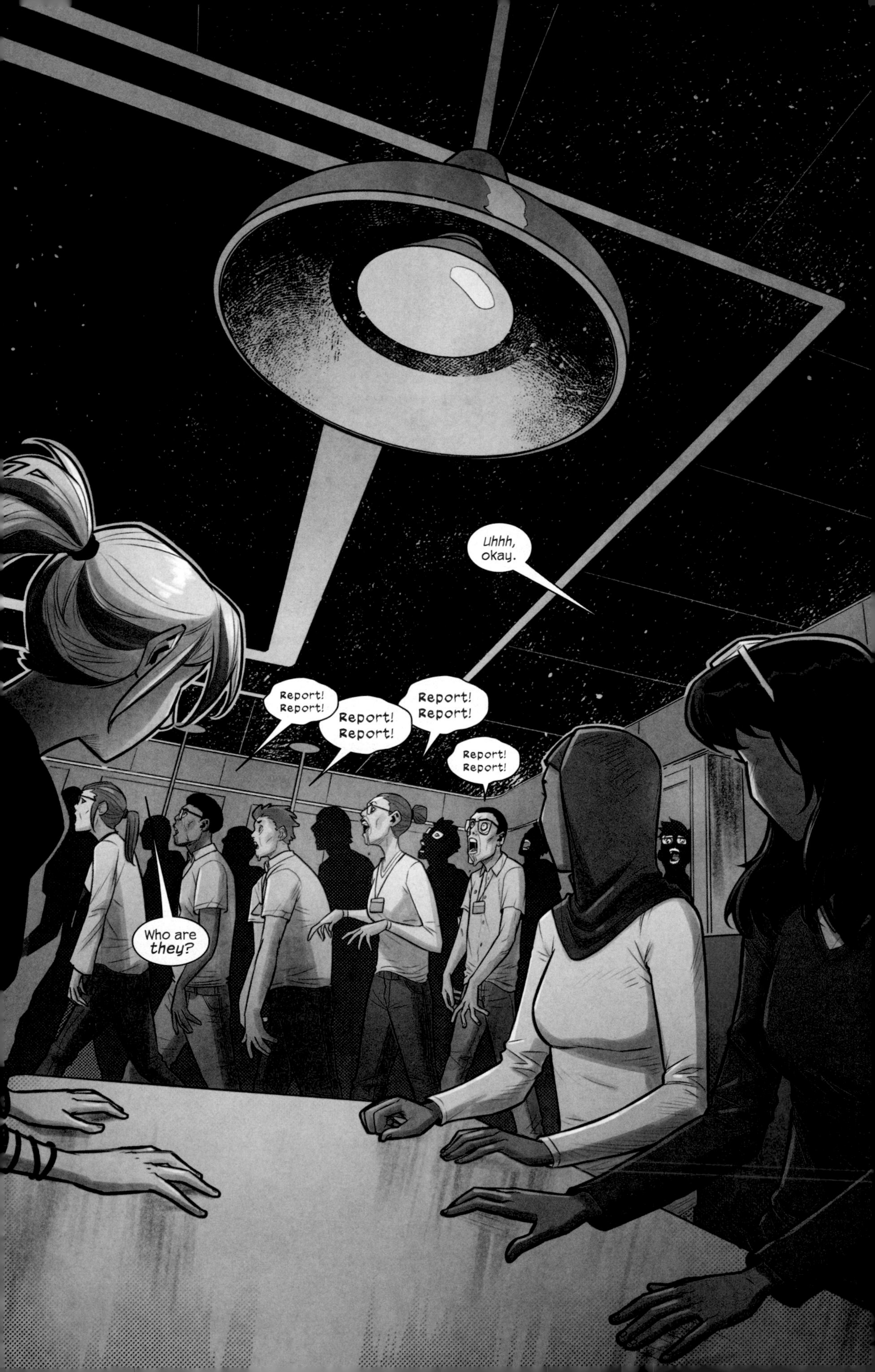
Uhhh, okay.
Report! Report!
Report! Report!
Report! Report!
Report! Report!
Who are they?

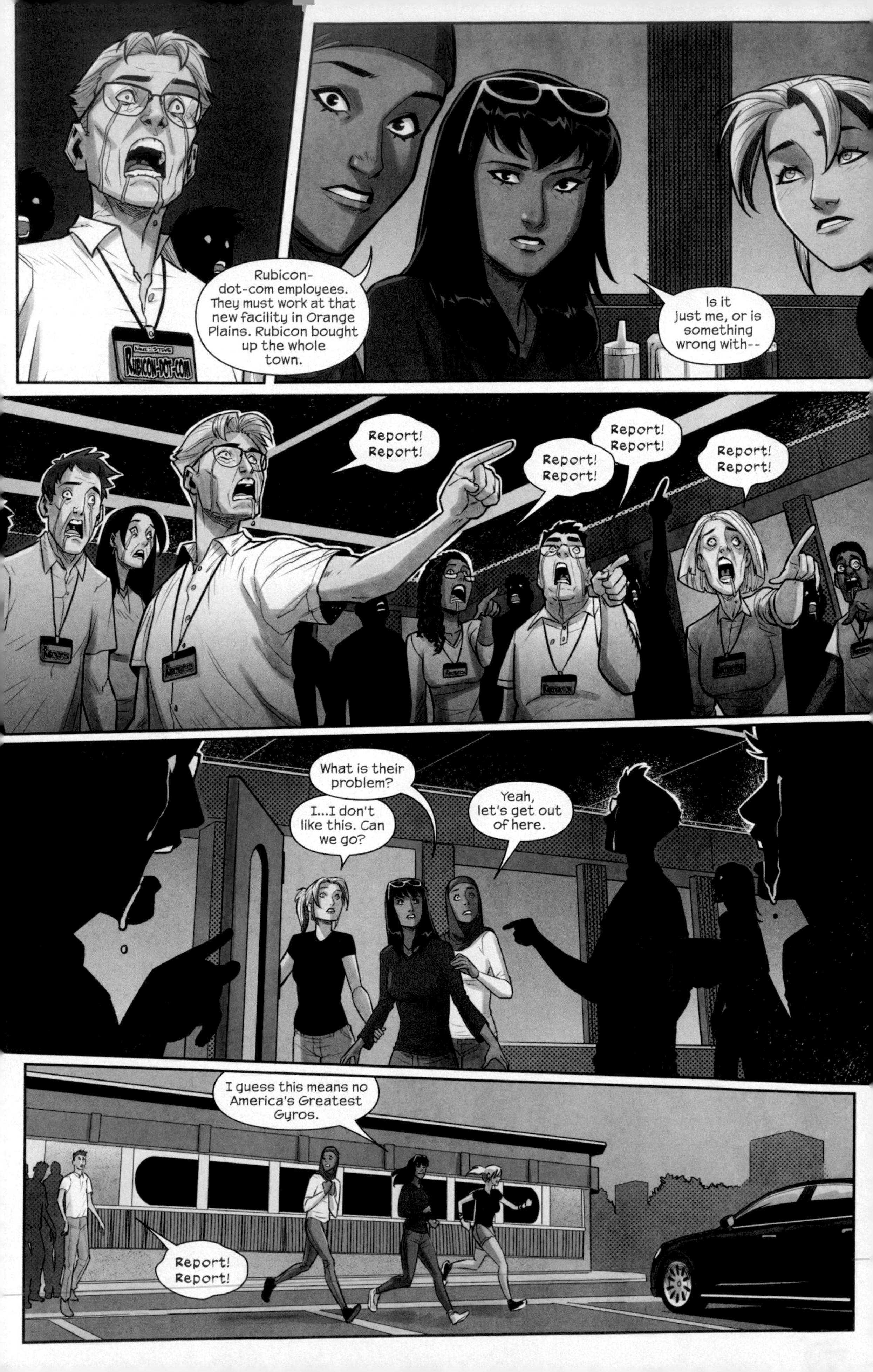
RUBICON-DOT-COM
Rubicon-dot-com employees. They must work at that new facility in Orange Plains. Rubicon bought up the whole town.
Is it just me, or is something wrong with--
Report! Report!
Report! Report!
Report! Report!
Report! Report!
What is their problem?
I...I don't like this. Can we go?
Yeah, let's get out of here.
I guess this means no America's Greatest Gyros.
Report! Report!

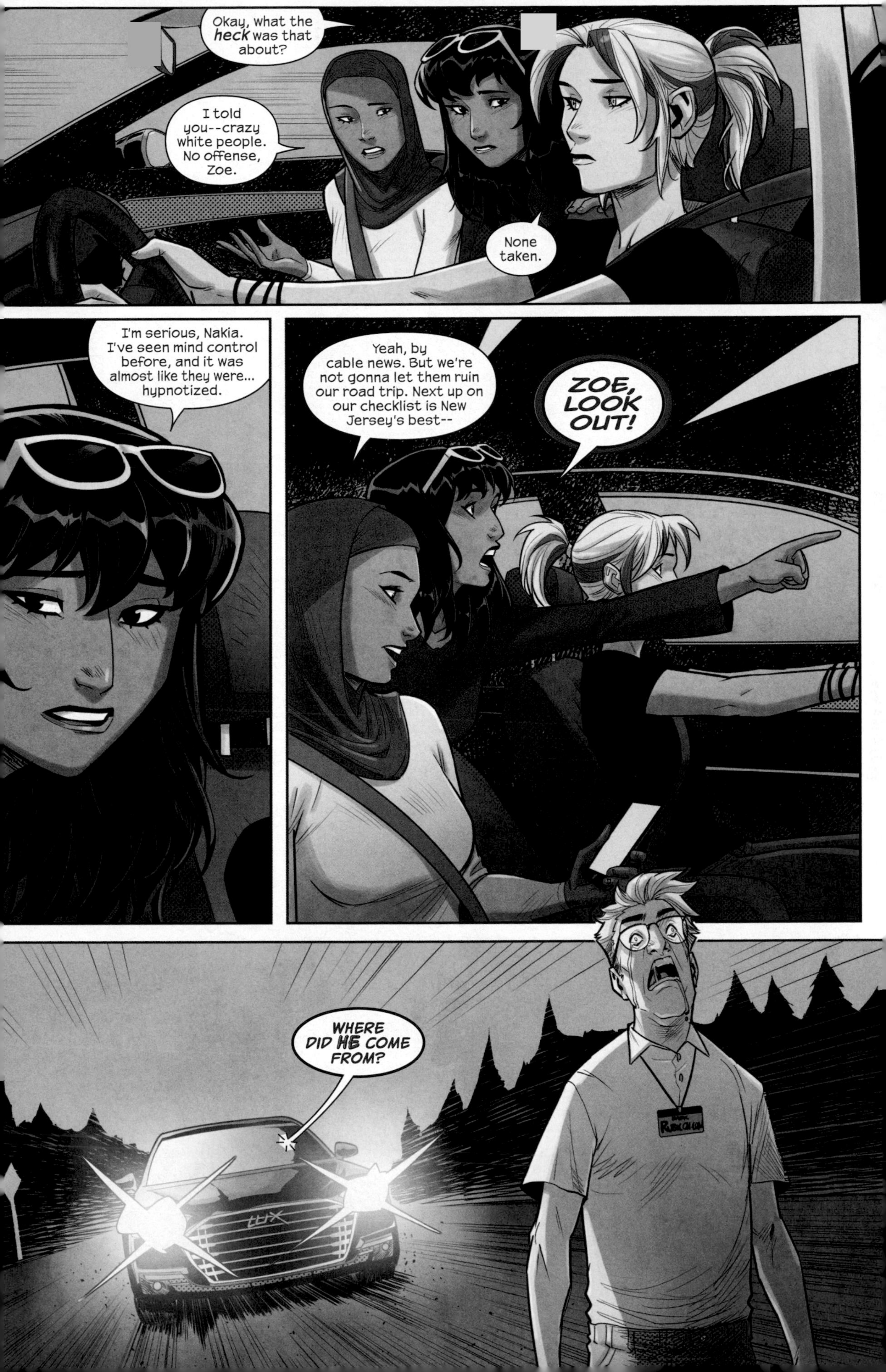

Okay, what the heck was that about?
I told you--crazy white people. No offense, Zoe.
None taken.
I'm serious, Nakia. I've seen mind control before, and it was almost like they were... hypnotized.
Yeah, by cable news. But we're not gonna let them ruin our road trip. Next up on our checklist is New Jersey's best--
ZOE, LOOK OUT!
WHERE DID HE COME FROM?

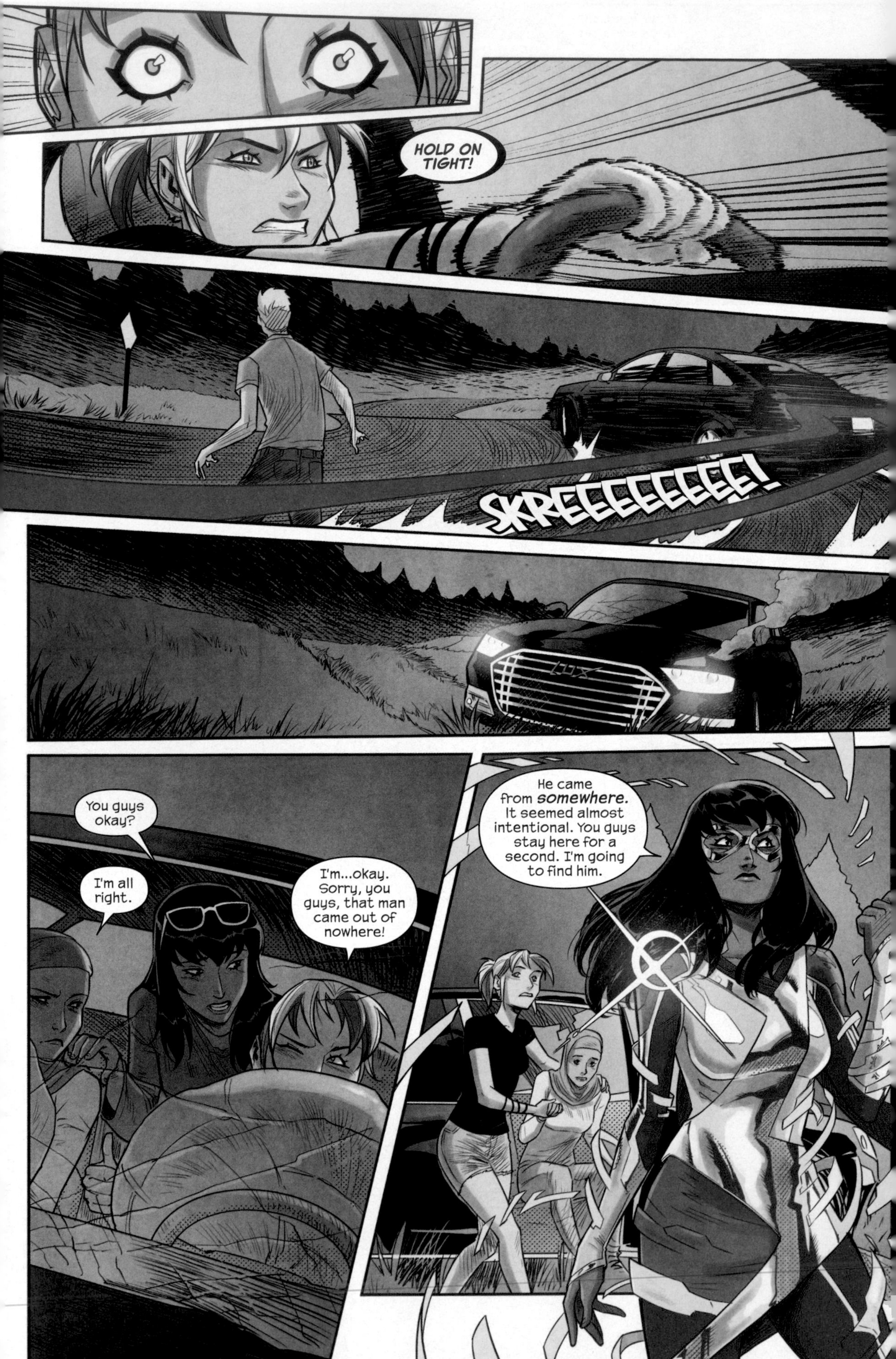

HOLD ON TIGHT!
SKREEEEEEEEE!
You guys okay?
I'm all right.
I'm...okay. Sorry, you guys, that man came out of nowhere!
He came from *somewhere.* It seemed almost intentional. You guys stay here for a second. I'm going to find him.

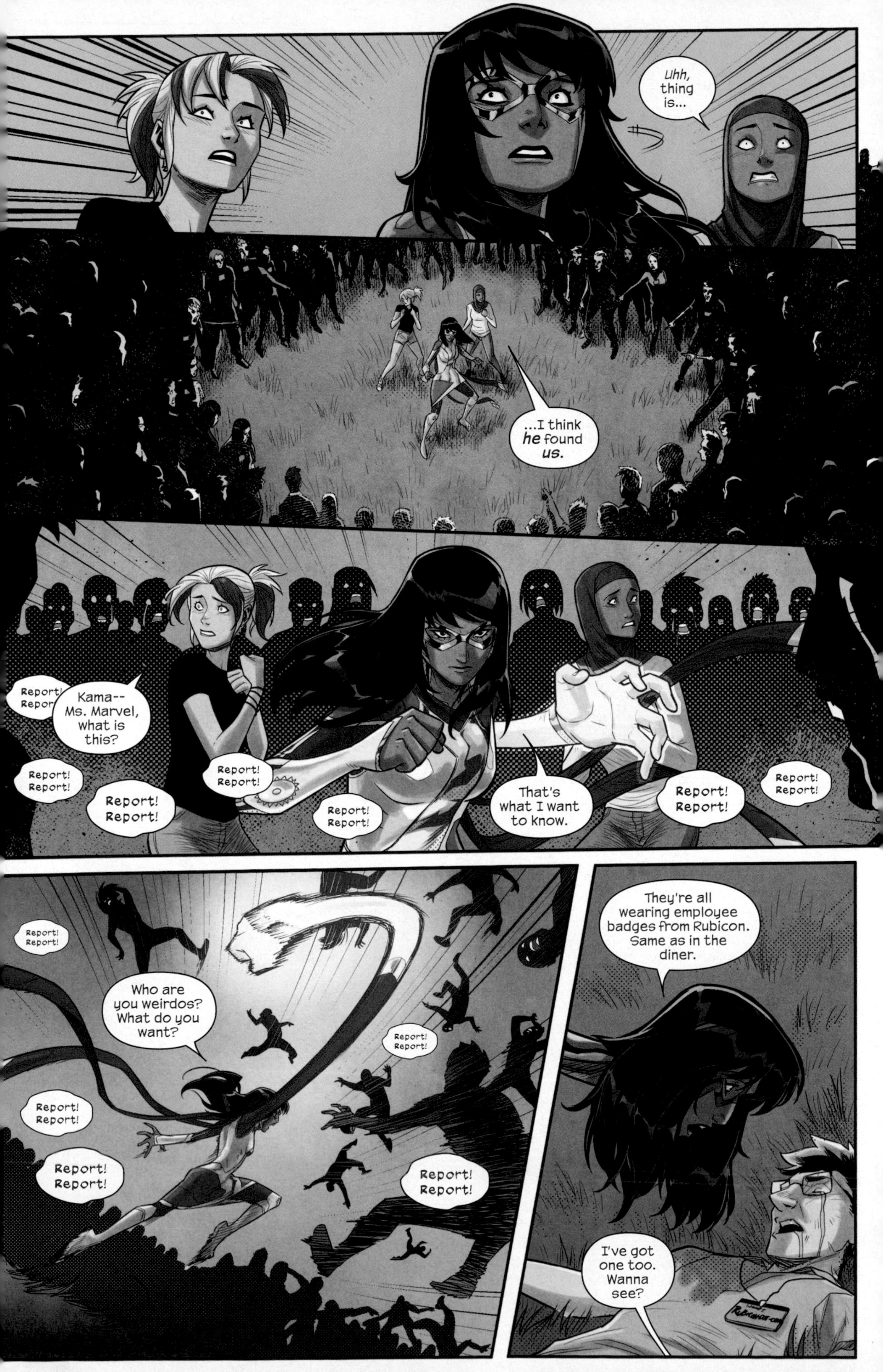

Uhh, thing is...
...I think he found us.
Kama-- Ms. Marvel, what is this?
Report! Report!
Report! Report!
Report! Report!
Report! Report!
Report! Report!
That's what I want to know.
Report! Report!
Report! Report!
Report! Report!
Who are you weirdos? What do you want?
Report! Report!
Report! Report!
Report! Report!
Report! Report!
They're all wearing employee badges from Rubicon. Same as in the diner.
I've got one too. Wanna see?

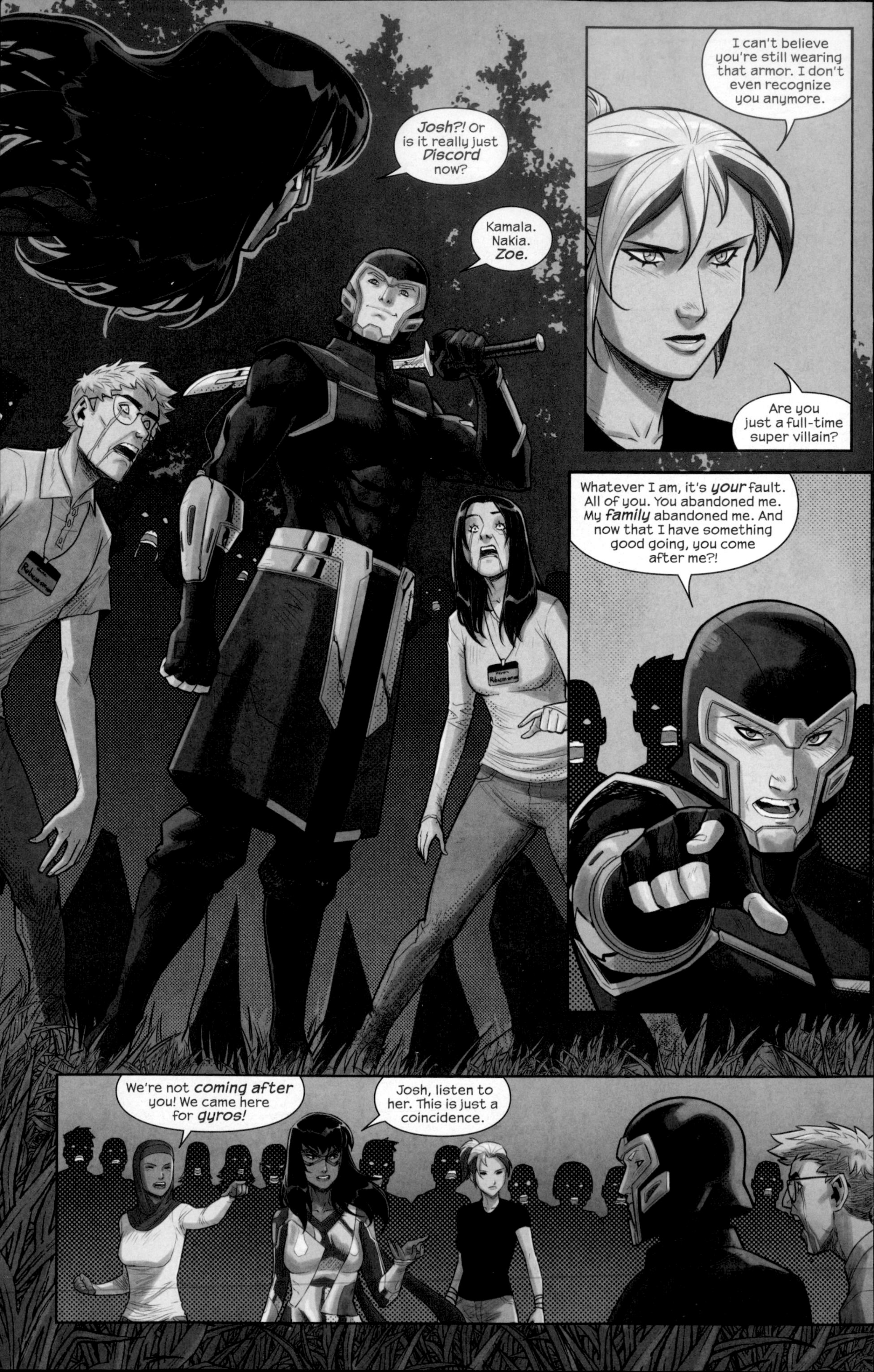
Josh?! Or is it really just Discord now?
Kamala. Nakia. Zoe.
I can't believe you're still wearing that armor. I don't even recognize you anymore.
Are you just a full-time super villain?
Whatever I am, it's your fault. All of you. You abandoned me. My family abandoned me. And now that I have something good going, you come after me?!
We're not coming after you! We came here for gyros!
Josh, listen to her. This is just a coincidence.

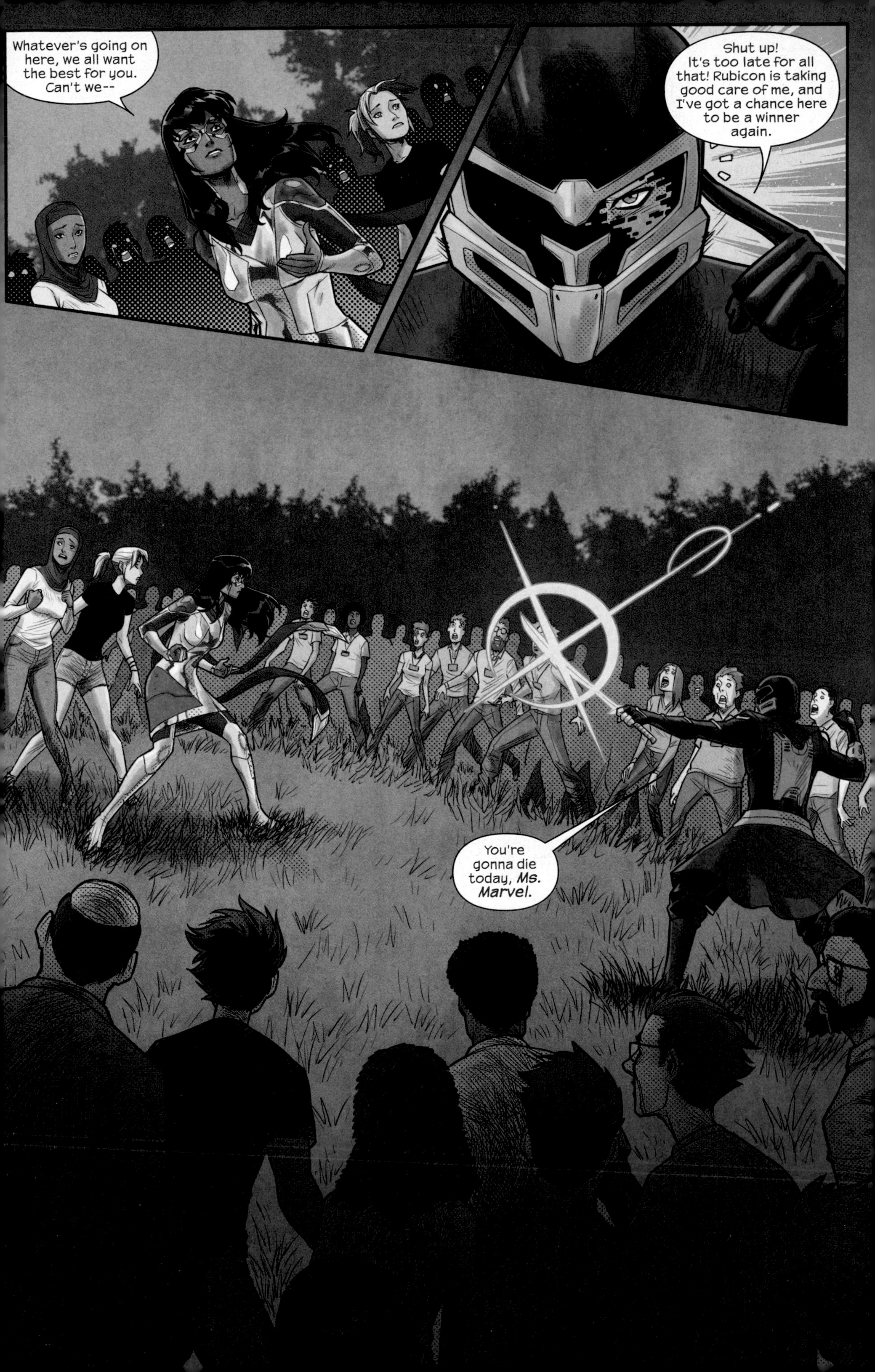
Whatever's going on here, we all want the best for you. Can't we--
Shut up! It's too late for all that! Rubicon is taking good care of me, and I've got a chance here to be a winner again.
You're gonna die today, *Ms. Marvel*.

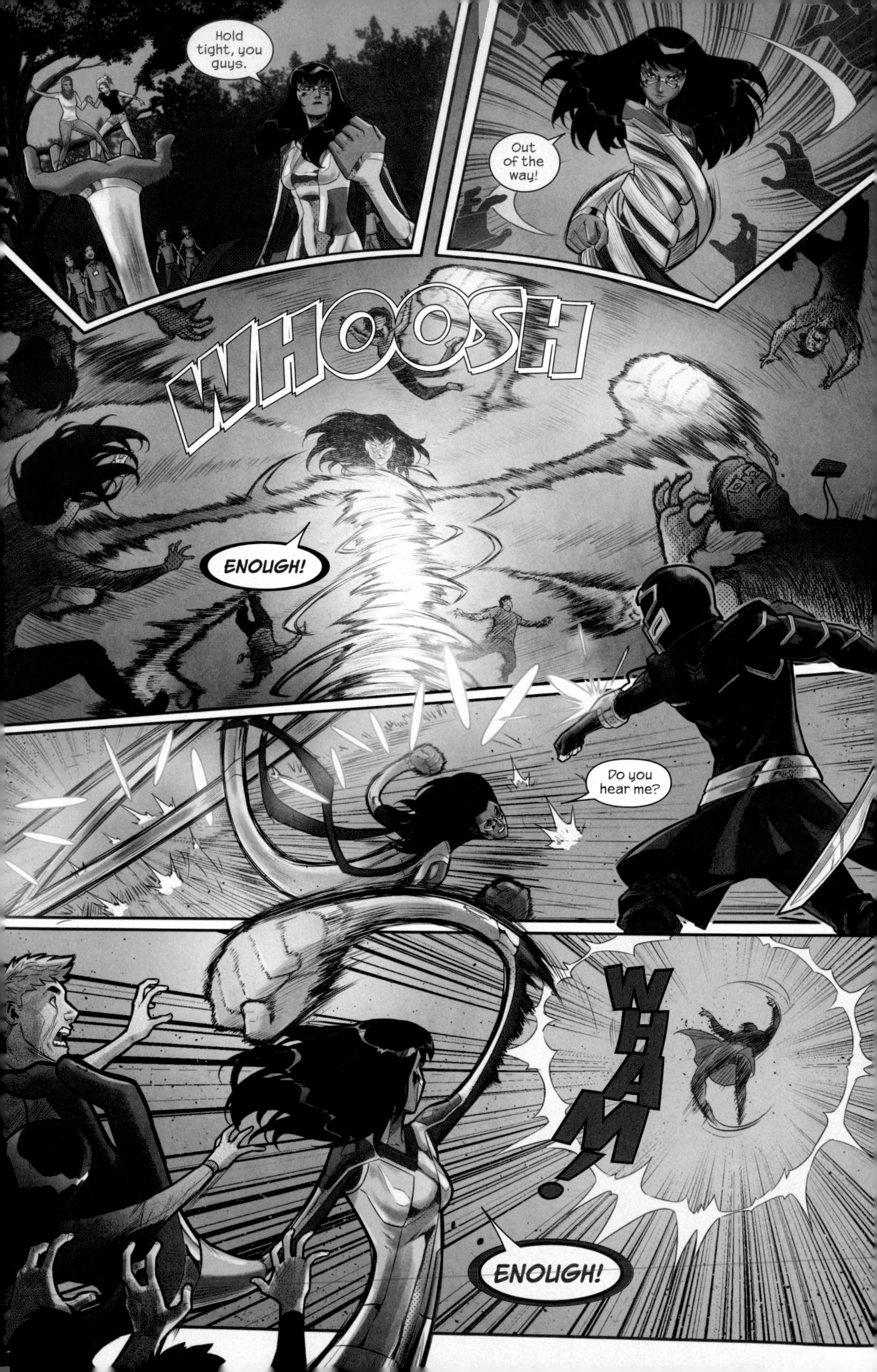
Hold tight, you guys.
Out of the way!
WHOOSH
ENOUGH!
Do you hear me?
WHAM!
ENOUGH!

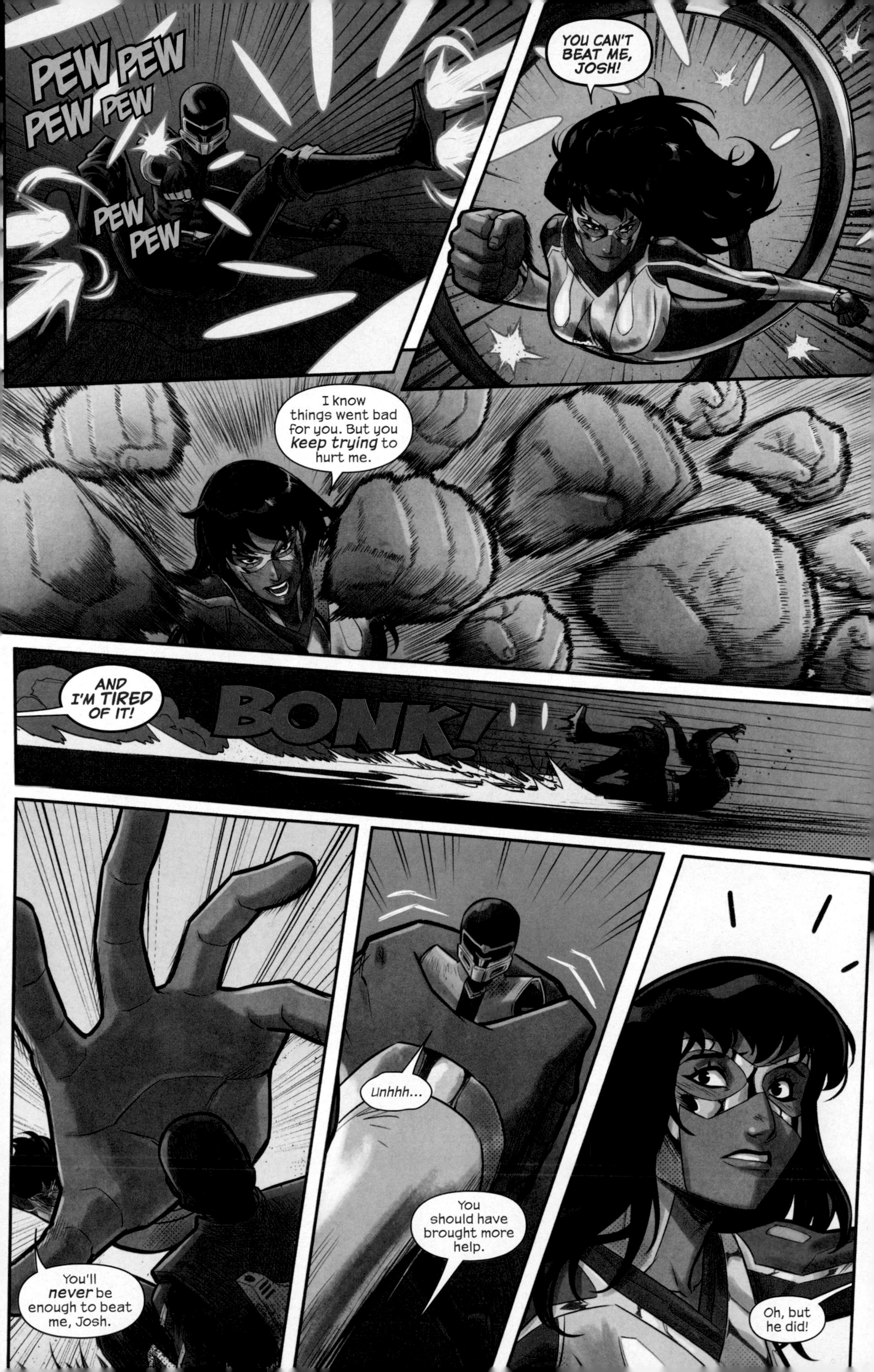
PEW PEW
PEW PEW
PEW
PEW
YOU CAN'T BEAT ME, JOSH!
I know things went bad for you. But you keep trying to hurt me.
AND I'M TIRED OF IT!
BONK!
You'll never be enough to beat me, Josh.
Unhhh...
You should have brought more help.
Oh, but he did!

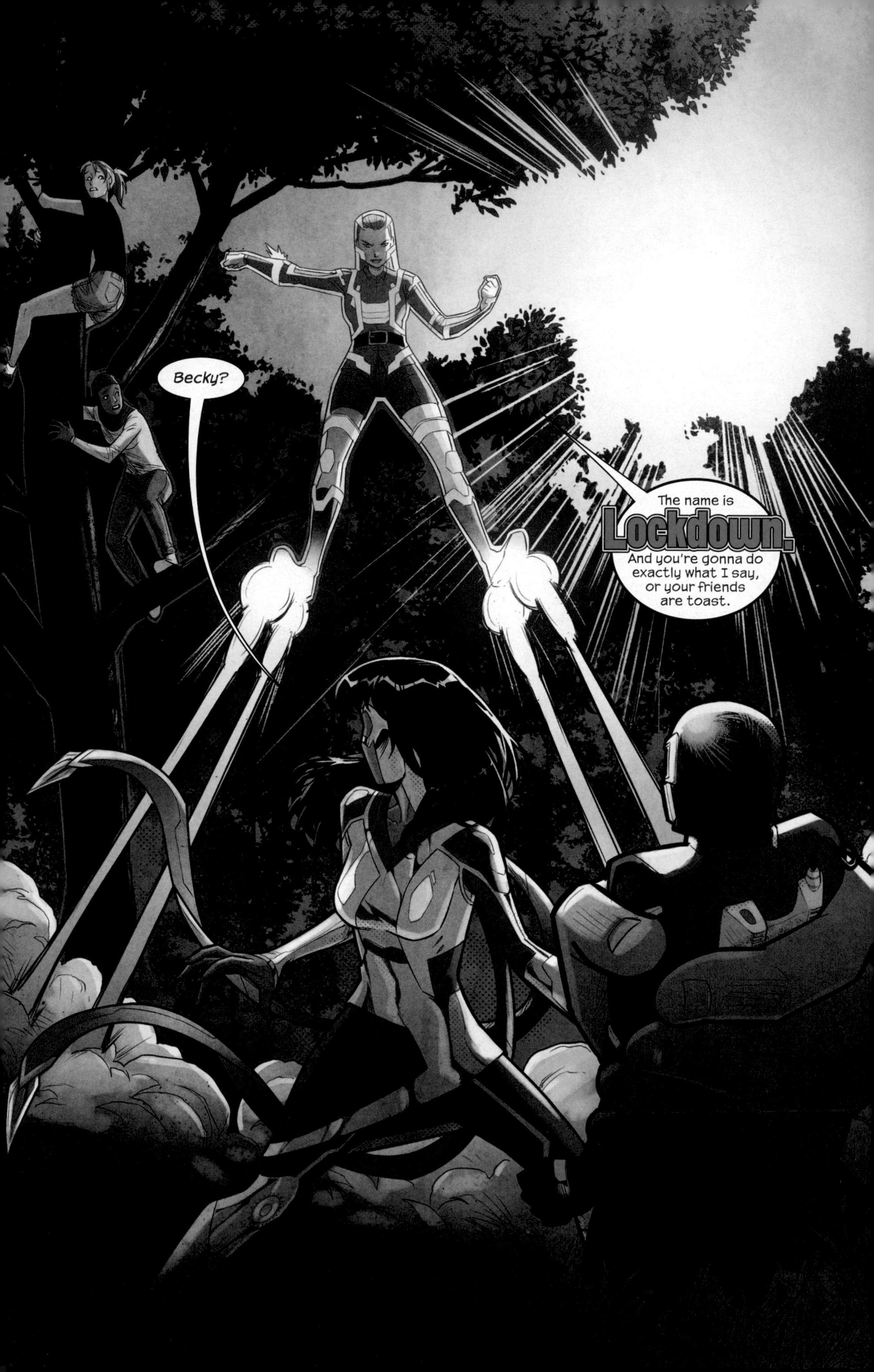
Becky?
The name is
Lockdown.
And you're gonna do exactly what I say, or your friends are toast.

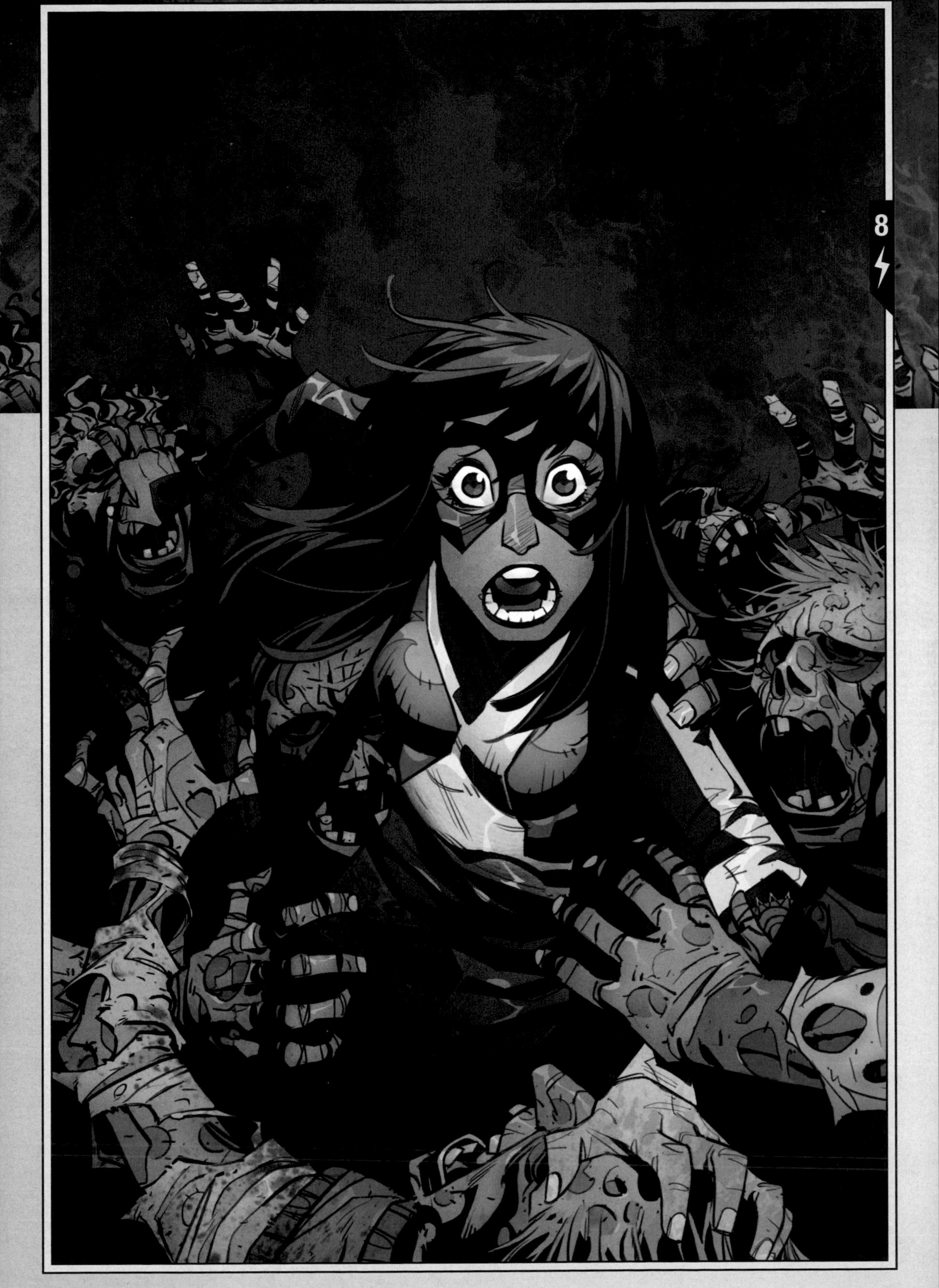

8

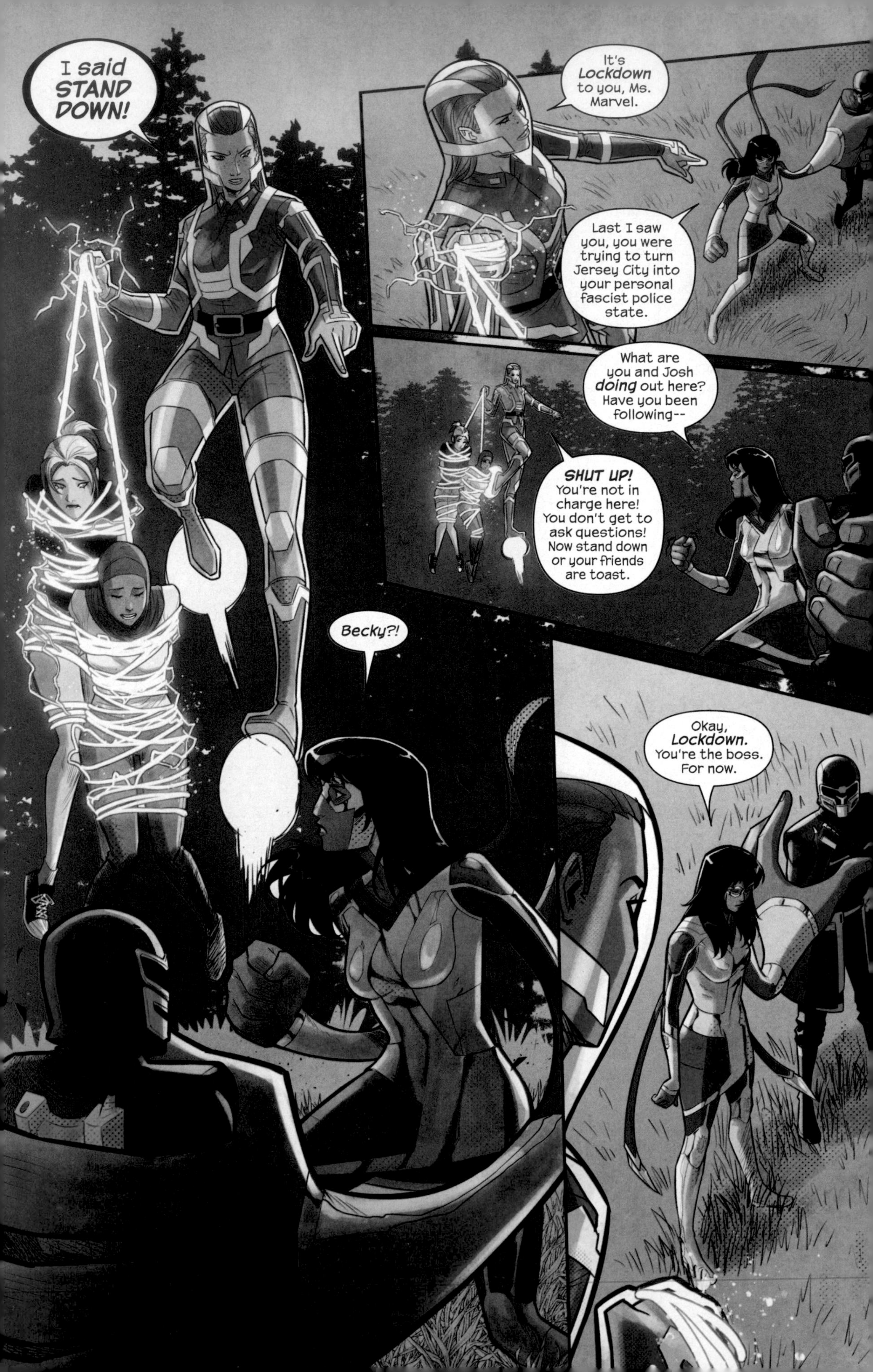
I said STAND DOWN!
It's Lockdown to you, Ms. Marvel.
Last I saw you, you were trying to turn Jersey City into your personal fascist police state.
What are you and Josh doing out here? Have you been following--
SHUT UP! You're not in charge here! You don't get to ask questions! Now stand down or your friends are toast.
Becky?!
Okay, Lockdown. You're the boss. For now.

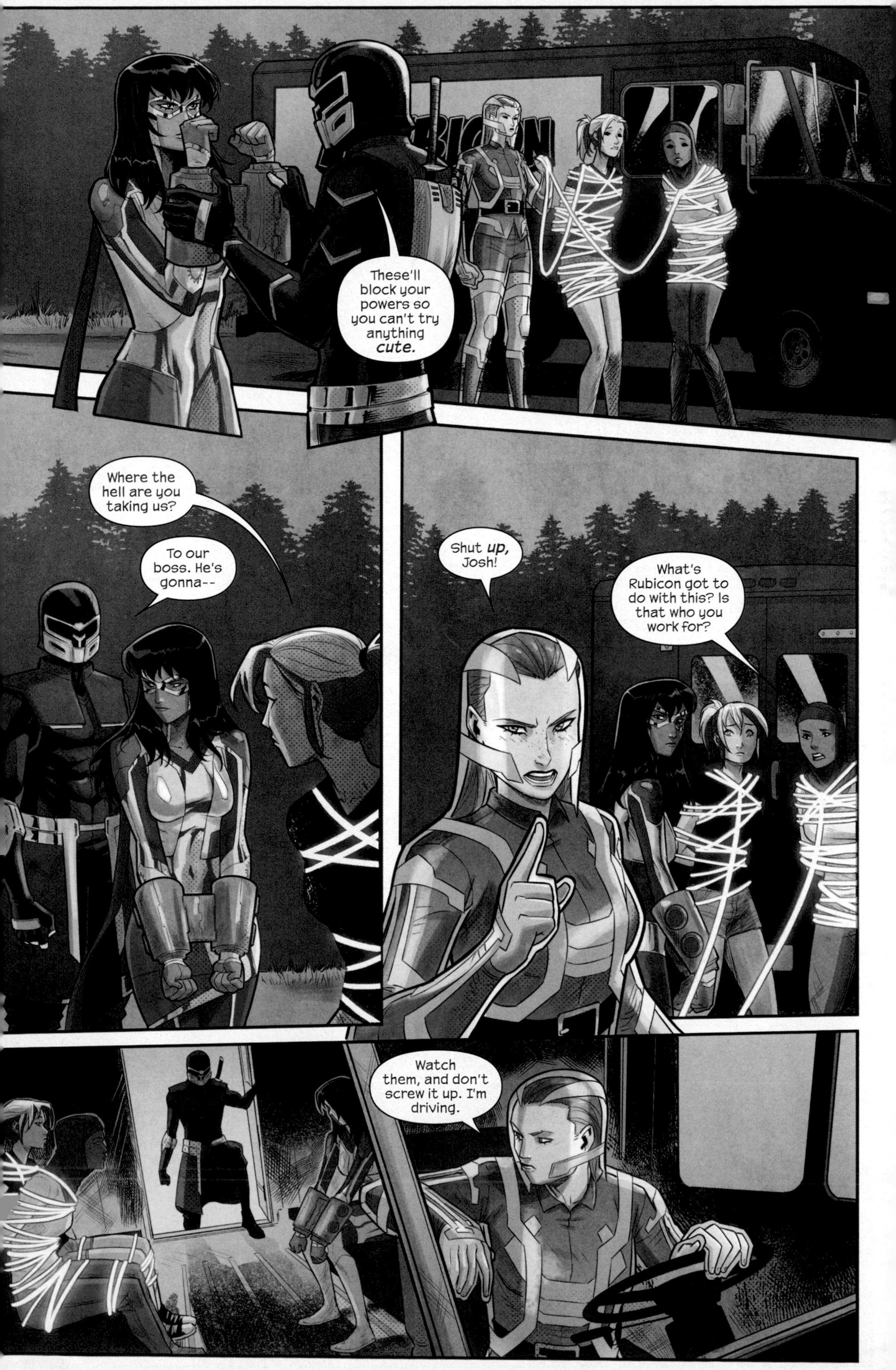

RUBICON
These'll block your powers so you can't try anything *cute.*
Where the hell are you taking us?
To our boss. He's gonna--
Shut *up,* Josh!
What's Rubicon got to do with this? Is that who you work for?
Watch them, and don't screw it up. I'm driving.

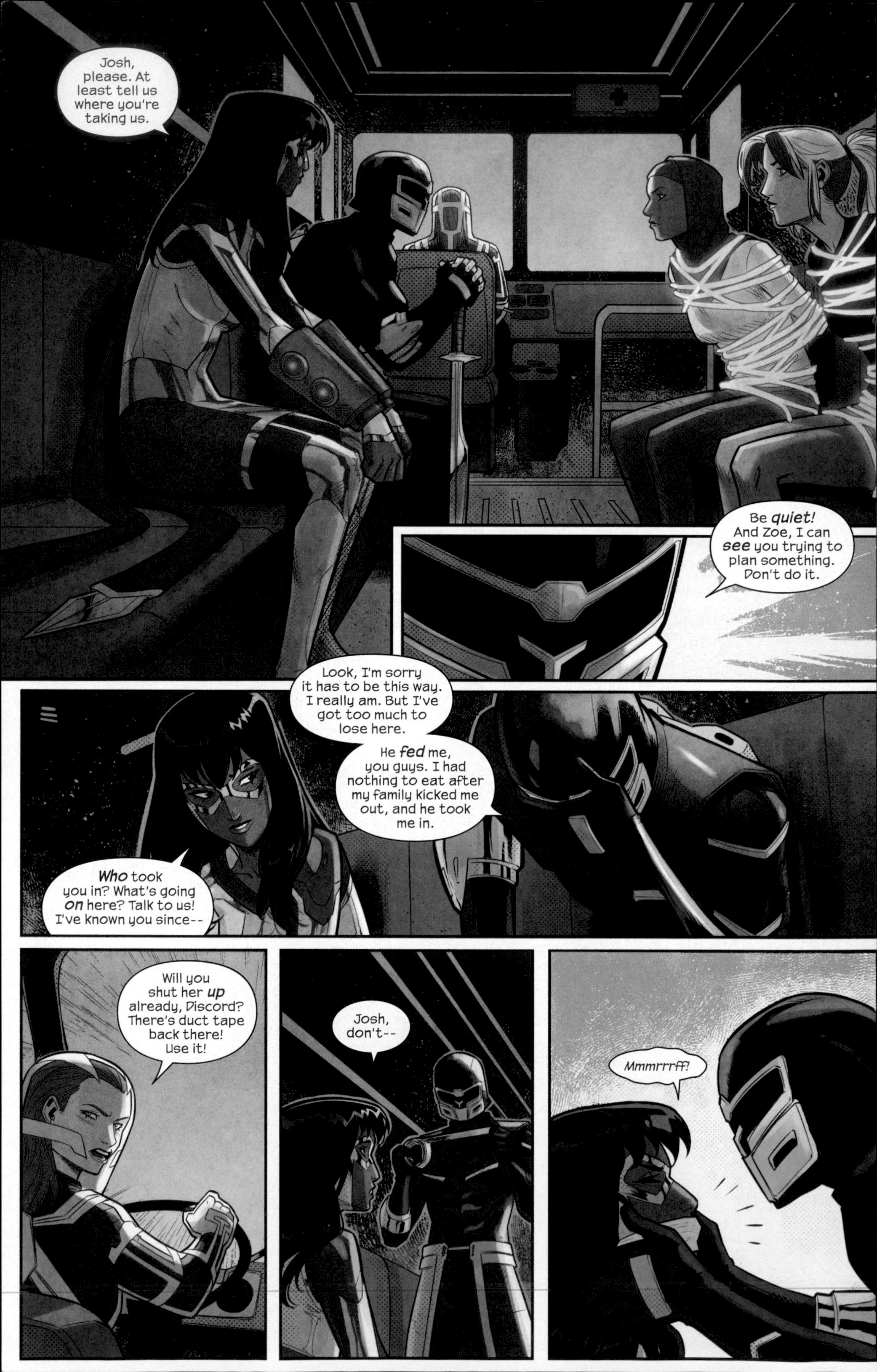
Josh, please. At least tell us where you're taking us.
Be *quiet!* And Zoe, I can *see* you trying to plan something. Don't do it.
Look, I'm sorry it has to be this way. I really am. But I've got too much to lose here.
He *fed* me, you guys. I had nothing to eat after my family kicked me out, and he took me in.
Who took you in? What's going *on* here? Talk to us! I've known you since--
Will you shut her *up* already, Discord? There's duct tape back there! Use it!
Josh, don't--
Mmmrrrff!

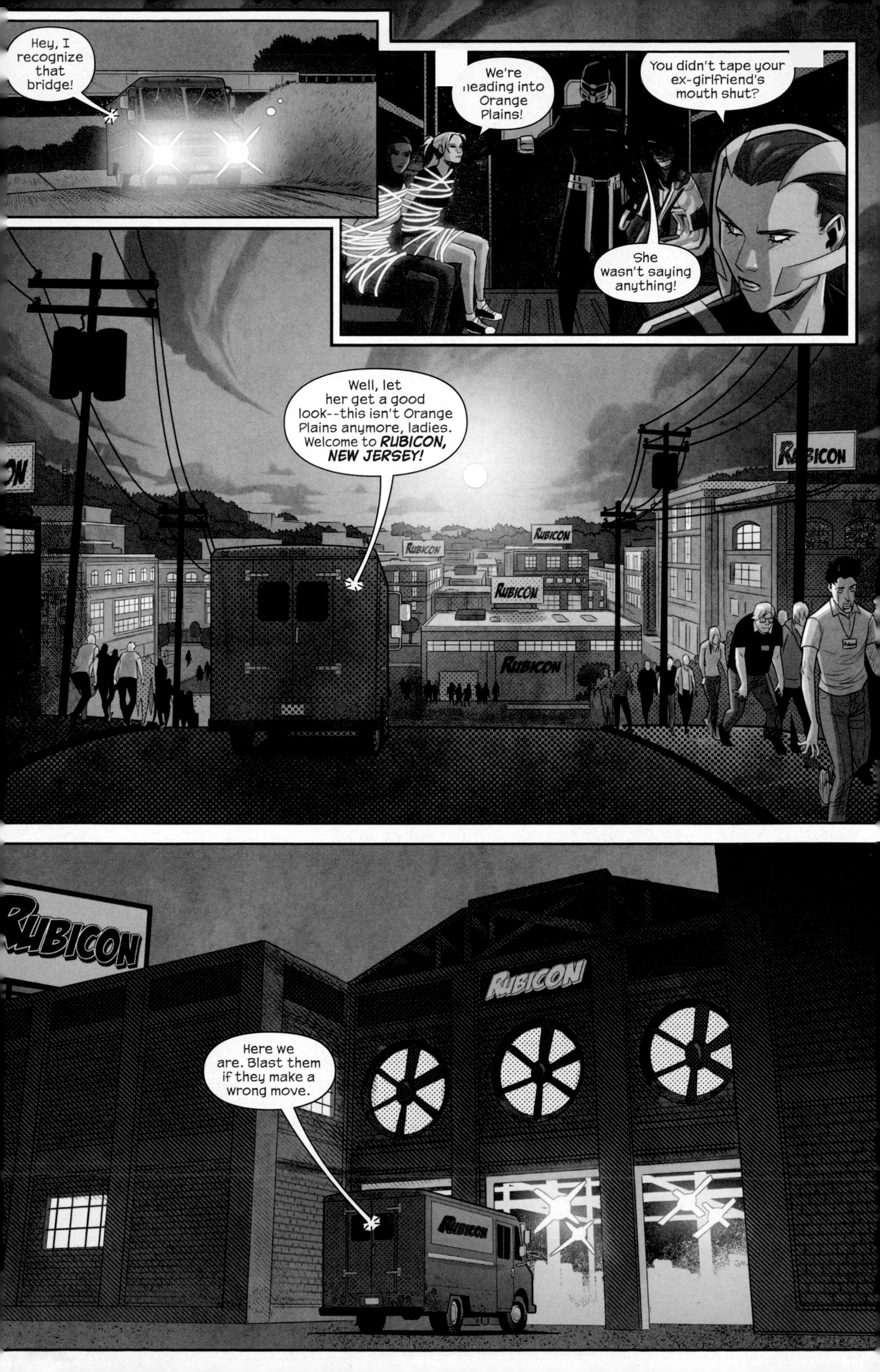
Hey, I recognize that bridge!
We're heading into Orange Plains!
You didn't tape your ex-girlfriend's mouth shut?
She wasn't saying anything!
Well, let her get a good look--this isn't Orange Plains anymore, ladies. Welcome to **RUBICON, NEW JERSEY!**
RUBICON
RUBICON
RUBICON
RUBICON
RUBICON
RUBICON
Here we are. Blast them if they make a wrong move.
RUBICON
RUBICON

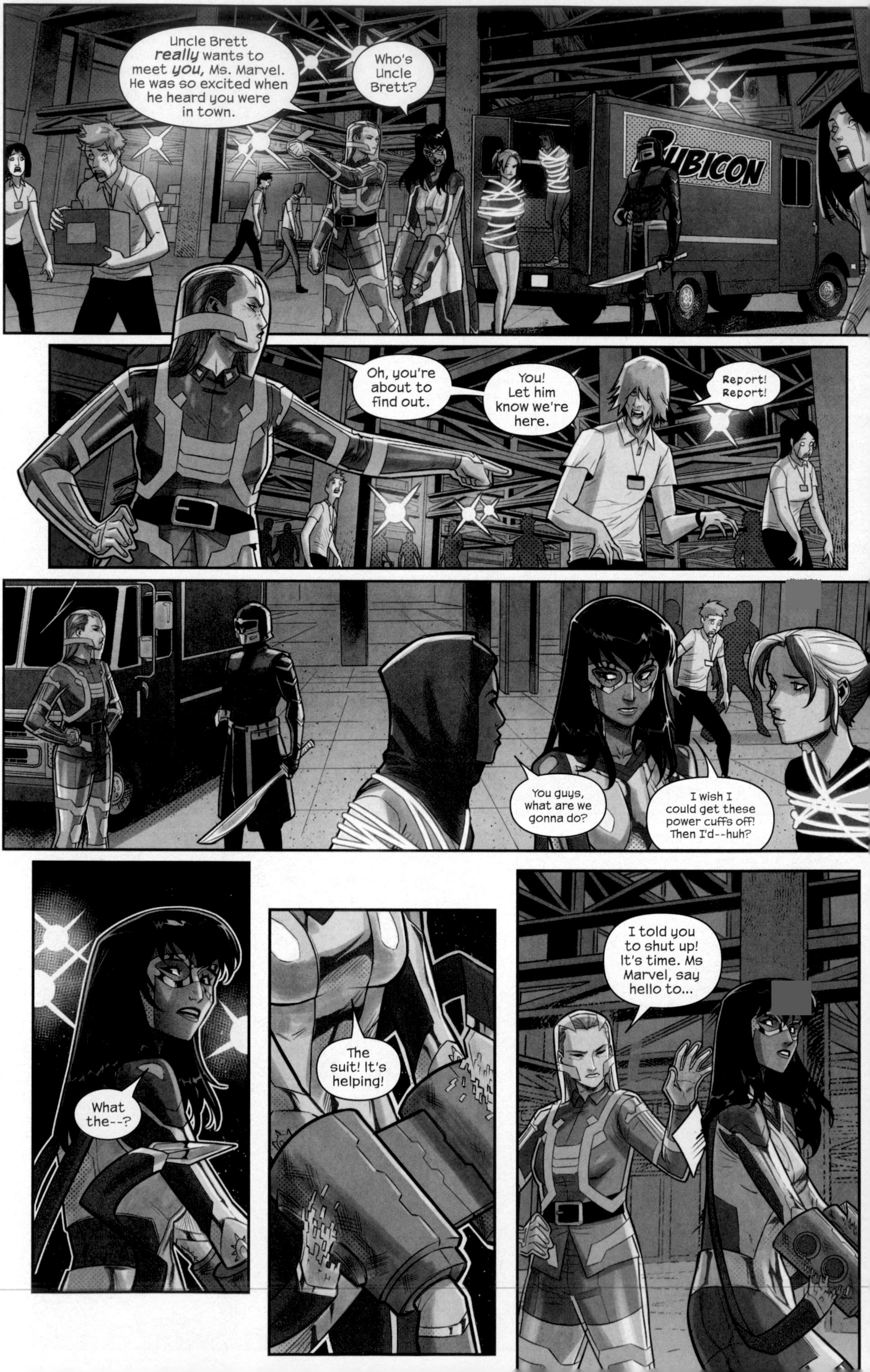
Uncle Brett *really* wants to meet *you,* Ms. Marvel. He was so excited when he heard you were in town.
Who's Uncle Brett?
Oh, you're about to find out.
You! Let him know we're here.
Report! Report!
You guys, what are we gonna do?
I wish I could get these power cuffs off! Then I'd--huh?
What the--?
The suit! It's helping!
I told you to shut up! It's time. Ms Marvel, say hello to...
RUBICON

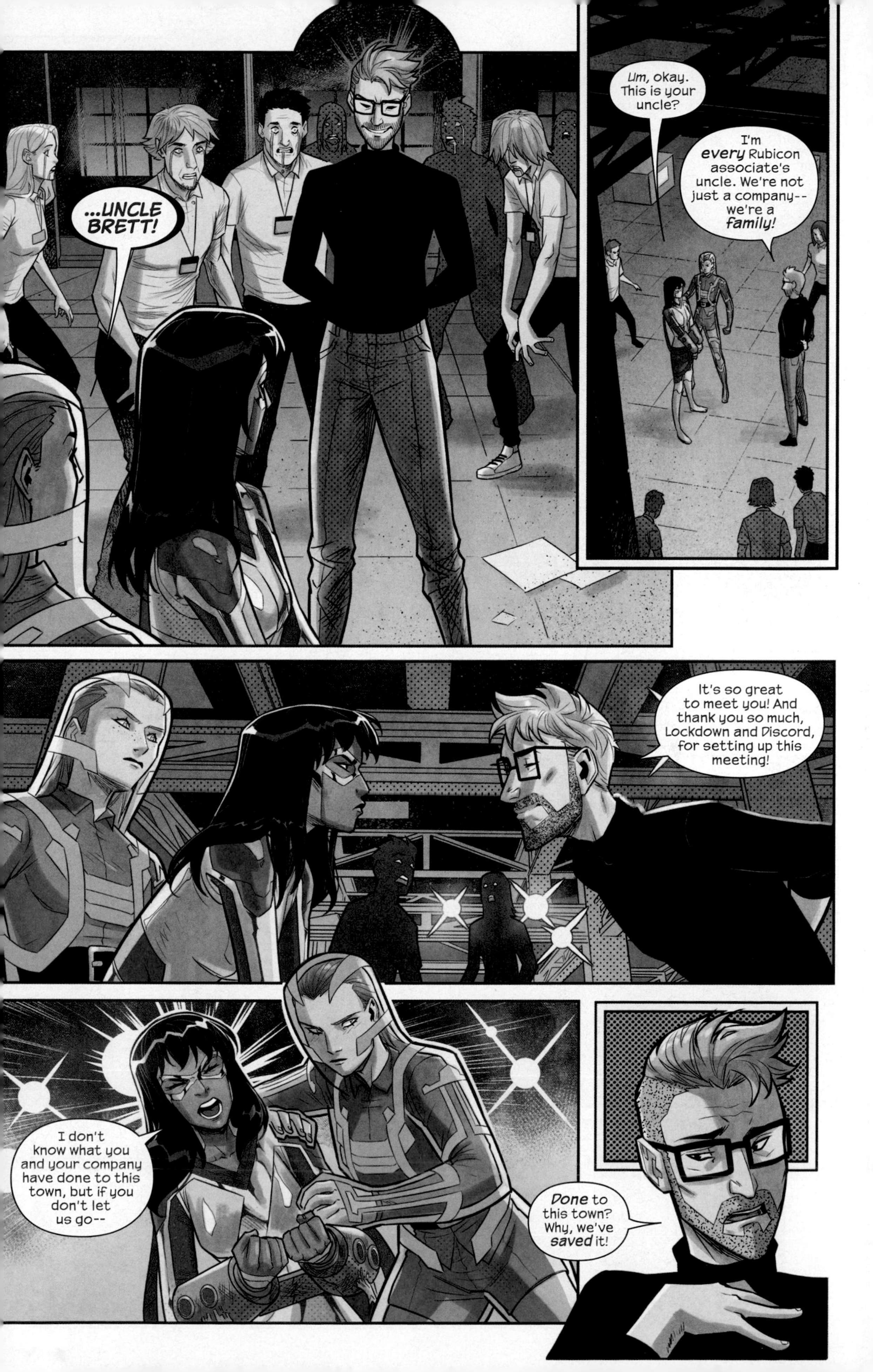
...UNCLE BRETT!
Um, okay. This is your uncle?
I'm every Rubicon associate's uncle. We're not just a company-- we're a family!
It's so great to meet you! And thank you so much, Lockdown and Discord, for setting up this meeting!
I don't know what you and your company have done to this town, but if you don't let us go--
Done to this town? Why, we've saved it!

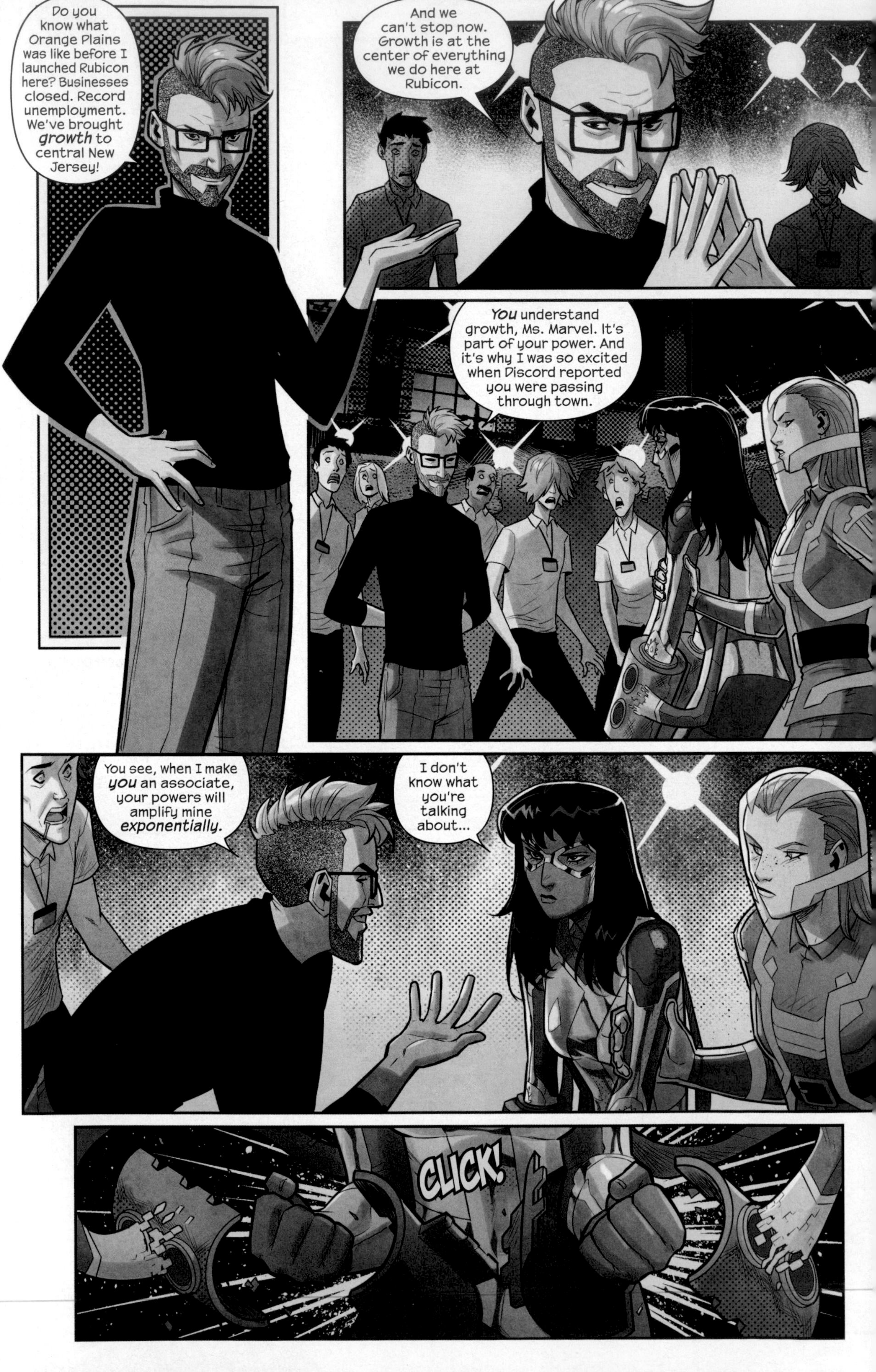

Do you know what Orange Plains was like before I launched Rubicon here? Businesses closed. Record unemployment. We've brought *growth* to central New Jersey!
And we can't stop now. Growth is at the center of everything we do here at Rubicon.
You understand growth, Ms. Marvel. It's part of your power. And it's why I was so excited when Discord reported you were passing through town.
You see, when I make *you* an associate, your powers will amplify mine *exponentially*.
I don't know what you're talking about...
CLICK!

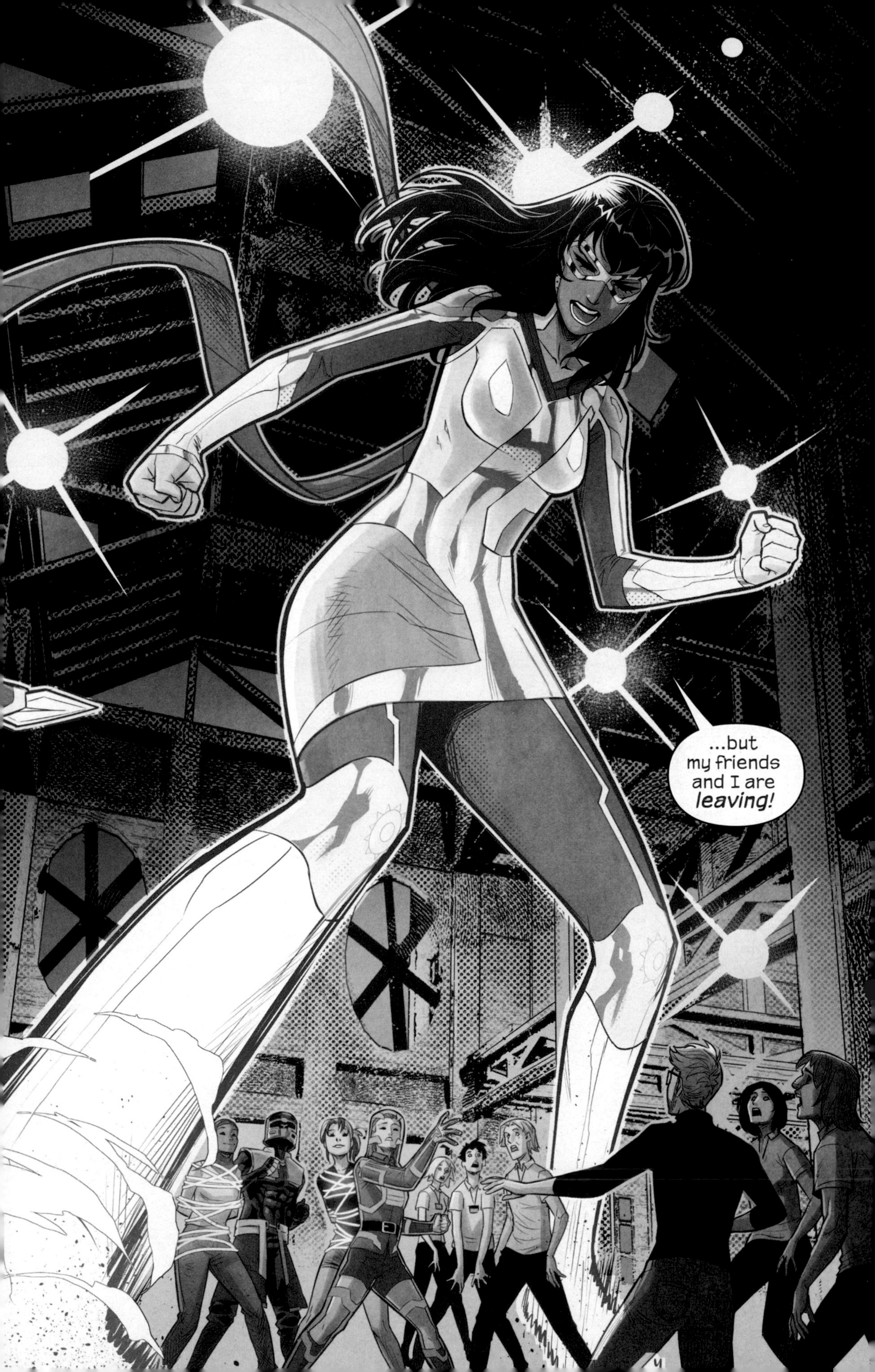
...but my friends and I are *leaving!*

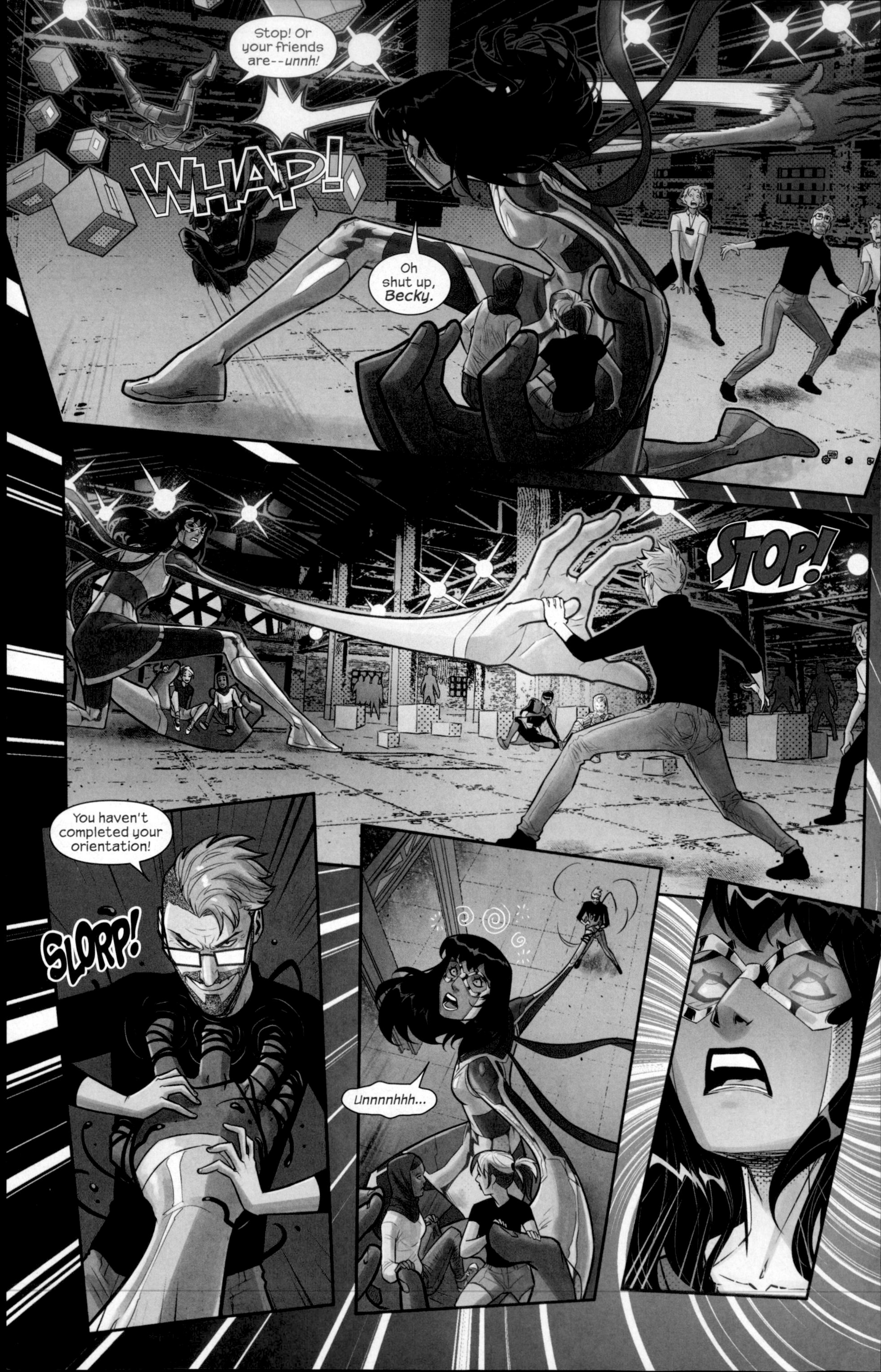
Stop! Or your friends are--unnh!
WHAP!
Oh shut up, Becky.
STOP!
You haven't completed your orientation!
SLORP!
Unnnnhhh...

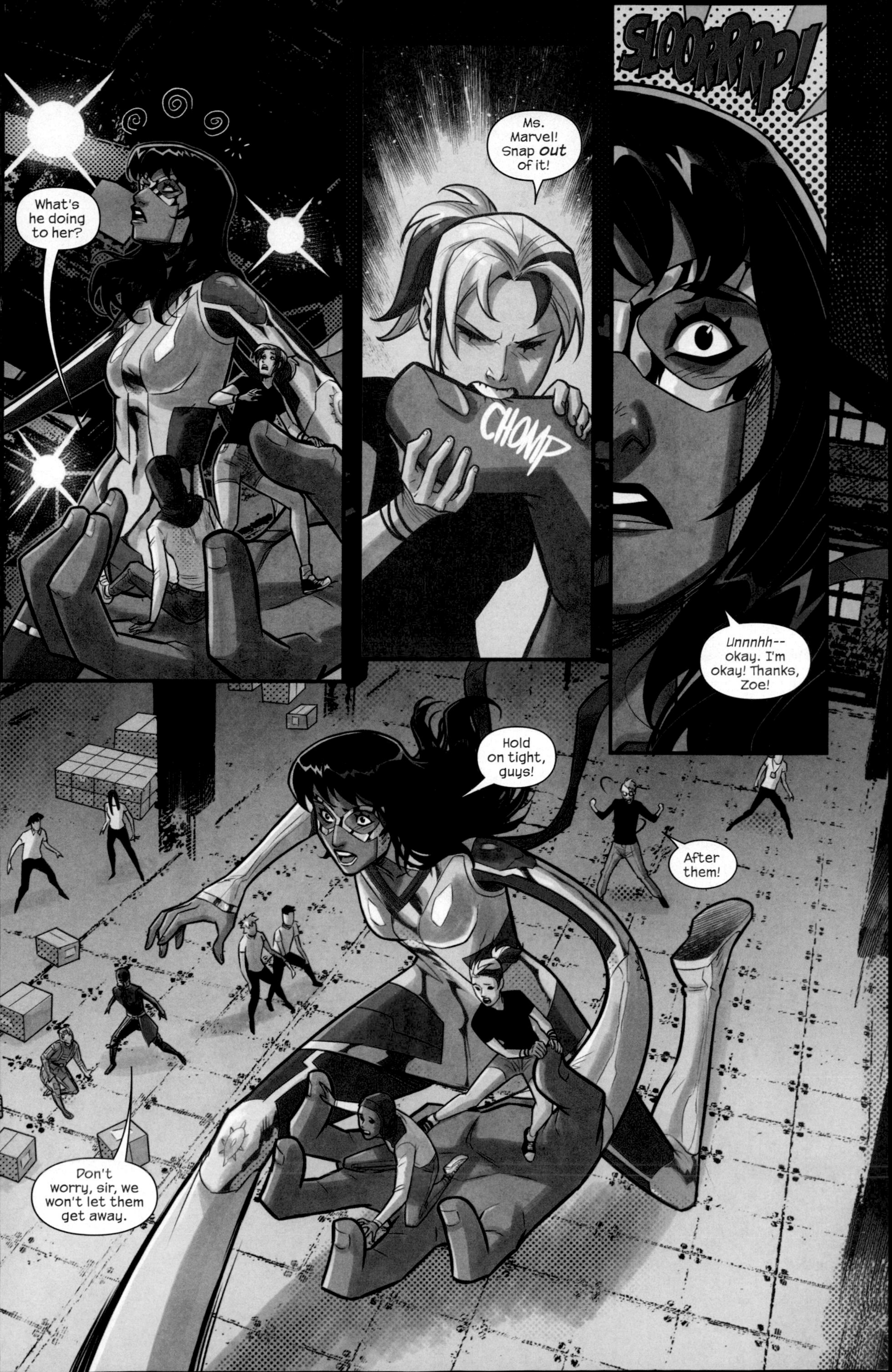
What's he doing to her?
Ms. Marvel! Snap out of it!
CHOMP
SLOORRRRP!
Unnnhh-- okay. I'm okay! Thanks, Zoe!
Hold on tight, guys!
After them!
Don't worry, sir, we won't let them get away.

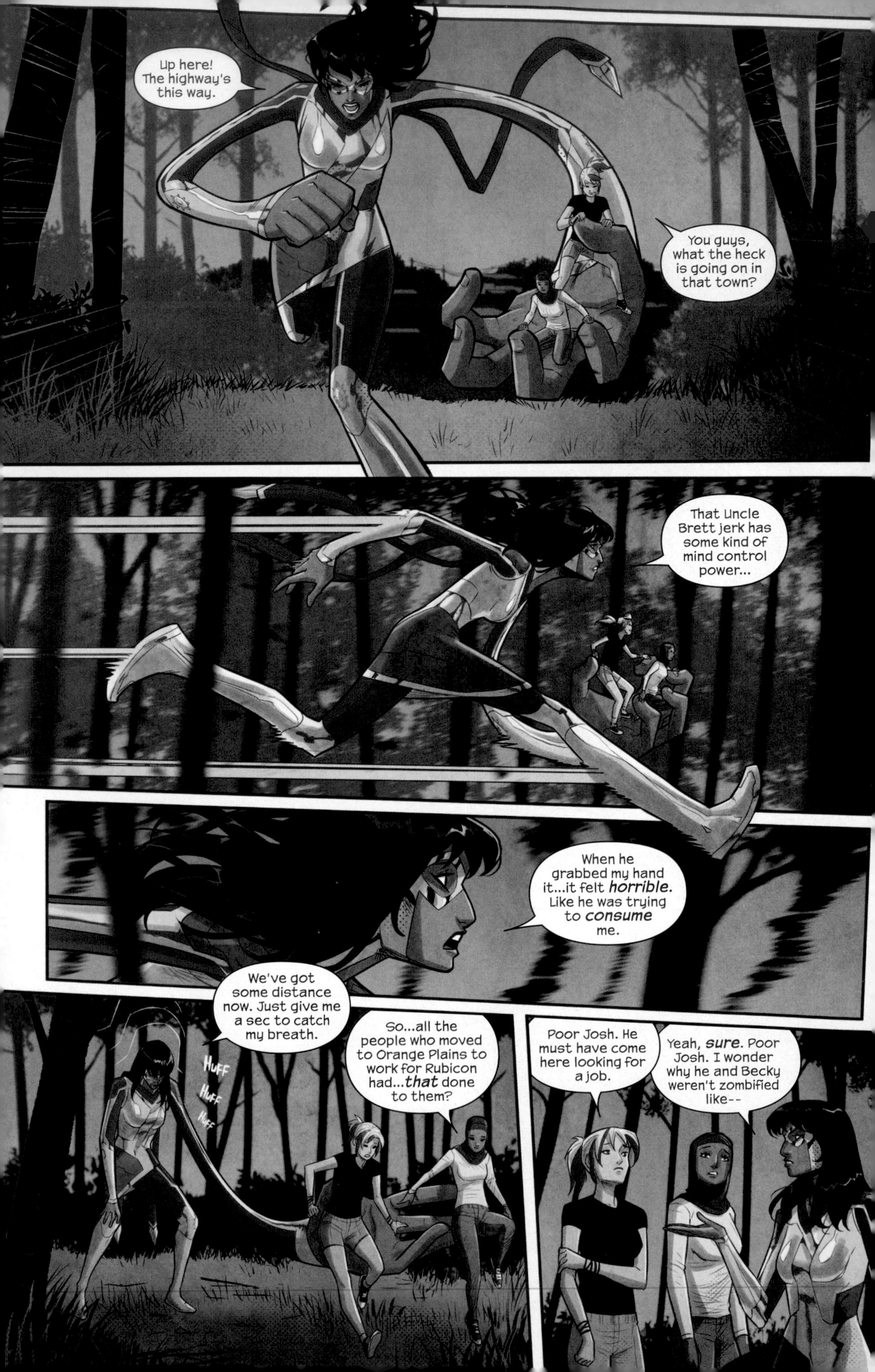
Up here! The highway's this way.
You guys, what the heck is going on in that town?
That Uncle Brett jerk has some kind of mind control power...
When he grabbed my hand it...it felt *horrible.* Like he was trying to *consume* me.
We've got some distance now. Just give me a sec to catch my breath.
HUFF HUFF HUFF
So...all the people who moved to Orange Plains to work for Rubicon had...*that* done to them?
Poor Josh. He must have come here looking for a job.
Yeah, *sure*. Poor Josh. I wonder why he and Becky weren't zombified like--

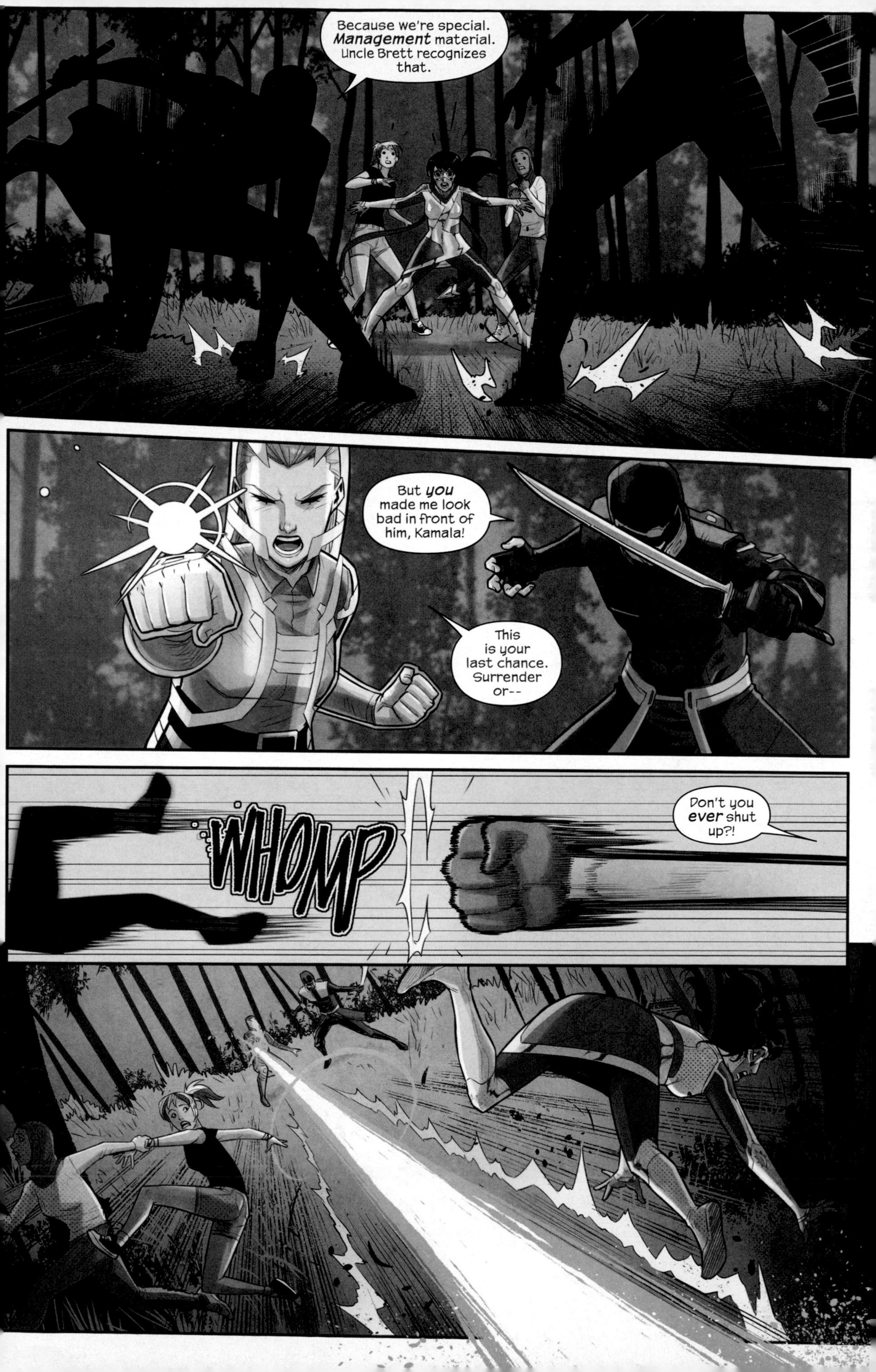

Because we're special. **Management** material. Uncle Brett recognizes that.
But **you** made me look bad in front of him, Kamala!
This is your last chance. Surrender or--
WHOMP
Don't you **ever** shut up?!

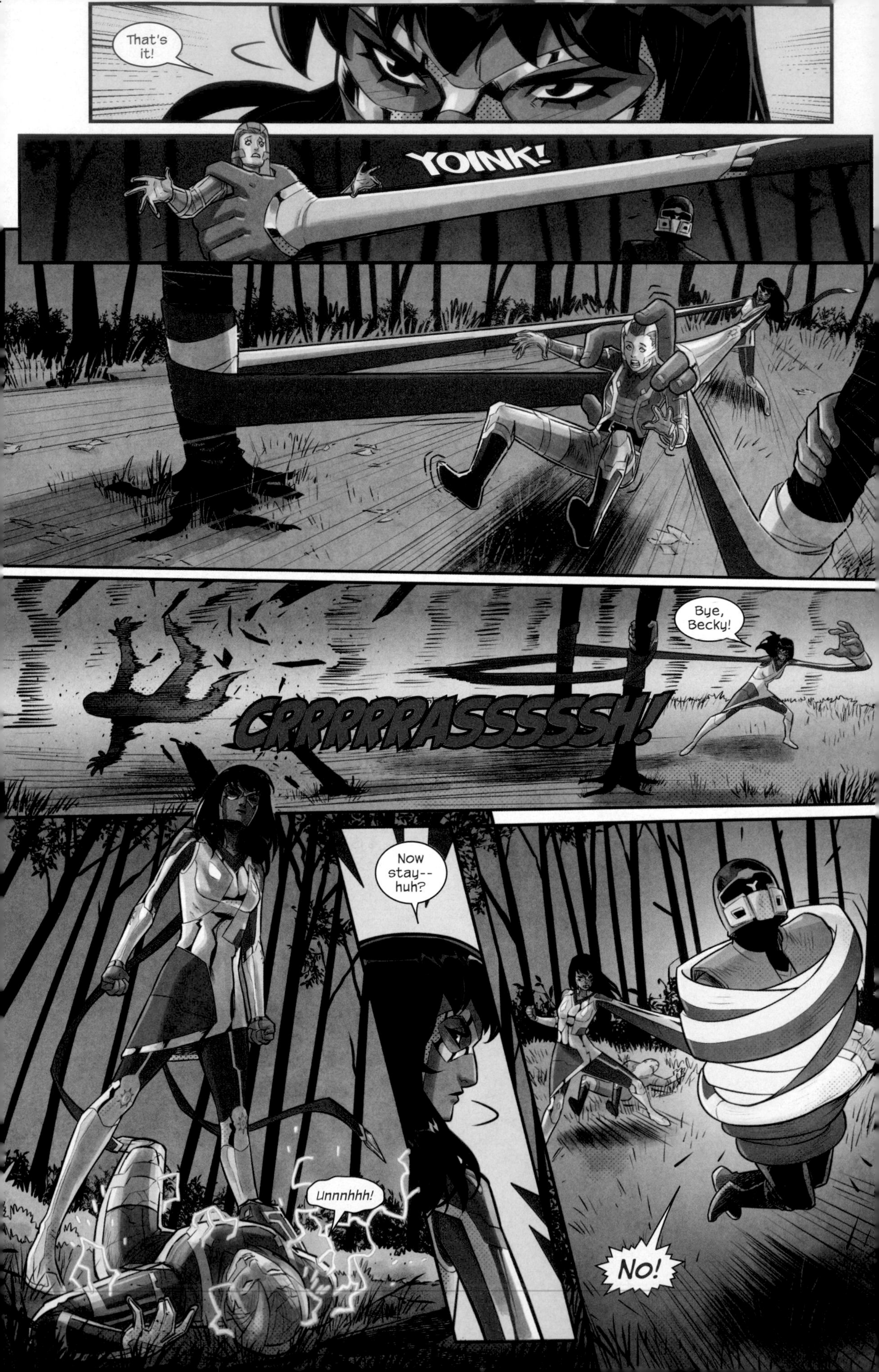
That's it!
YOINK!
Bye, Becky!
CRRRRRASSSSSH!
Now stay--huh?
Unnnhhh!
NO!

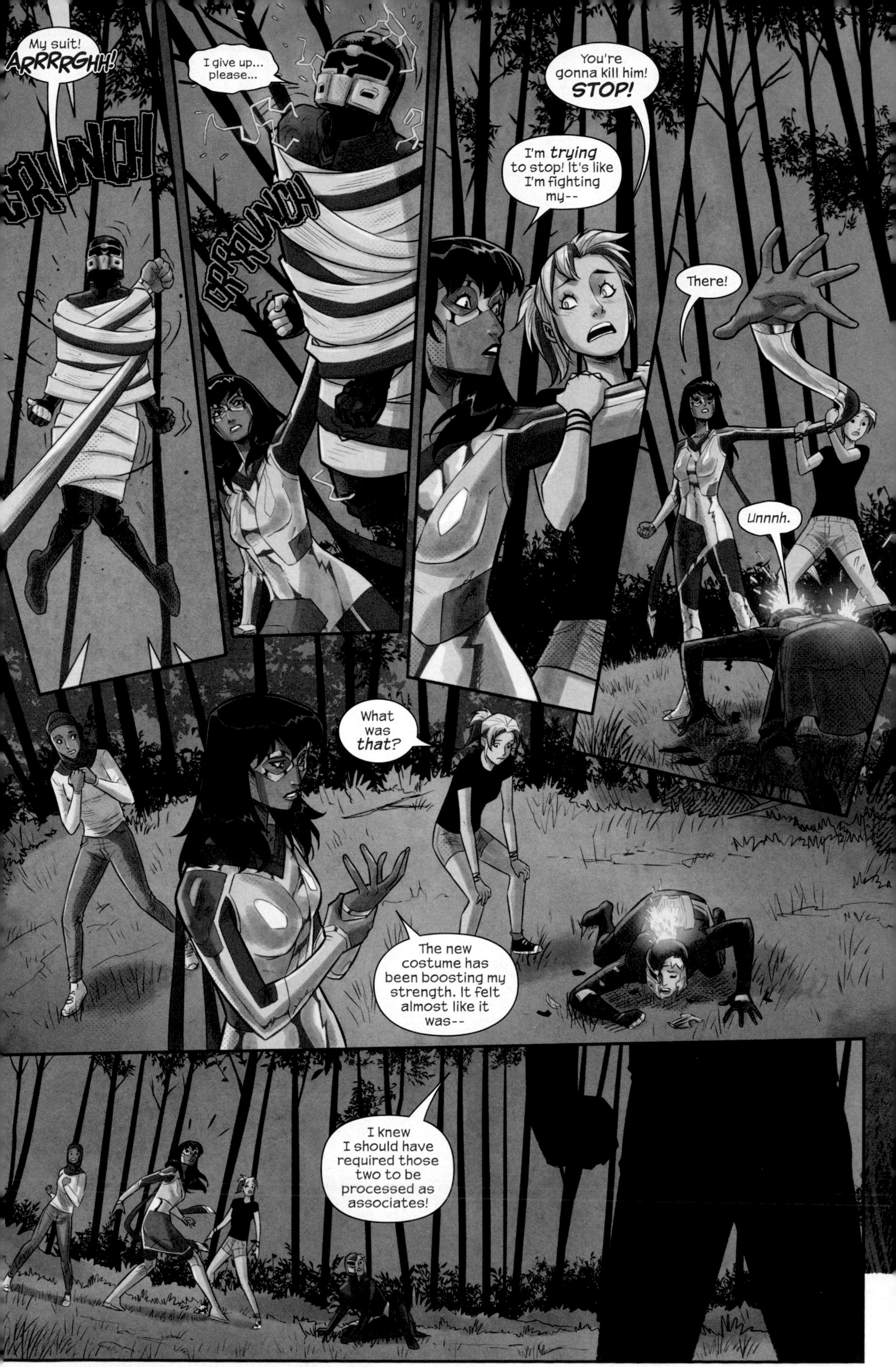
My suit! ARRRRGHH!
CRUNCH
I give up... please...
CRRUNCH
You're gonna kill him! STOP!
I'm trying to stop! It's like I'm fighting my--
There!
Unnnh.
What was that?
The new costume has been boosting my strength. It felt almost like it was--
I knew I should have required those two to be processed as associates!

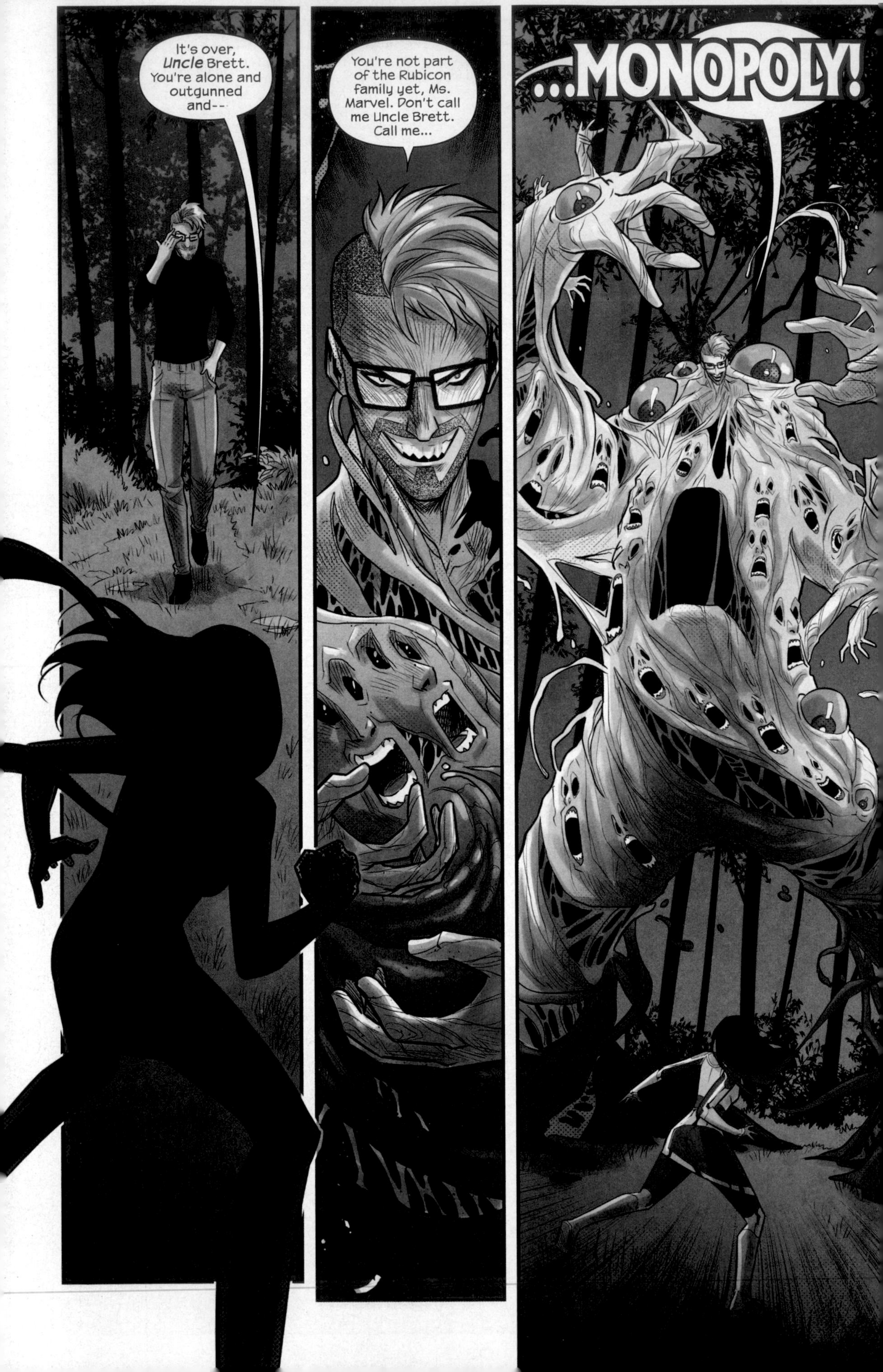

It's over, Uncle Brett. You're alone and outgunned and--
You're not part of the Rubicon family yet, Ms. Marvel. Don't call me Uncle Brett. Call me...
...MONOPOLY!

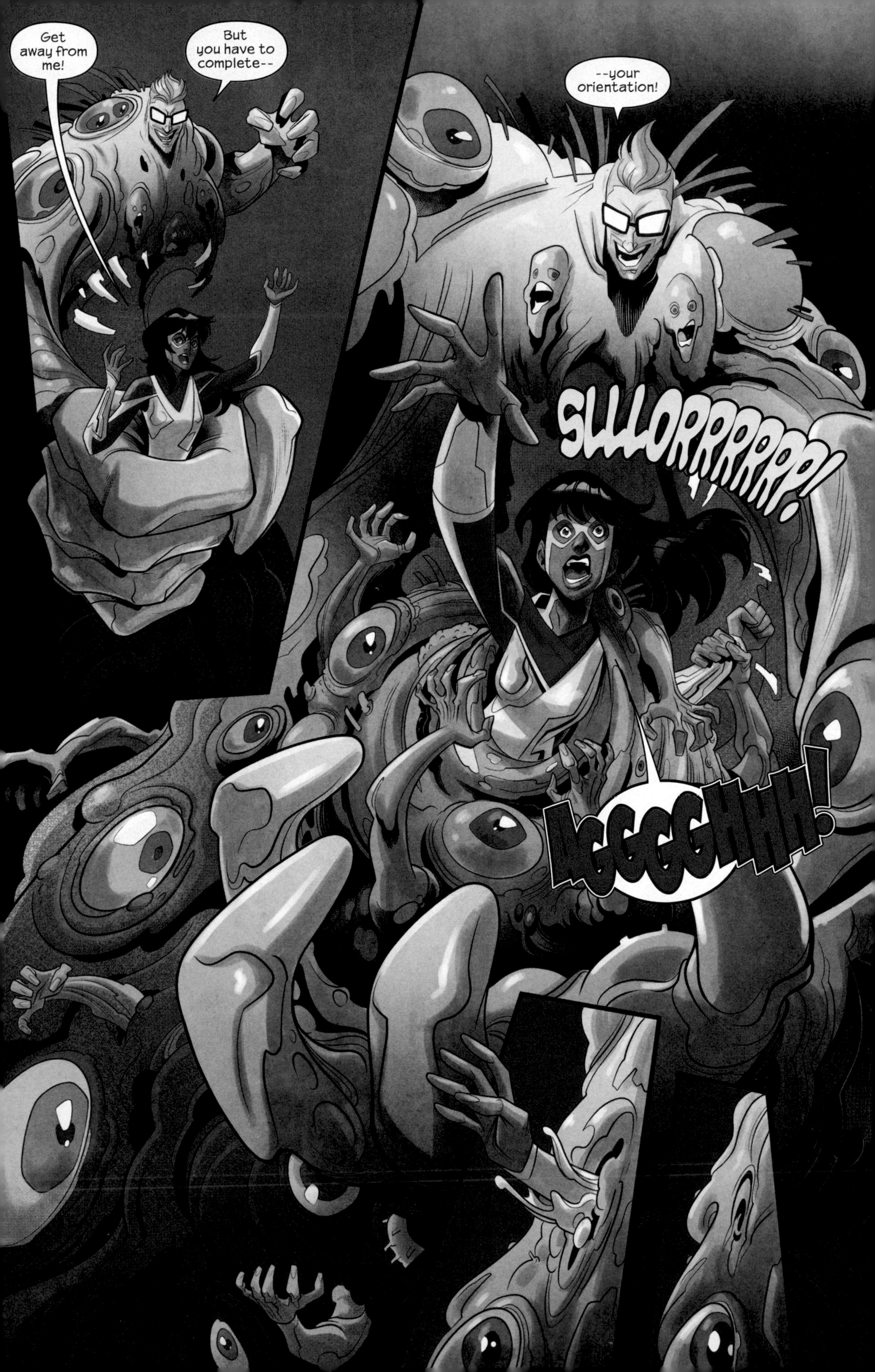
Get away from me!
But you have to complete--
--your orientation!
SLLLORRRRRRP!
AGGGHHHH!

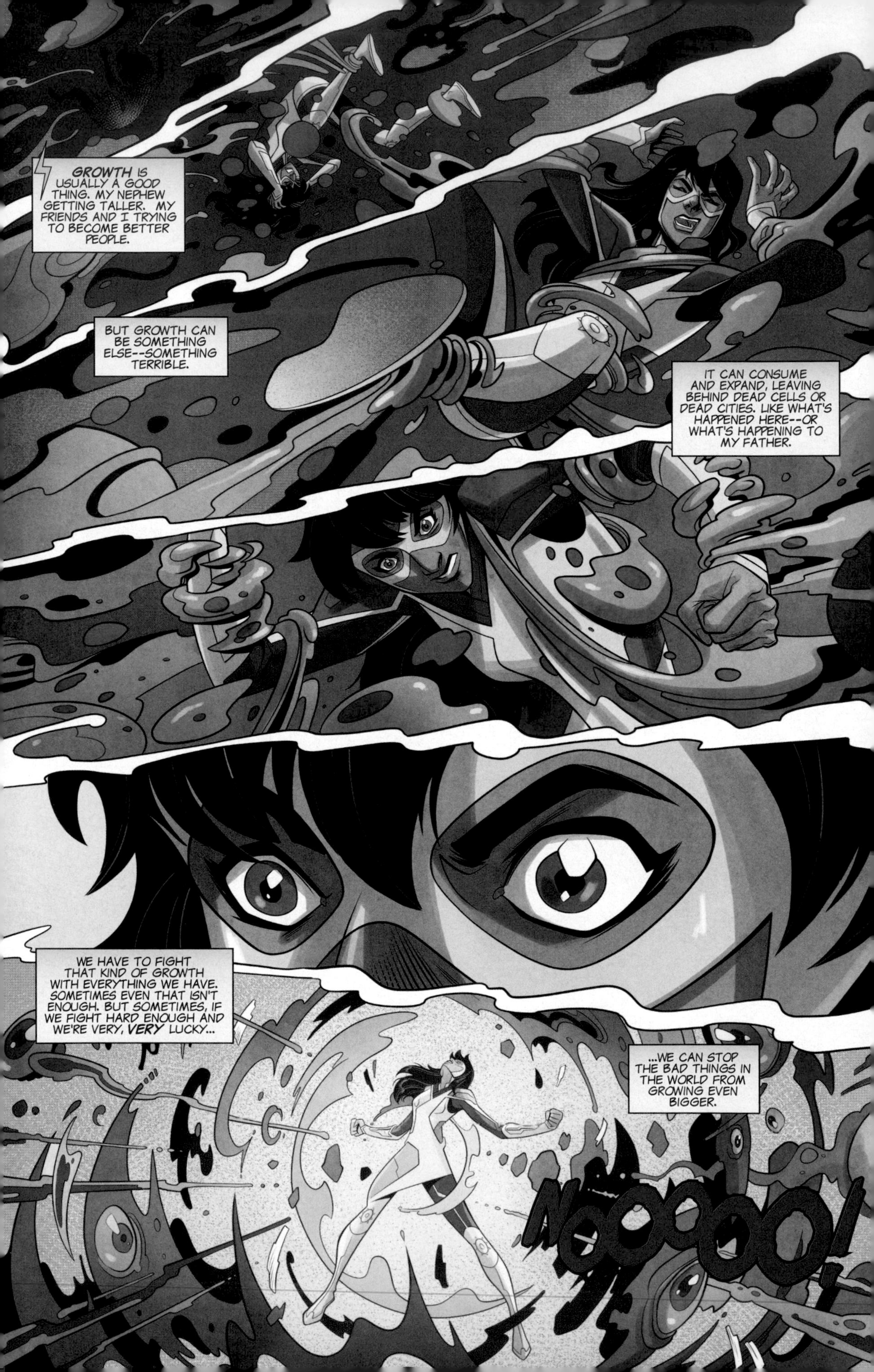
GROWTH IS USUALLY A GOOD THING. MY NEPHEW GETTING TALLER. MY FRIENDS AND I TRYING TO BECOME BETTER PEOPLE.
BUT GROWTH CAN BE SOMETHING ELSE--SOMETHING TERRIBLE.
IT CAN CONSUME AND EXPAND, LEAVING BEHIND DEAD CELLS OR DEAD CITIES. LIKE WHAT'S HAPPENED HERE--OR WHAT'S HAPPENING TO MY FATHER.
WE HAVE TO FIGHT THAT KIND OF GROWTH WITH EVERYTHING WE HAVE. SOMETIMES EVEN THAT ISN'T ENOUGH. BUT SOMETIMES, IF WE FIGHT HARD ENOUGH AND WE'RE VERY, VERY LUCKY...
...WE CAN STOP THE BAD THINGS IN THE WORLD FROM GROWING EVEN BIGGER.
NOOOOOO!

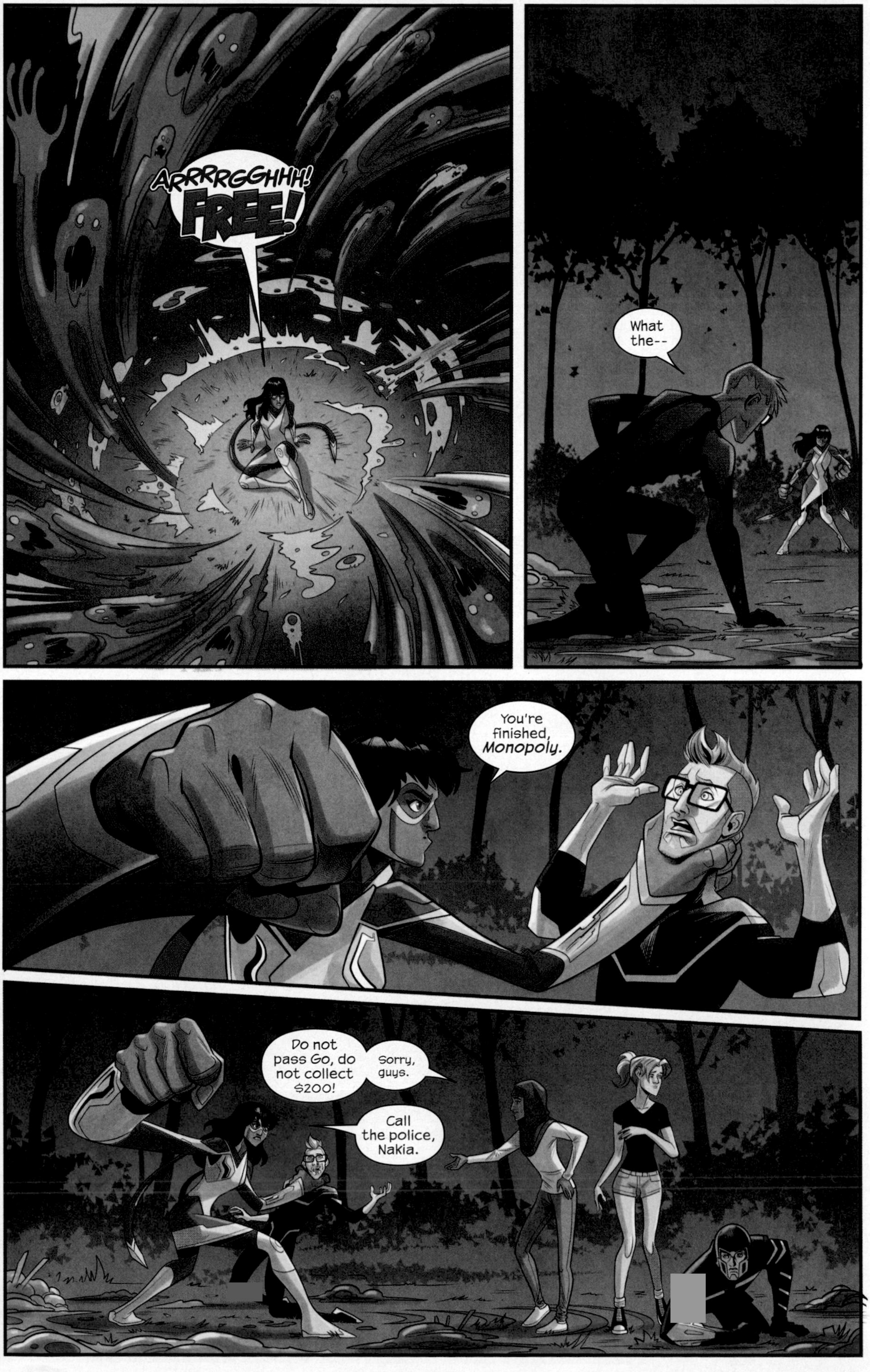
ARRRRGGHHH! FREE!
What the--
You're finished, *Monopoly.*
Do not pass Go, do not collect $200!
Sorry, guys.
Call the police, Nakia.

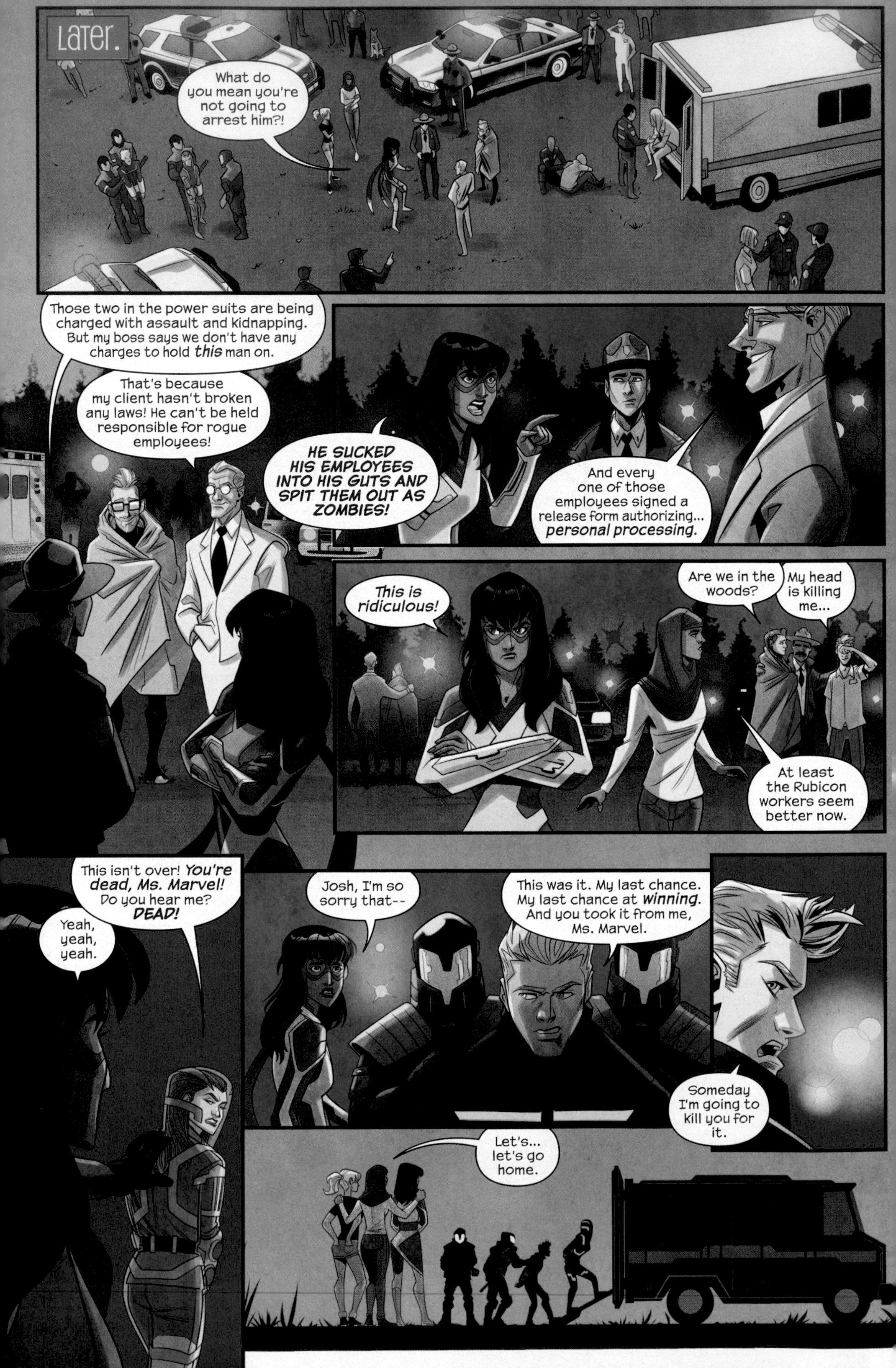
LATER.
What do you mean you're not going to arrest him?!
Those two in the power suits are being charged with assault and kidnapping. But my boss says we don't have any charges to hold *this* man on.
That's because my client hasn't broken any laws! He can't be held responsible for rogue employees!
HE SUCKED HIS EMPLOYEES INTO HIS GUTS AND SPIT THEM OUT AS ZOMBIES!
And every one of those employees signed a release form authorizing... *personal processing.*
This is ridiculous!
Are we in the woods?
My head is killing me...
At least the Rubicon workers seem better now.
This isn't over! *You're dead, Ms. Marvel!* Do you hear me? *DEAD!*
Yeah, yeah, yeah.
Josh, I'm so sorry that--
This was it. My last chance. My last chance at *winning*. And you took it from me, Ms. Marvel.
Someday I'm going to kill you for it.
Let's... let's go home.

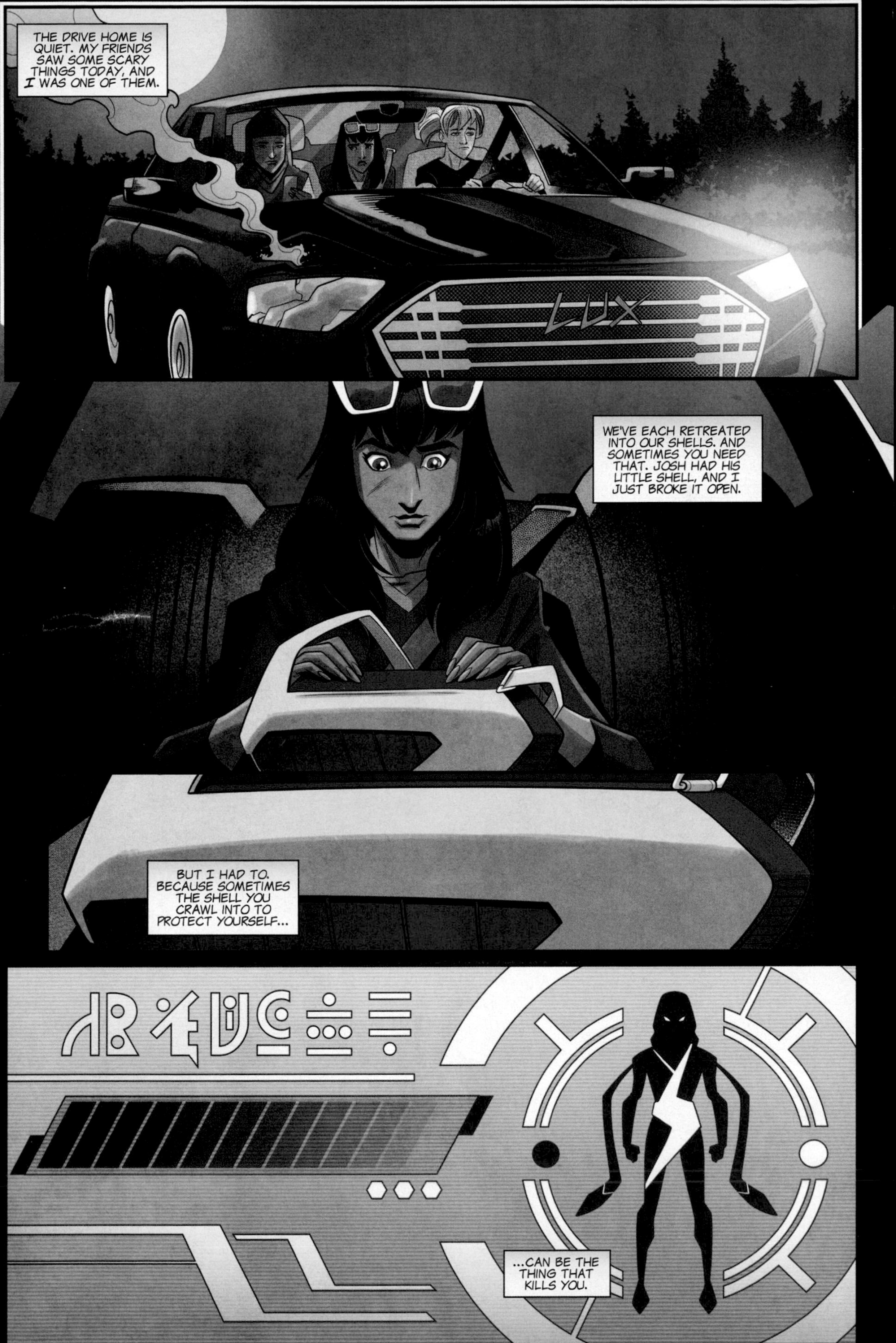
THE DRIVE HOME IS QUIET. MY FRIENDS SAW SOME SCARY THINGS TODAY, AND I WAS ONE OF THEM.
LUX
WE'VE EACH RETREATED INTO OUR SHELLS. AND SOMETIMES YOU NEED THAT. JOSH HAD HIS LITTLE SHELL, AND I JUST BROKE IT OPEN.
BUT I HAD TO. BECAUSE SOMETIMES THE SHELL YOU CRAWL INTO TO PROTECT YOURSELF...
...CAN BE THE THING THAT KILLS YOU.

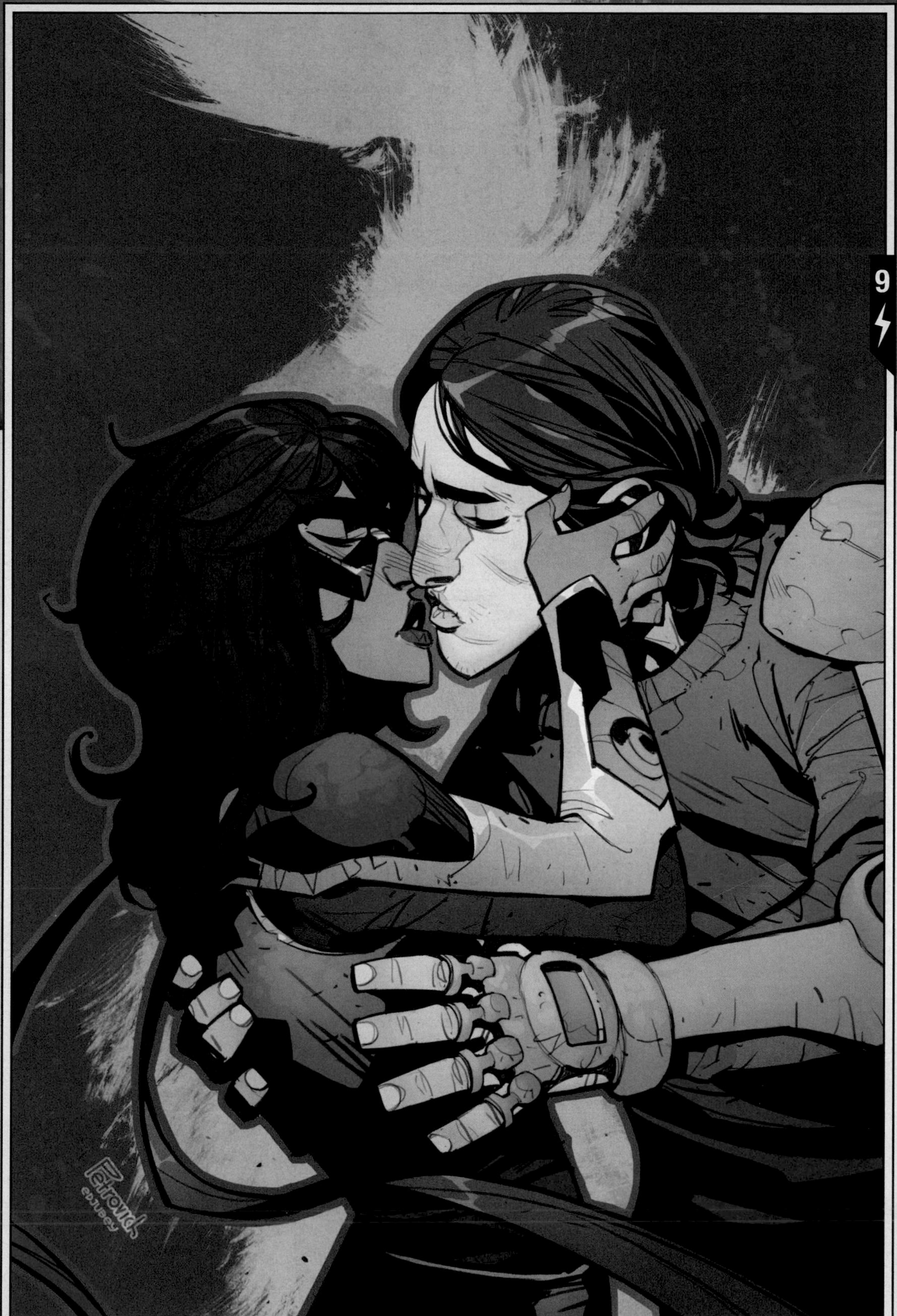

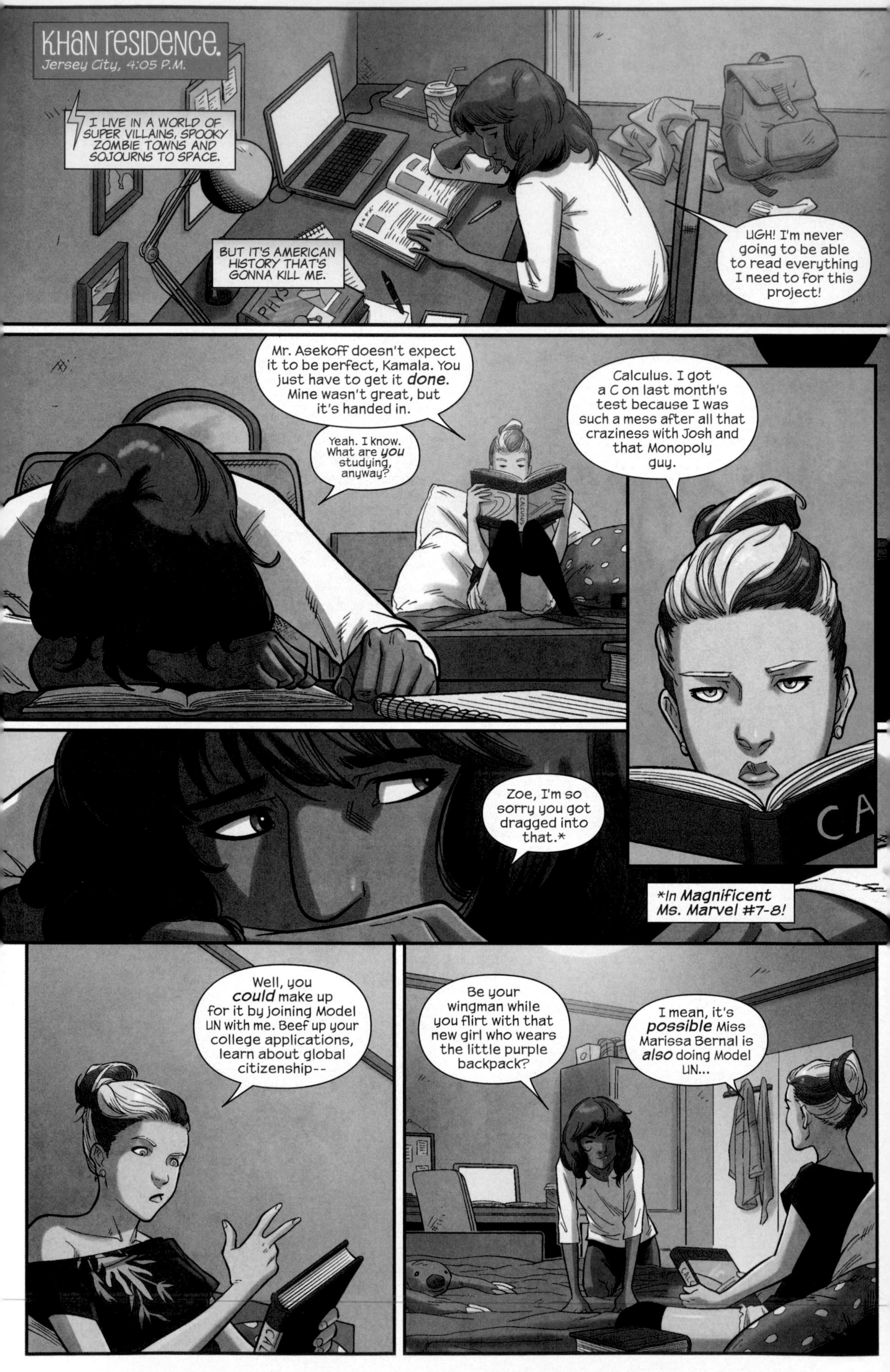

Khan residence.
Jersey City, 4:05 P.M.
I LIVE IN A WORLD OF SUPER VILLAINS, SPOOKY ZOMBIE TOWNS AND SOJOURNS TO SPACE.
BUT IT'S AMERICAN HISTORY THAT'S GONNA KILL ME.
UGH! I'm never going to be able to read everything I need to for this project!
Mr. Asekoff doesn't expect it to be perfect, Kamala. You just have to get it done. Mine wasn't great, but it's handed in.
Yeah. I know. What are you studying, anyway?
Calculus. I got a C on last month's test because I was such a mess after all that craziness with Josh and that Monopoly guy.
Zoe, I'm so sorry you got dragged into that.*
*In Magnificent Ms. Marvel #7-8!
Well, you could make up for it by joining Model UN with me. Beef up your college applications, learn about global citizenship--
Be your wingman while you flirt with that new girl who wears the little purple backpack?
I mean, it's possible Miss Marissa Bernal is also doing Model UN...

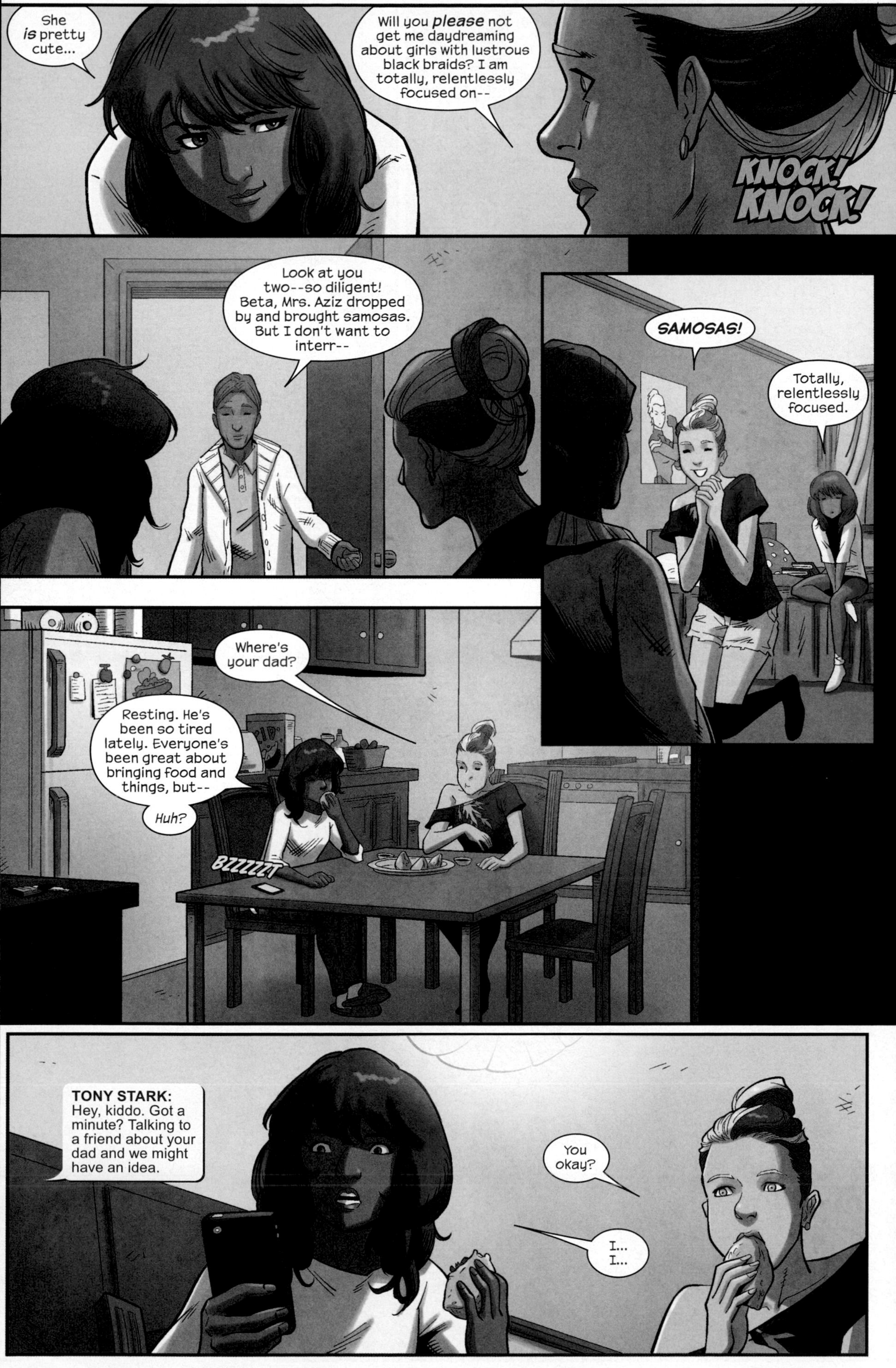

She *is* pretty cute...
Will you *please* not get me daydreaming about girls with lustrous black braids? I am totally, relentlessly focused on--
KNOCK! KNOCK!
Look at you two--so diligent! Beta, Mrs. Aziz dropped by and brought samosas. But I don't want to interr--
SAMOSAS!
Totally, relentlessly focused.
Where's your dad?
Resting. He's been so tired lately. Everyone's been great about bringing food and things, but--
Huh?
BZZZZZT
TONY STARK: Hey, kiddo. Got a minute? Talking to a friend about your dad and we might have an idea.
You okay?
I... I...

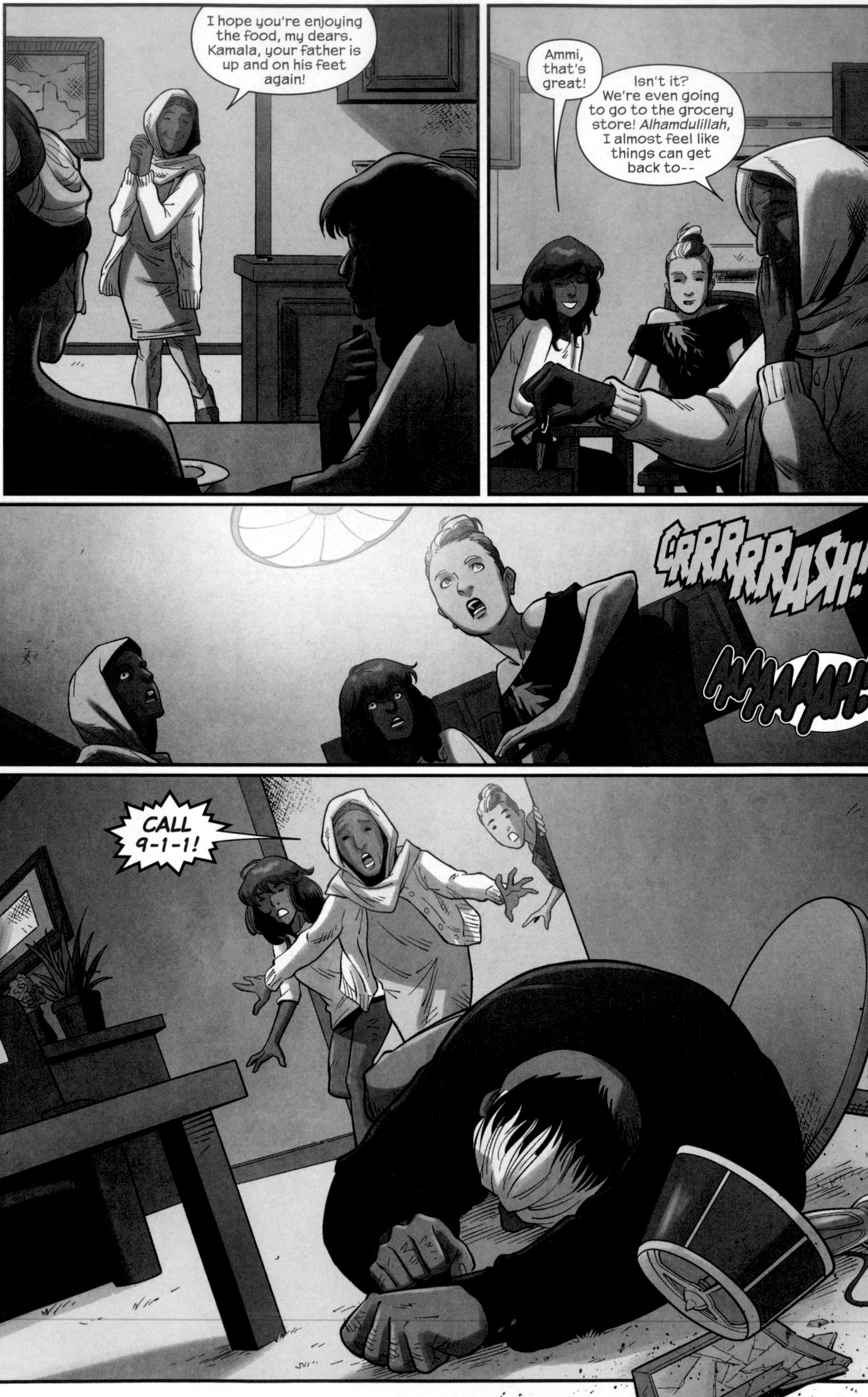
I hope you're enjoying the food, my dears. Kamala, your father is up and on his feet again!
Ammi, that's great!
Isn't it? We're even going to go to the grocery store! *Alhamdulillah*, I almost feel like things can get back to--
CRRRRRASH!
AAAAAAH!
CALL 9-1-1!

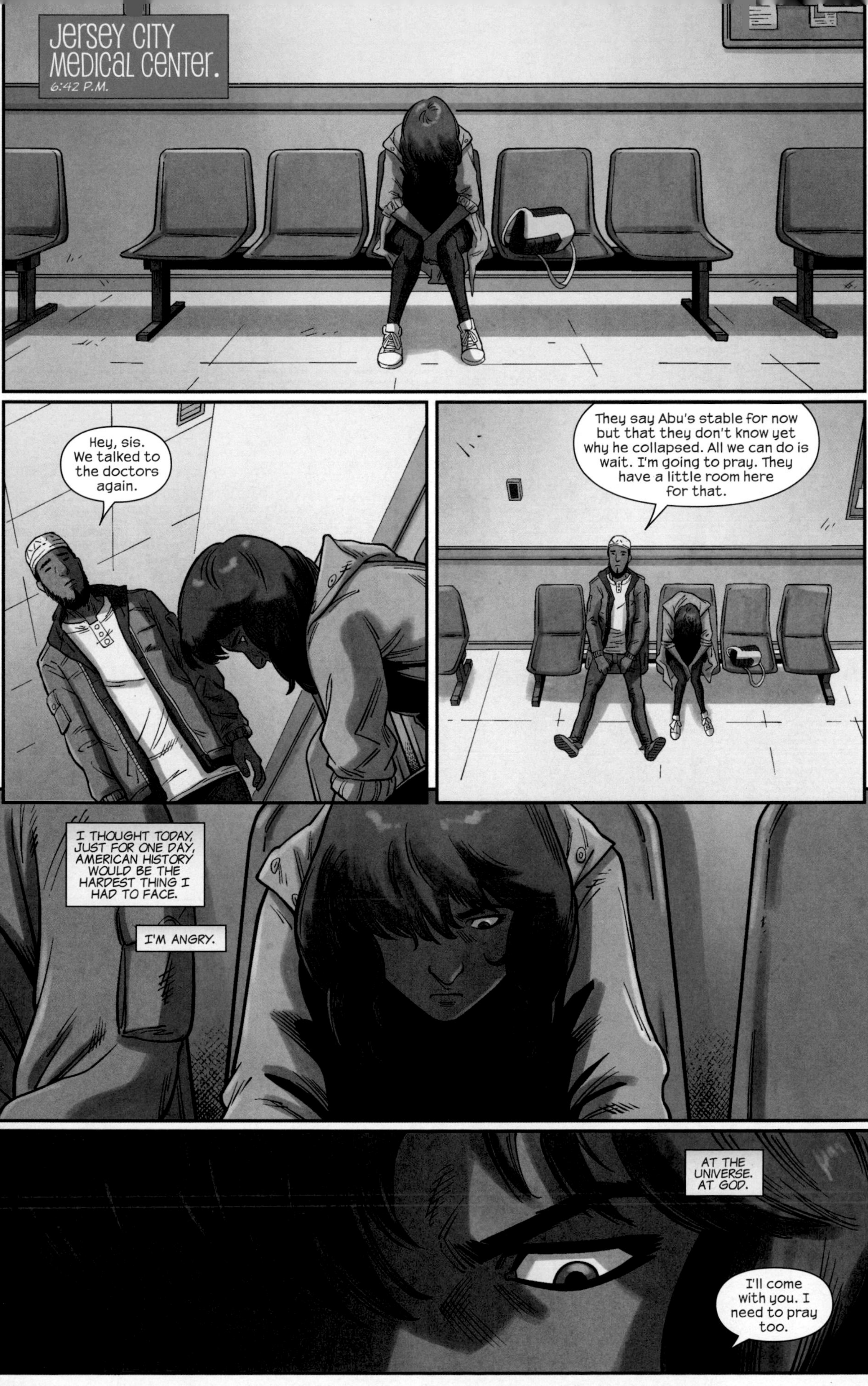
Jersey City Medical Center.
6:42 P.M.
Hey, sis. We talked to the doctors again.
They say Abu's stable for now but that they don't know yet why he collapsed. All we can do is wait. I'm going to pray. They have a little room here for that.
I THOUGHT TODAY, JUST FOR ONE DAY, AMERICAN HISTORY WOULD BE THE HARDEST THING I HAD TO FACE.
I'M ANGRY.
AT THE UNIVERSE. AT GOD.
I'll come with you. I need to pray too.

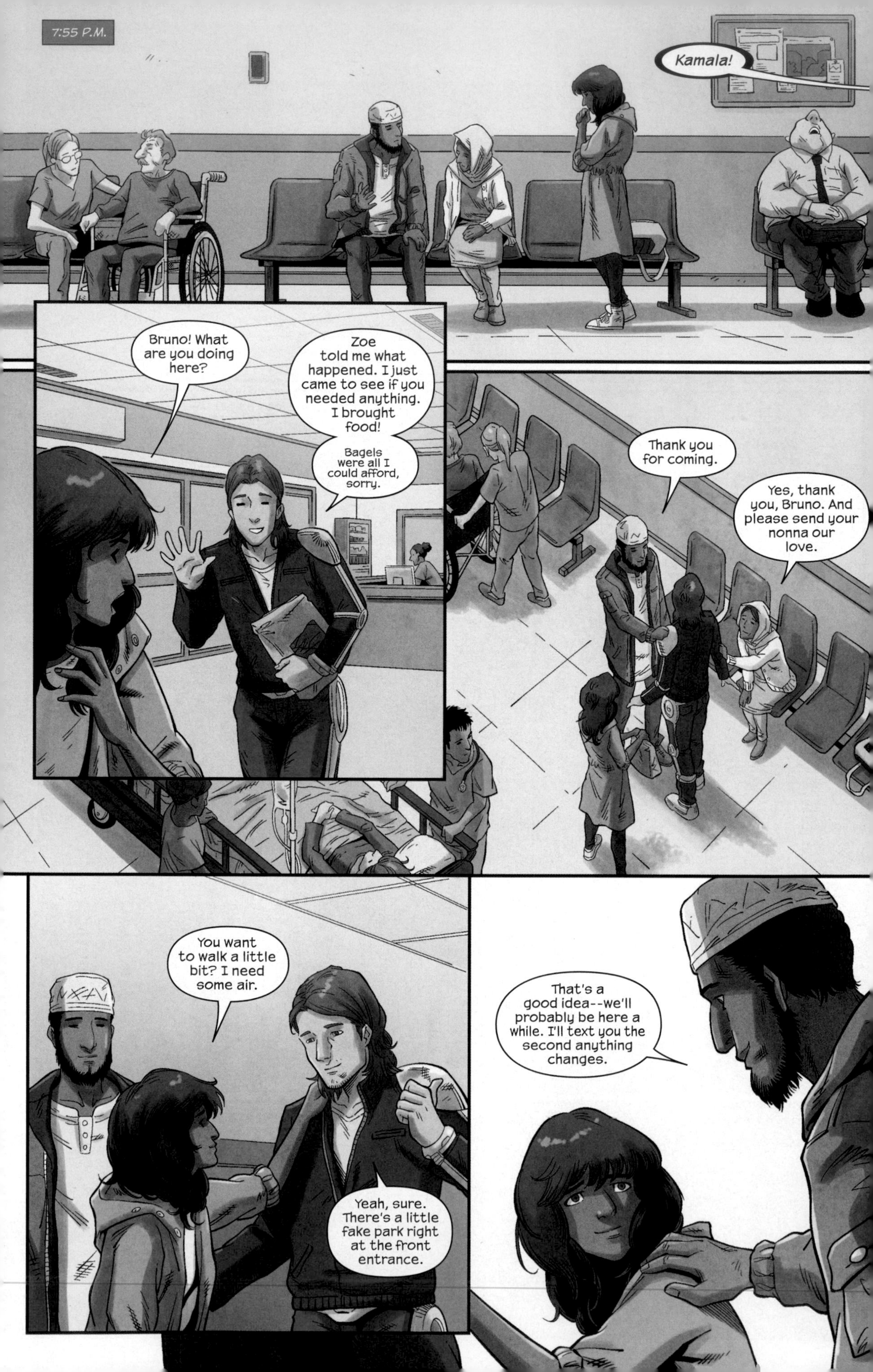
7:55 P.M.
Kamala!
Bruno! What are you doing here?
Zoe told me what happened. I just came to see if you needed anything. I brought food!
Bagels were all I could afford, sorry.
Thank you for coming.
Yes, thank you, Bruno. And please send your nonna our love.
You want to walk a little bit? I need some air.
Yeah, sure. There's a little fake park right at the front entrance.
That's a good idea--we'll probably be here a while. I'll text you the second anything changes.

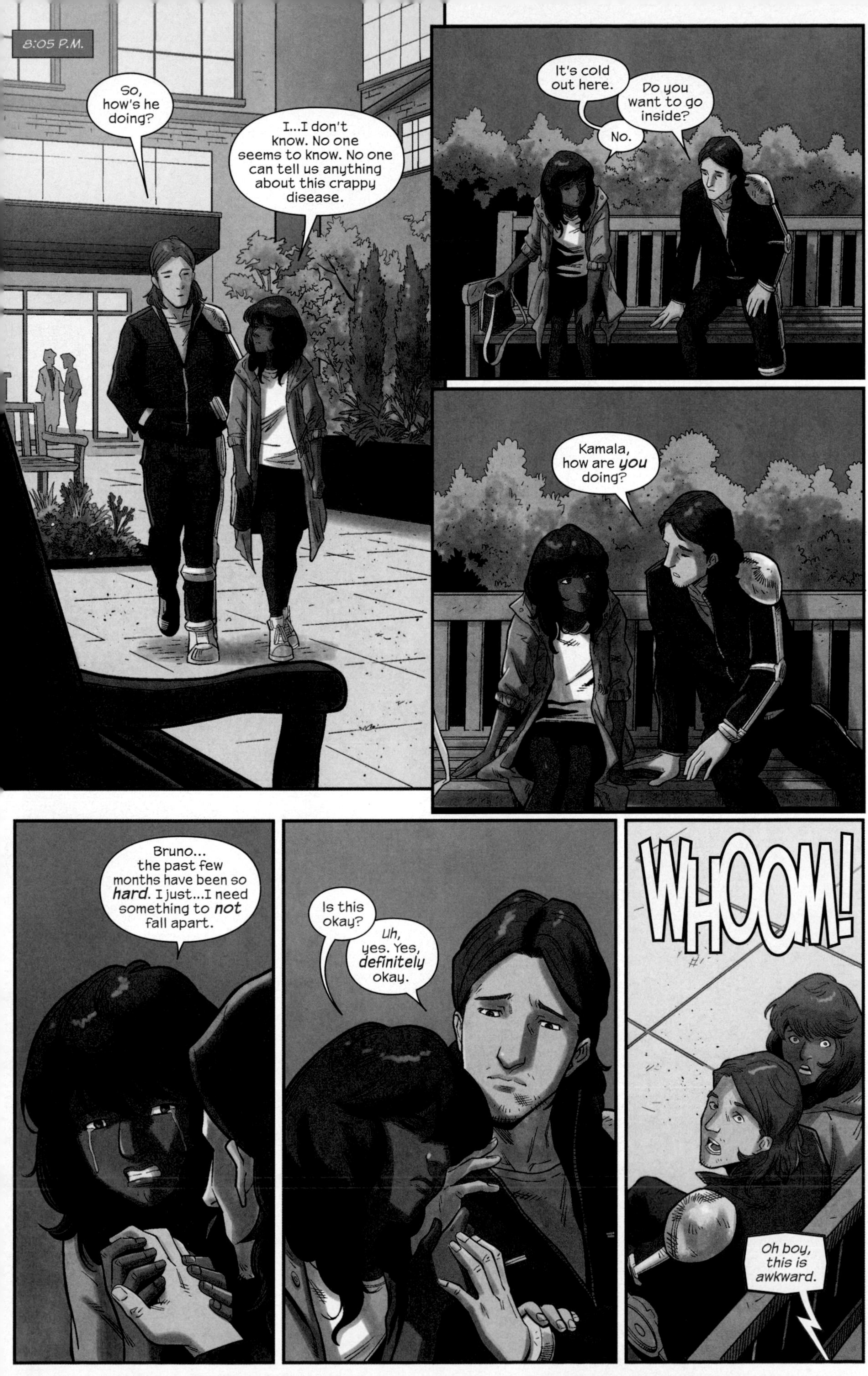
8:05 P.M.
So, how's he doing?
I...I don't know. No one seems to know. No one can tell us anything about this crappy disease.
It's cold out here.
Do you want to go inside?
No.
Kamala, how are *you* doing?
Bruno... the past few months have been so ***hard***. I just...I need something to ***not*** fall apart.
Is this okay?
Uh, yes. Yes, *definitely* okay.
WHOOM!
Oh boy, this is awkward.

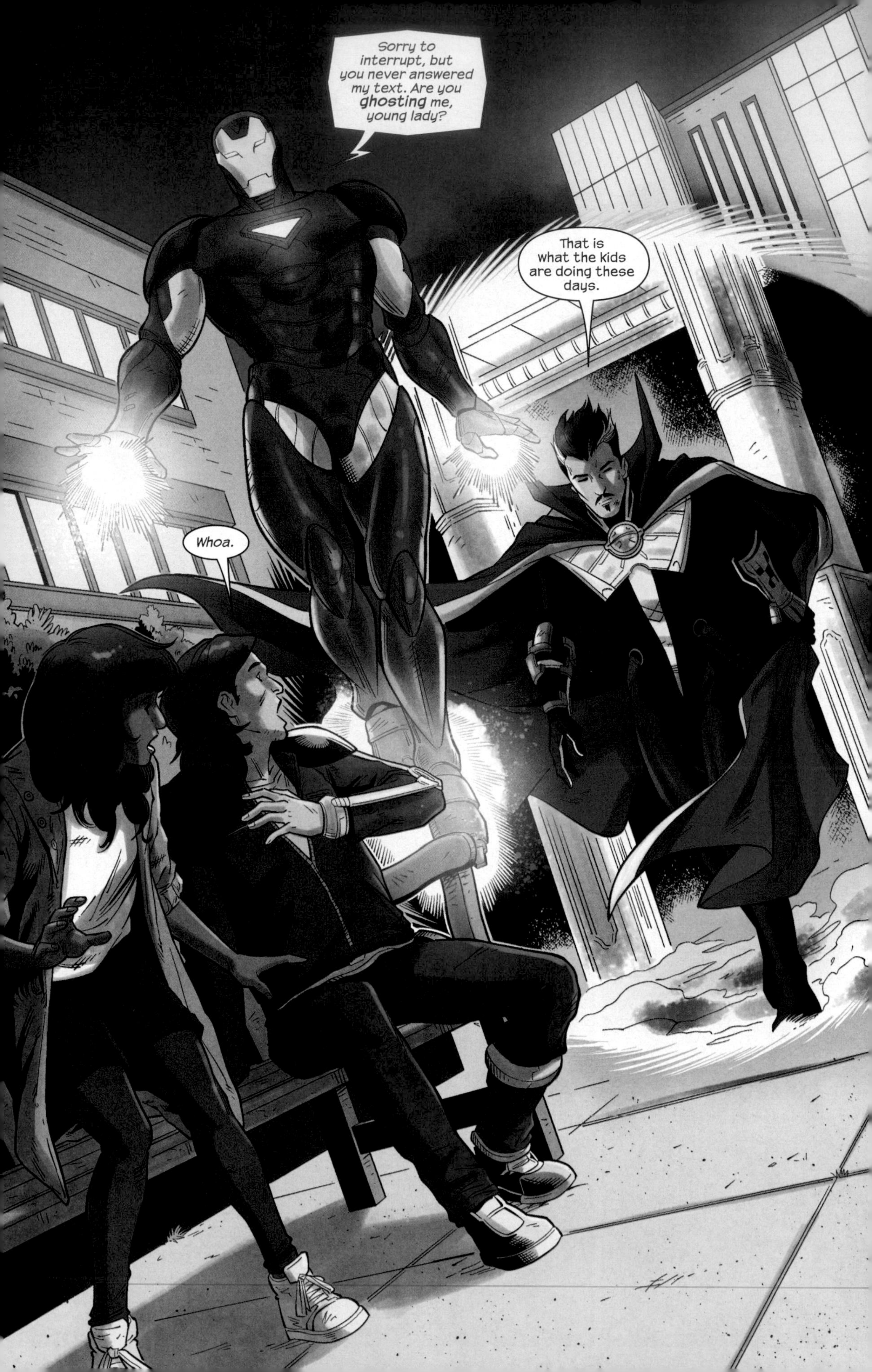
Sorry to interrupt, but you never answered my text. Are you **ghosting** me, young lady?
That is what the kids are doing these days.
Whoa.

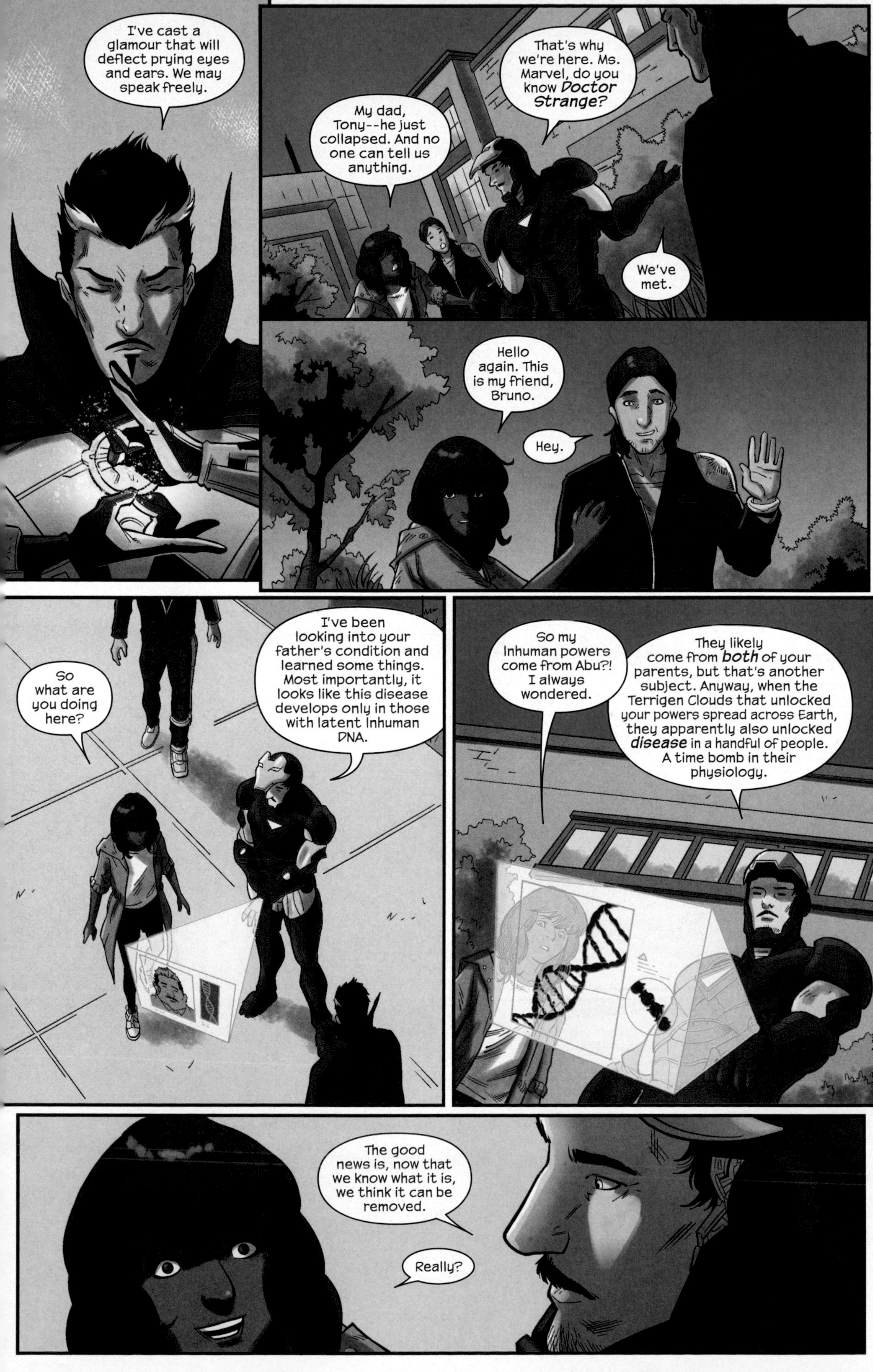
I've cast a glamour that will deflect prying eyes and ears. We may speak freely.
My dad, Tony--he just collapsed. And no one can tell us anything.
That's why we're here. Ms. Marvel, do you know *Doctor Strange*?
We've met.
Hello again. This is my friend, Bruno.
Hey.
So what are you doing here?
I've been looking into your father's condition and learned some things. Most importantly, it looks like this disease develops only in those with latent Inhuman DNA.
So my Inhuman powers come from Abu?! I always wondered.
They likely come from ***both*** of your parents, but that's another subject. Anyway, when the Terrigen Clouds that unlocked your powers spread across Earth, they apparently also unlocked ***disease*** in a handful of people. A time bomb in their physiology.
The good news is, now that we know what it is, we think it can be removed.
Really?

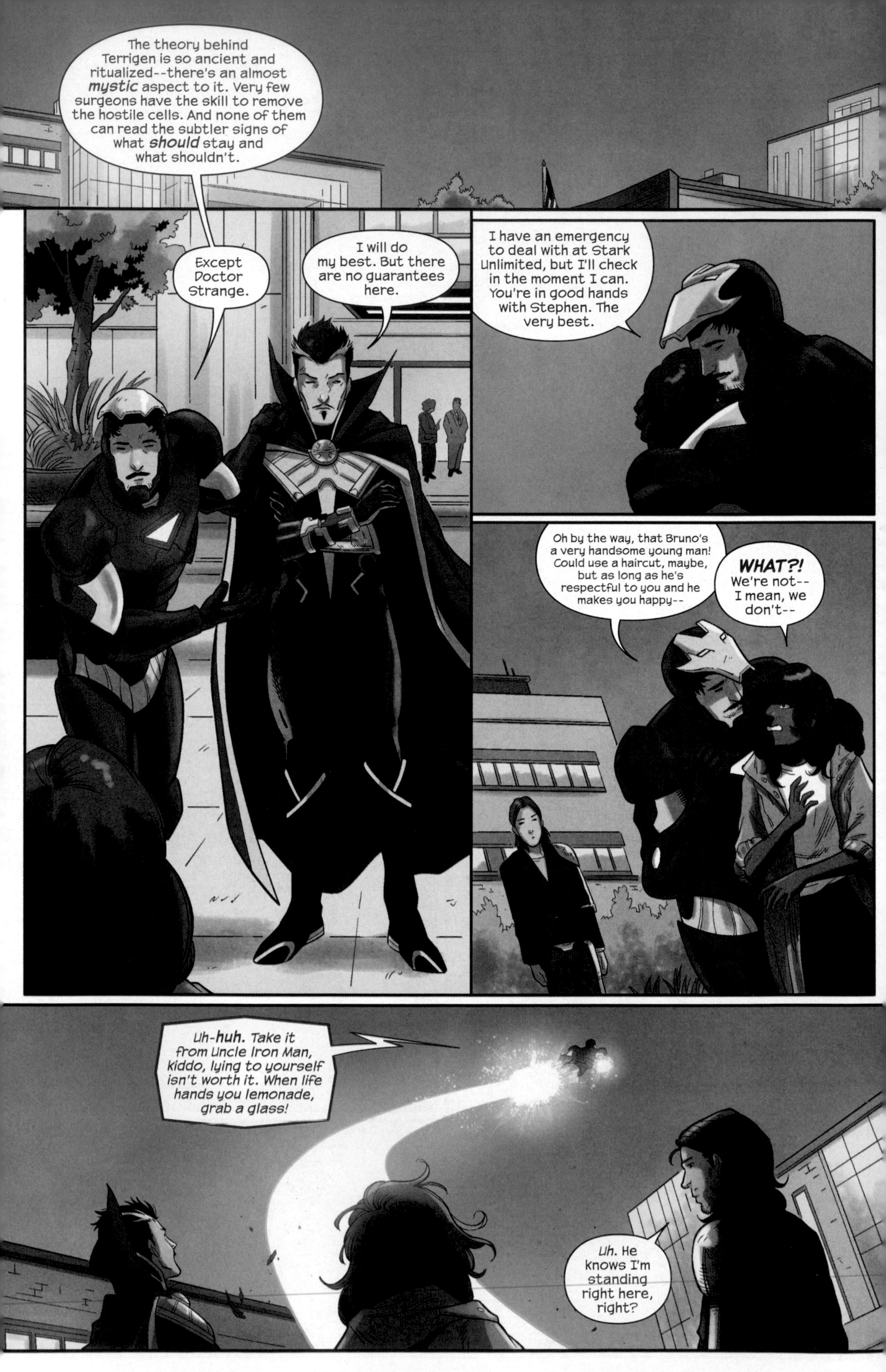
The theory behind Terrigen is so ancient and ritualized--there's an almost *mystic* aspect to it. Very few surgeons have the skill to remove the hostile cells. And none of them can read the subtler signs of what *should* stay and what shouldn't.
Except Doctor Strange.
I will do my best. But there are no guarantees here.
I have an emergency to deal with at Stark Unlimited, but I'll check in the moment I can. You're in good hands with Stephen. The very best.
Oh by the way, that Bruno's a very handsome young man! Could use a haircut, maybe, but as long as he's respectful to you and he makes you happy--
WHAT?! We're not-- I mean, we don't--
*Uh-**huh.** Take it from Uncle Iron Man, kiddo, lying to yourself isn't worth it. When life hands you lemonade, grab a glass!*
Uh. He knows I'm standing right here, right?

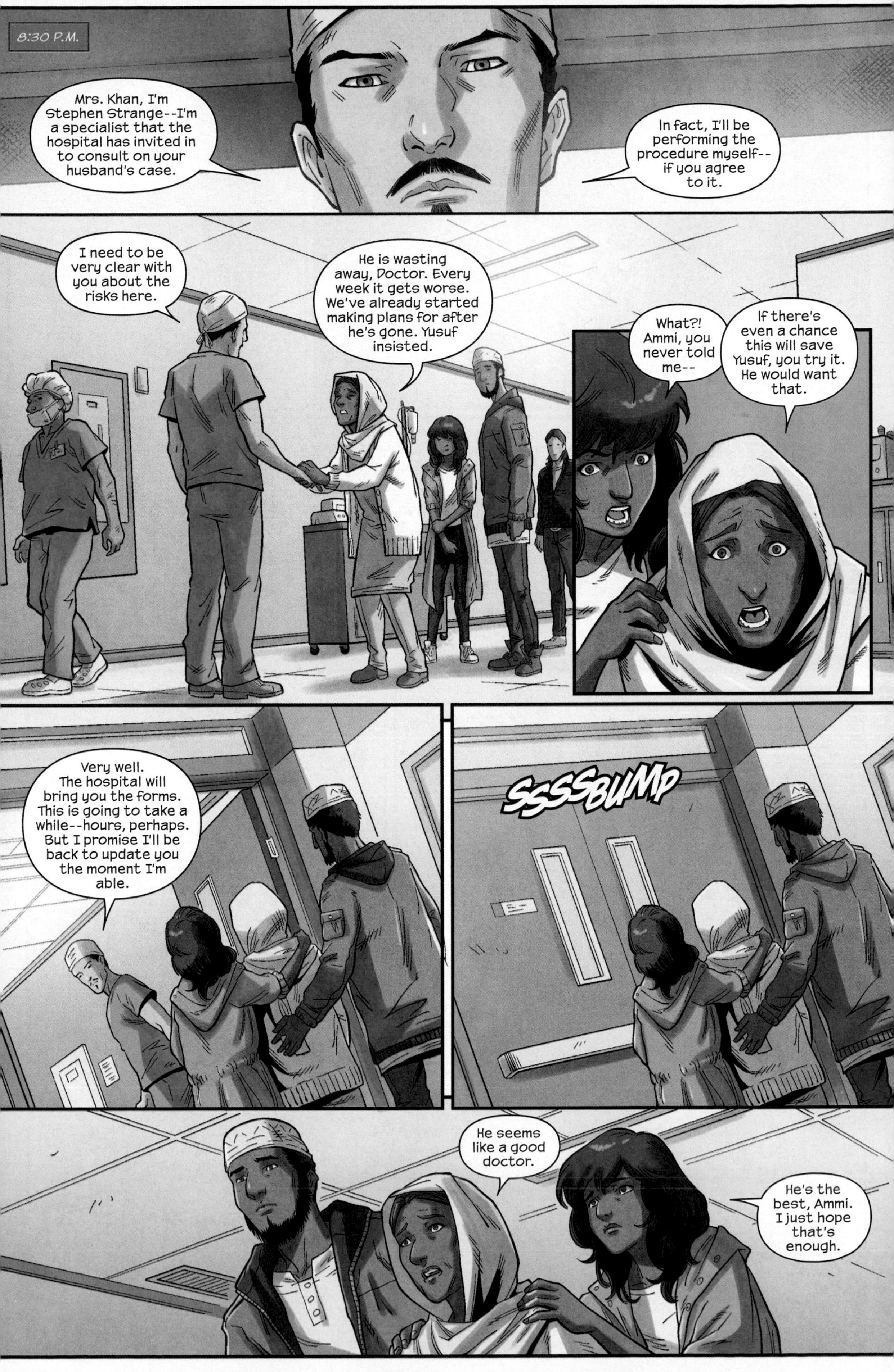
8:30 P.M.
Mrs. Khan, I'm Stephen Strange--I'm a specialist that the hospital has invited in to consult on your husband's case.
In fact, I'll be performing the procedure myself--if you agree to it.
I need to be very clear with you about the risks here.
He is wasting away, Doctor. Every week it gets worse. We've already started making plans for after he's gone. Yusuf insisted.
What?! Ammi, you never told me--
If there's even a chance this will save Yusuf, you try it. He would want that.
Very well. The hospital will bring you the forms. This is going to take a while--hours, perhaps. But I promise I'll be back to update you the moment I'm able.
SSSSBUMP
He seems like a good doctor.
He's the best, Ammi. I just hope that's enough.

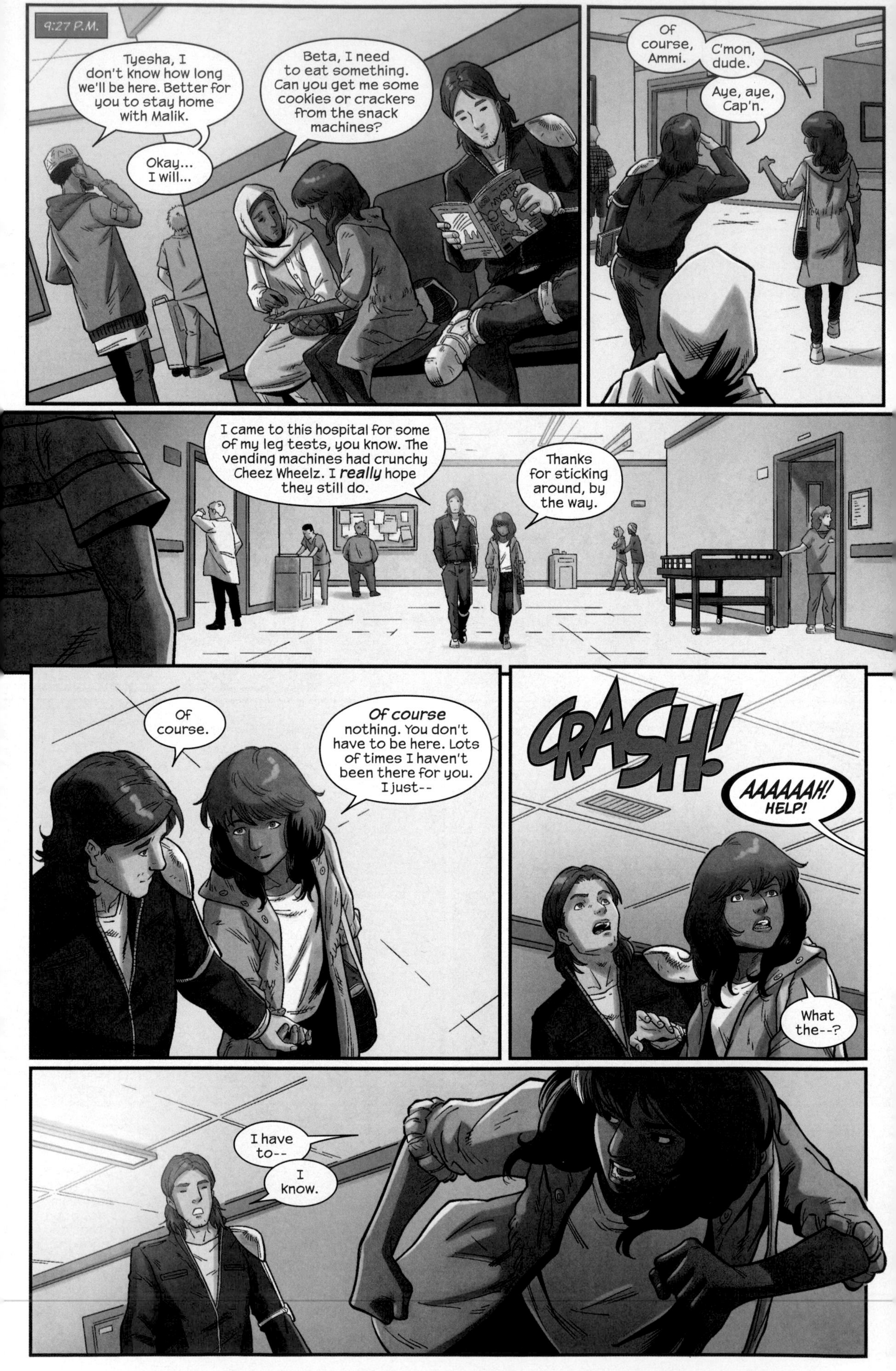
9:27 P.M.
Tyesha, I don't know how long we'll be here. Better for you to stay home with Malik.
Okay... I will...
Beta, I need to eat something. Can you get me some cookies or crackers from the snack machines?
Of course, Ammi.
C'mon, dude.
Aye, aye, Cap'n.
I came to this hospital for some of my leg tests, you know. The vending machines had crunchy Cheez Wheelz. I *really* hope they still do.
Thanks for sticking around, by the way.
Of course.
Of course nothing. You don't have to be here. Lots of times I haven't been there for you. I just--
CRASH!
AAAAAAH! HELP!
What the--?
I have to--
I know.

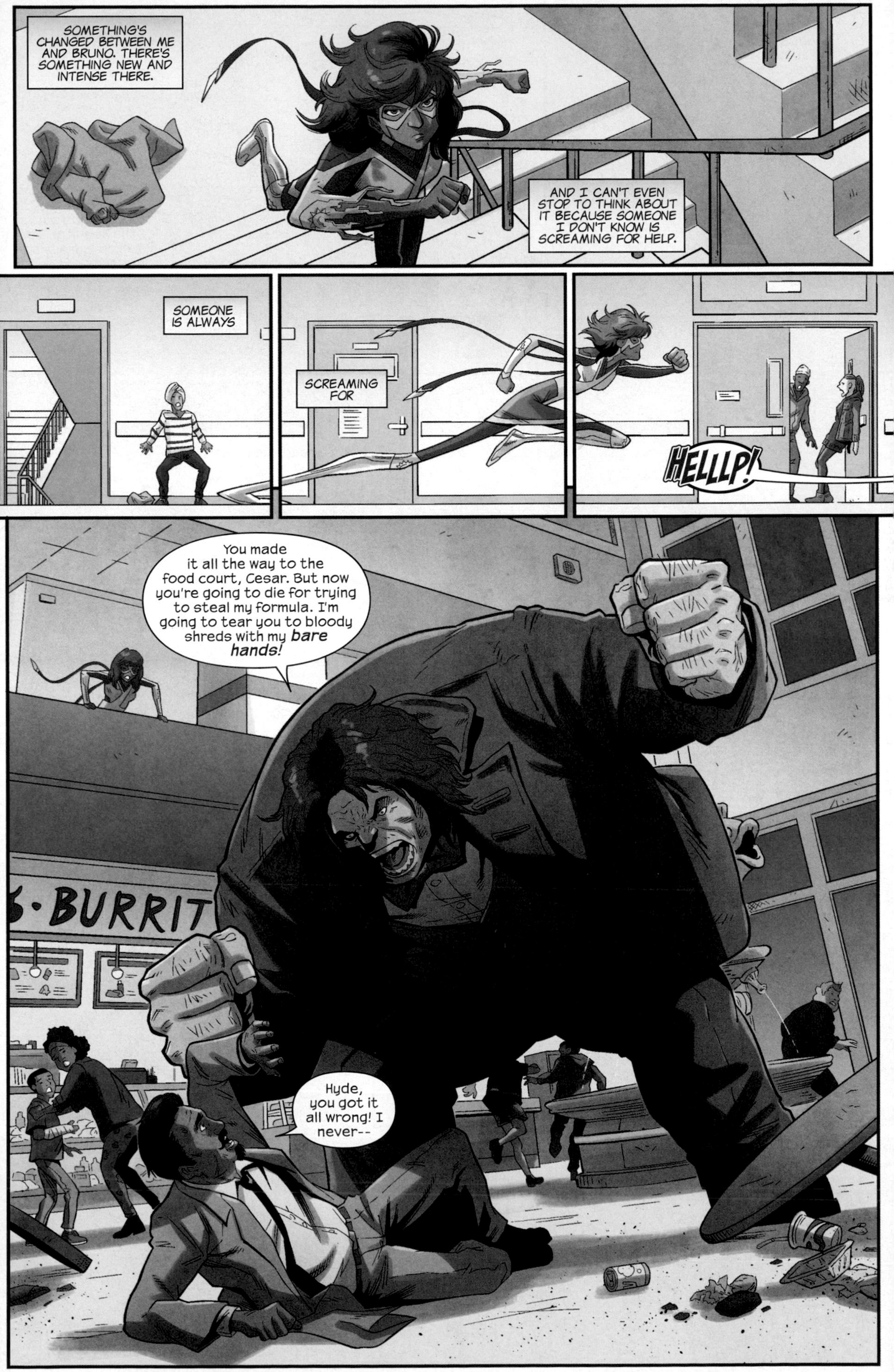

SOMETHING'S CHANGED BETWEEN ME AND BRUNO. THERE'S SOMETHING NEW AND INTENSE THERE.
AND I CAN'T EVEN STOP TO THINK ABOUT IT BECAUSE SOMEONE I DON'T KNOW IS SCREAMING FOR HELP.
SOMEONE IS ALWAYS
SCREAMING FOR
HELLLP!
You made it all the way to the food court, Cesar. But now you're going to die for trying to steal my formula. I'm going to tear you to bloody shreds with my bare hands!
Hyde, you got it all wrong! I never--
BURRIT

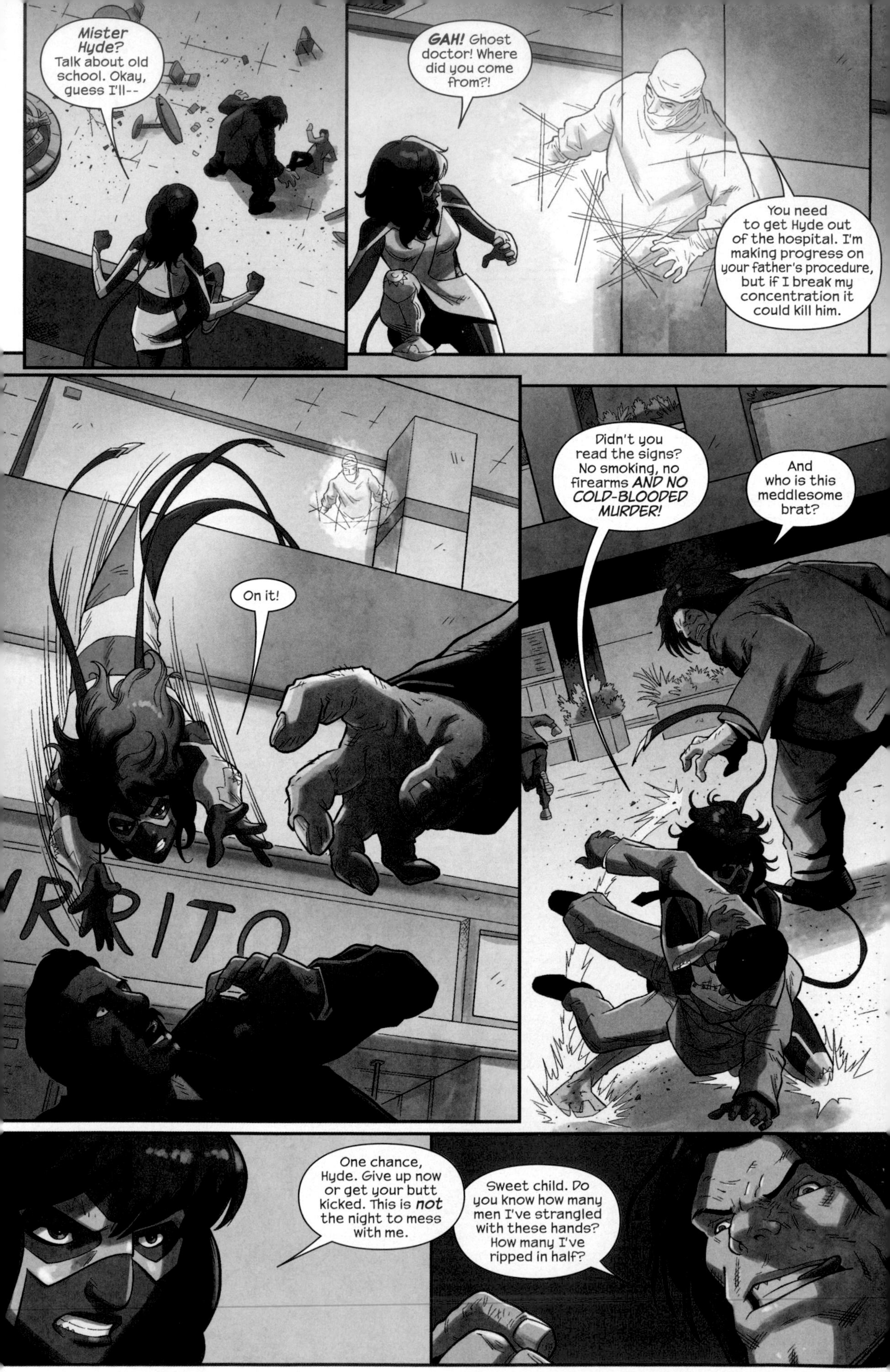
Mister Hyde? Talk about old school. Okay, guess I'll--
GAH! Ghost doctor! Where did you come from?!
You need to get Hyde out of the hospital. I'm making progress on your father's procedure, but if I break my concentration it could kill him.
On it!
RRITO
Didn't you read the signs? No smoking, no firearms AND NO COLD-BLOODED MURDER!
And who is this meddlesome brat?
One chance, Hyde. Give up now or get your butt kicked. This is not the night to mess with me.
Sweet child. Do you know how many men I've strangled with these hands? How many I've ripped in half?

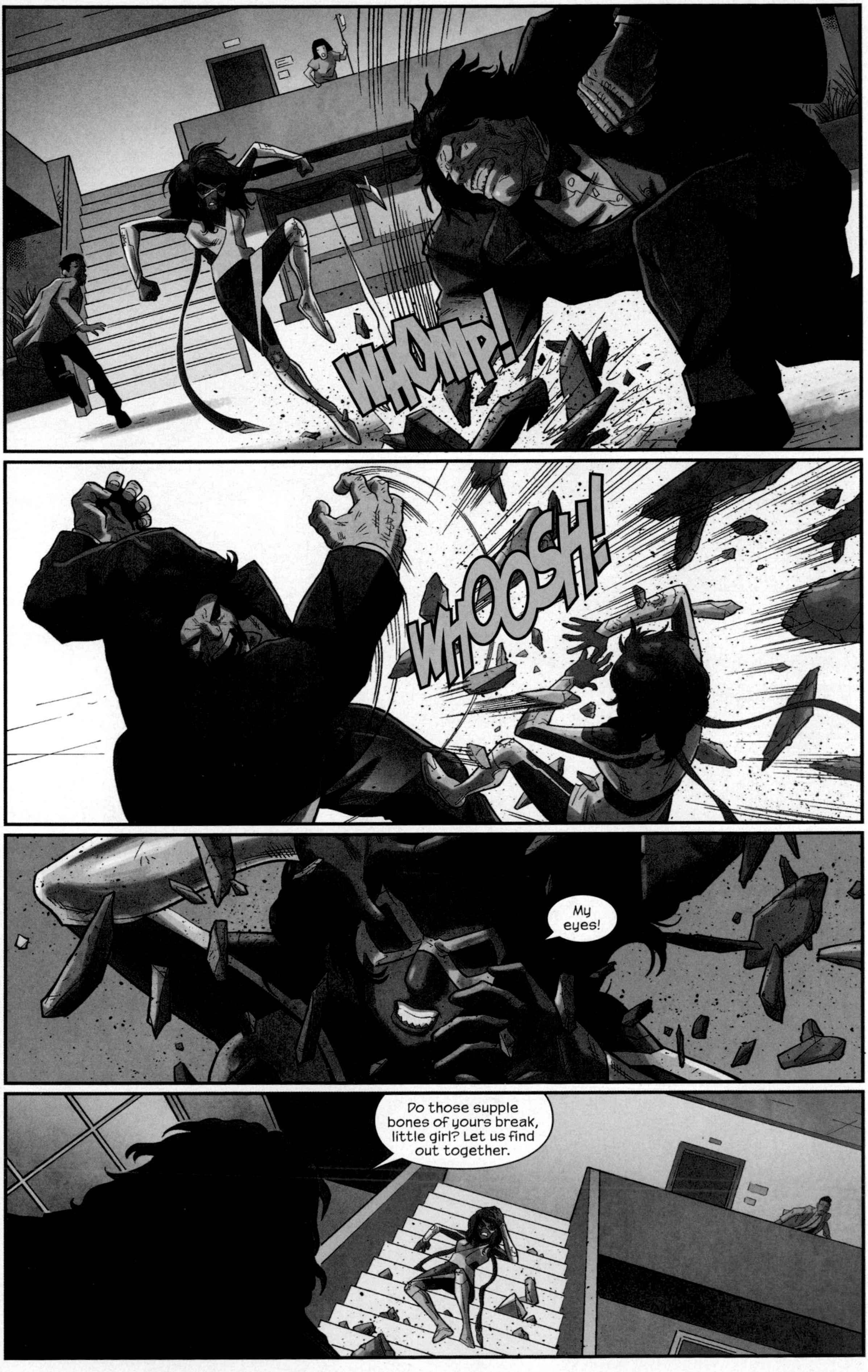
WHOMP!
WHOOSH!
My eyes!
Do those supple bones of yours break, little girl? Let us find out together.

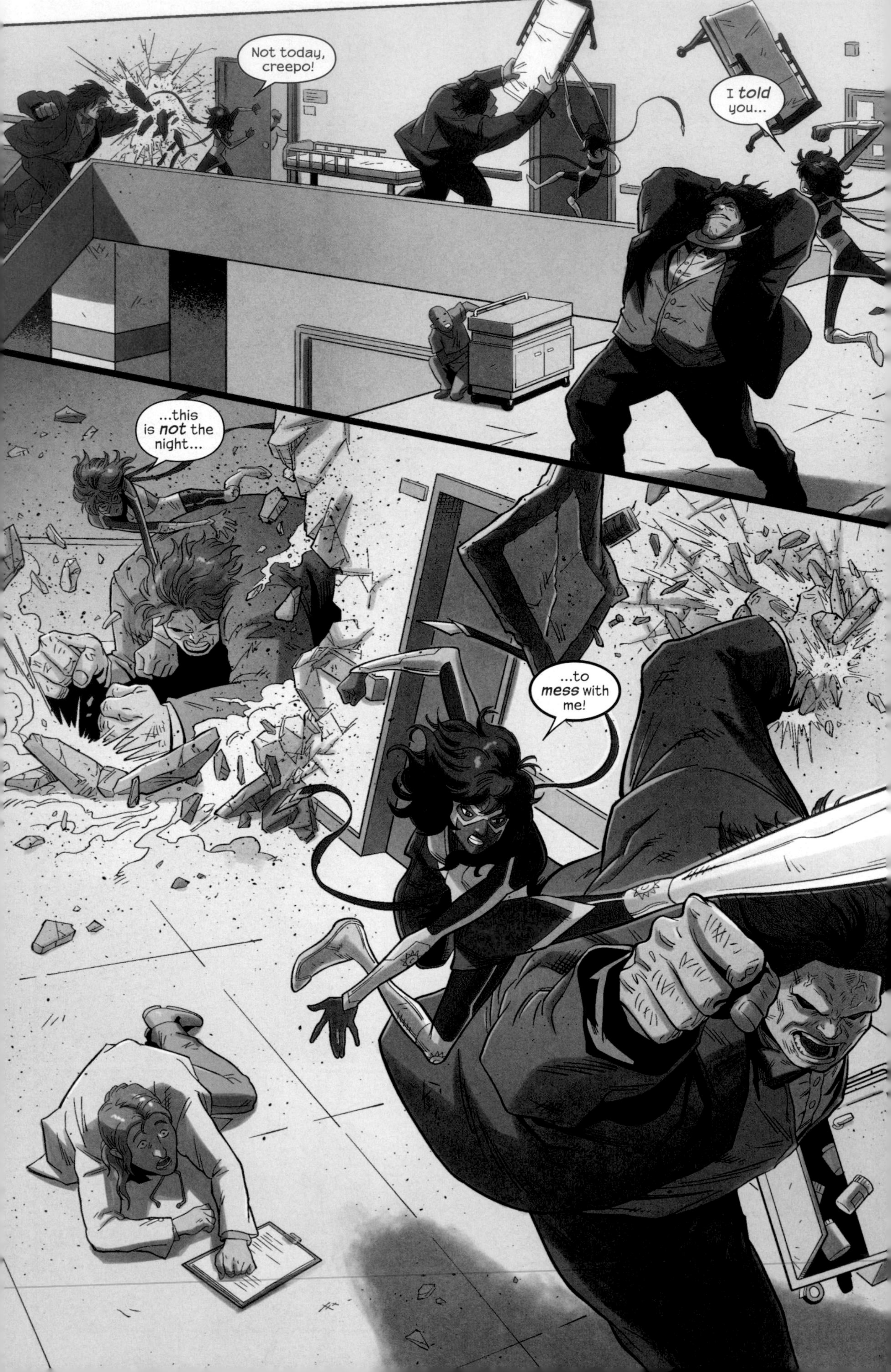
Not today, creepo!
I told you...
...this is not the night...
...to mess with me!

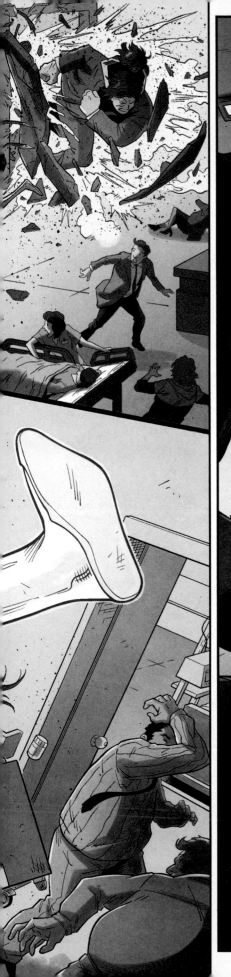

Bah! This annoyance grows tiresome. And more authorities will no doubt arrive soon.

I shall seek prey elsewhere.

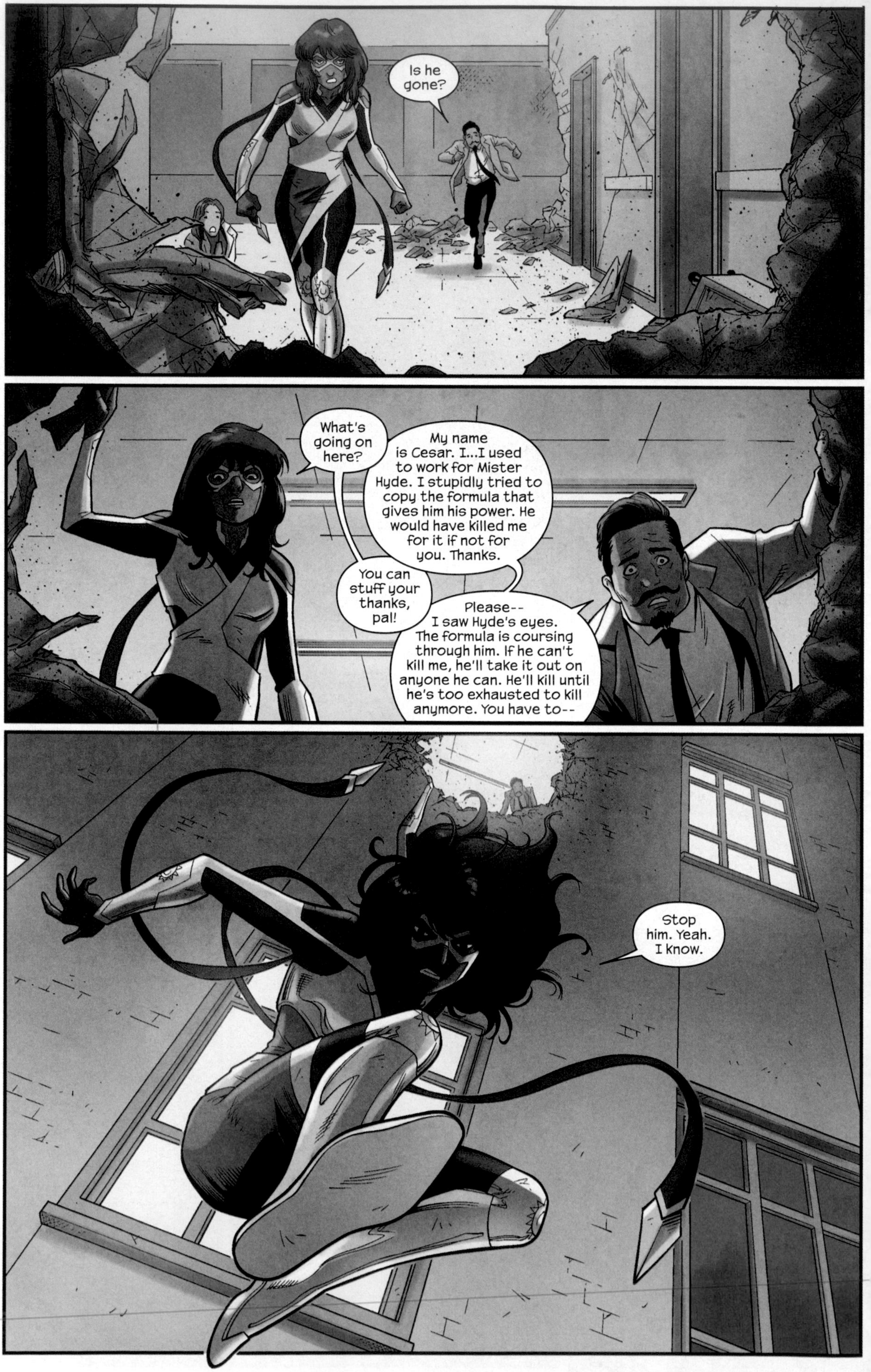
Is he gone?
What's going on here?
My name is Cesar. I...I used to work for Mister Hyde. I stupidly tried to copy the formula that gives him his power. He would have killed me for it if not for you. Thanks.
You can stuff your thanks, pal!
Please-- I saw Hyde's eyes. The formula is coursing through him. If he can't kill me, he'll take it out on anyone he can. He'll kill until he's too exhausted to kill anymore. You have to--
Stop him. Yeah. I know.

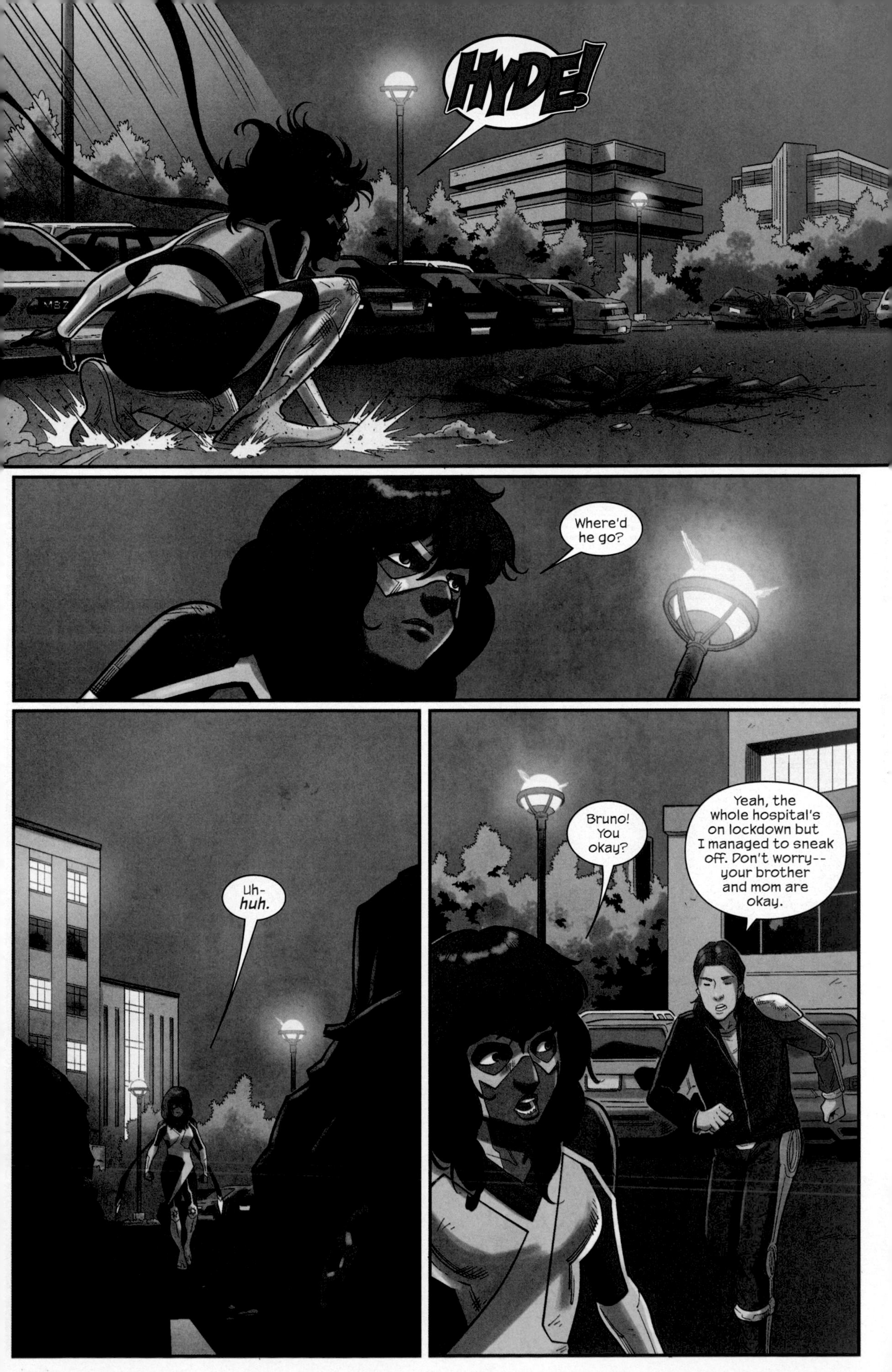
HYDE!
Where'd he go?
Uh-huh.
Bruno! You okay?
Yeah, the whole hospital's on lockdown but I managed to sneak off. Don't worry-- your brother and mom are okay.

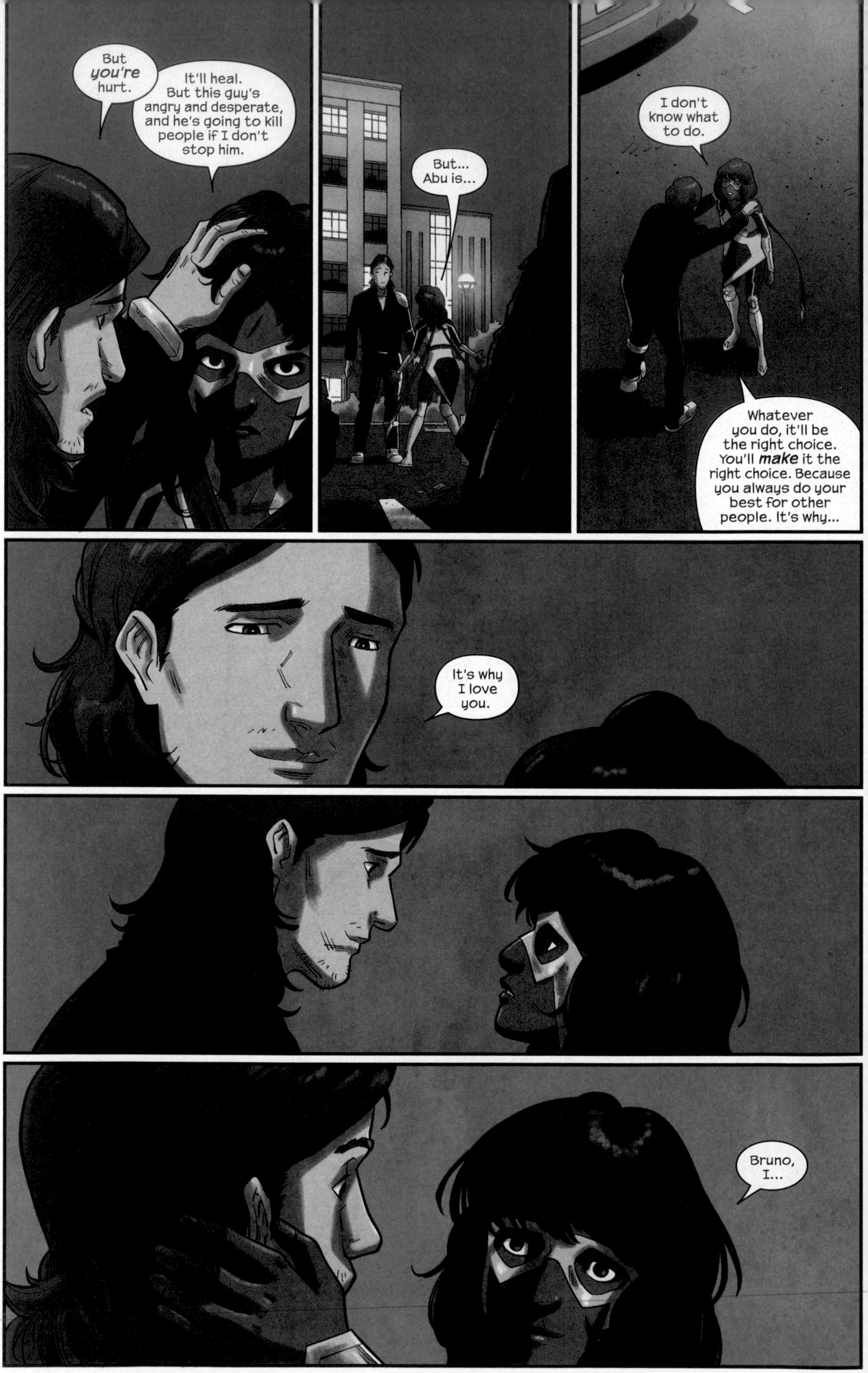
But *you're* hurt.
It'll heal. But this guy's angry and desperate, and he's going to kill people if I don't stop him.
But... Abu is...
I don't know what to do.
Whatever you do, it'll be the right choice. You'll *make* it the right choice. Because you always do your best for other people. It's why...
It's why I love you.
Bruno, I...

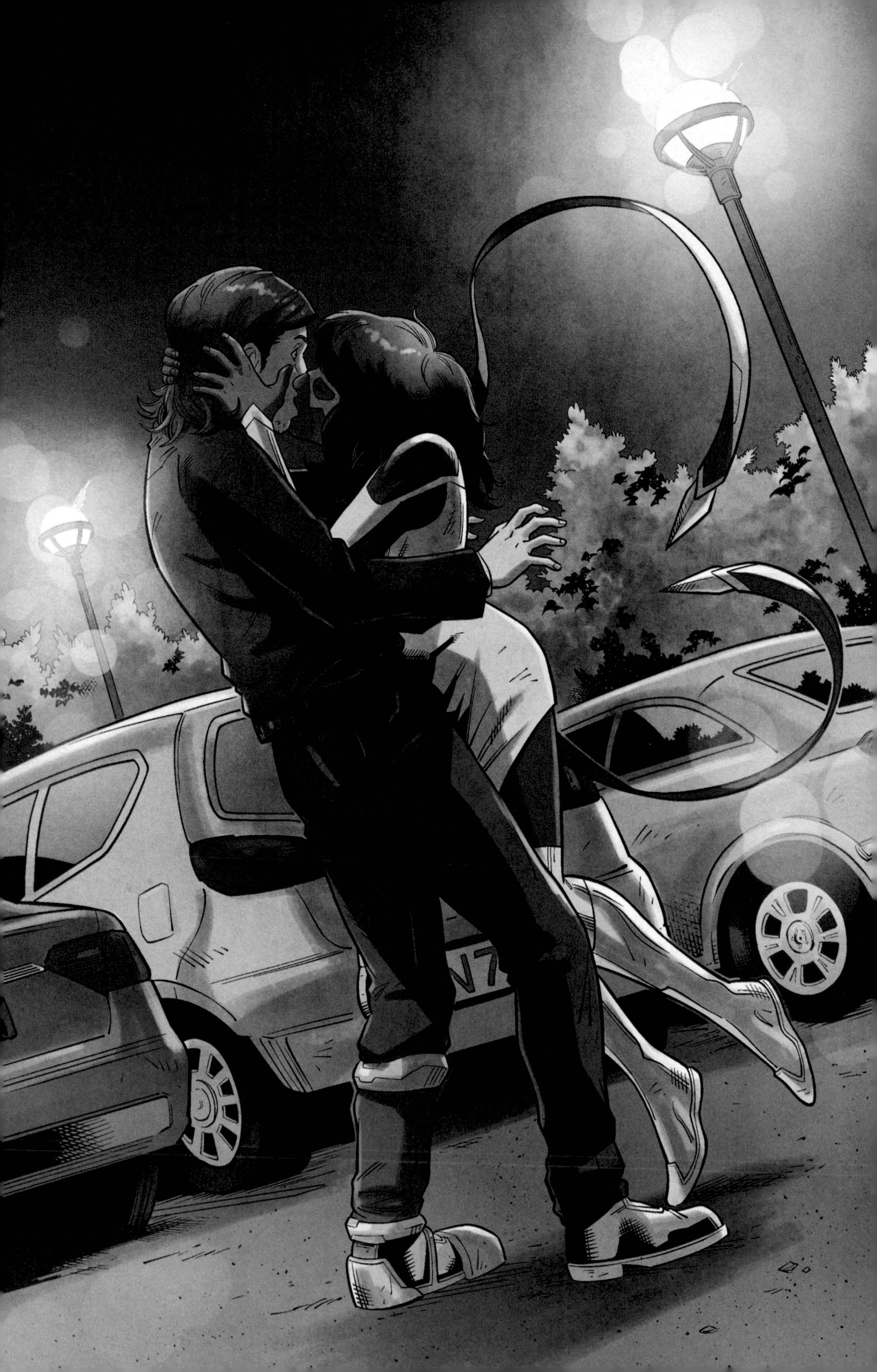

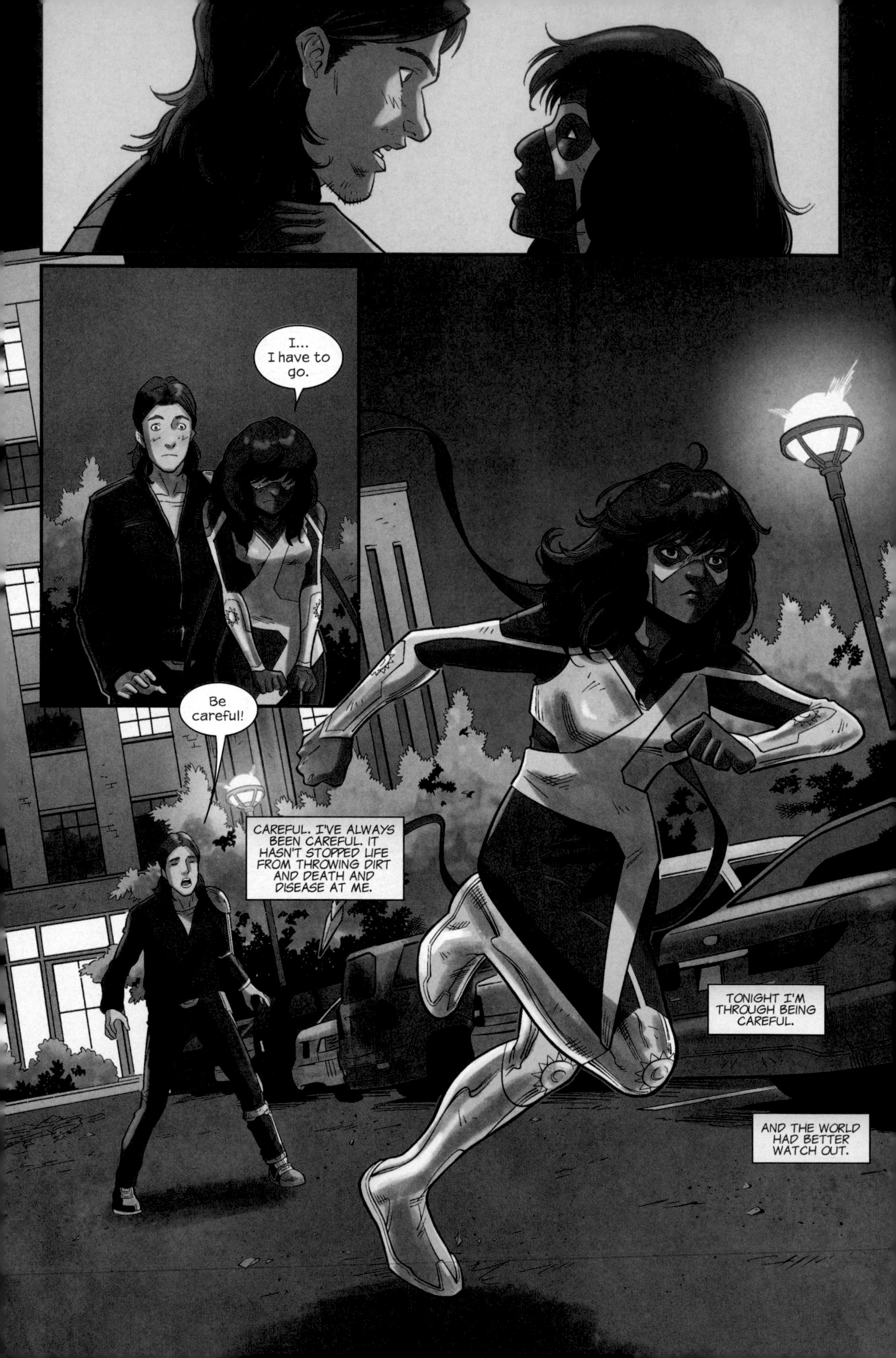

I... I have to go.
Be careful!
CAREFUL. I'VE ALWAYS BEEN CAREFUL. IT HASN'T STOPPED LIFE FROM THROWING DIRT AND DEATH AND DISEASE AT ME.
TONIGHT I'M THROUGH BEING CAREFUL.
AND THE WORLD HAD BETTER WATCH OUT.

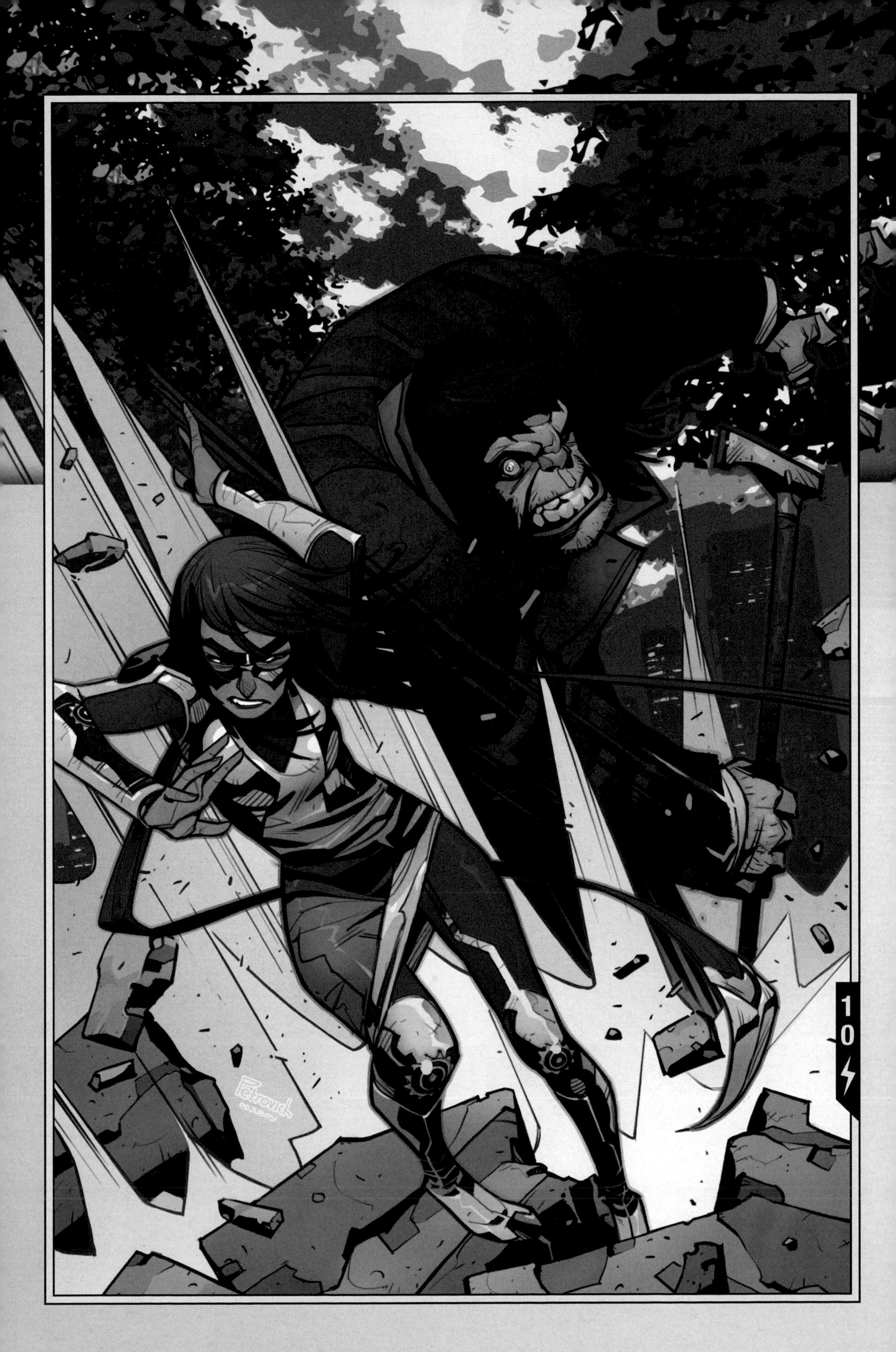
10

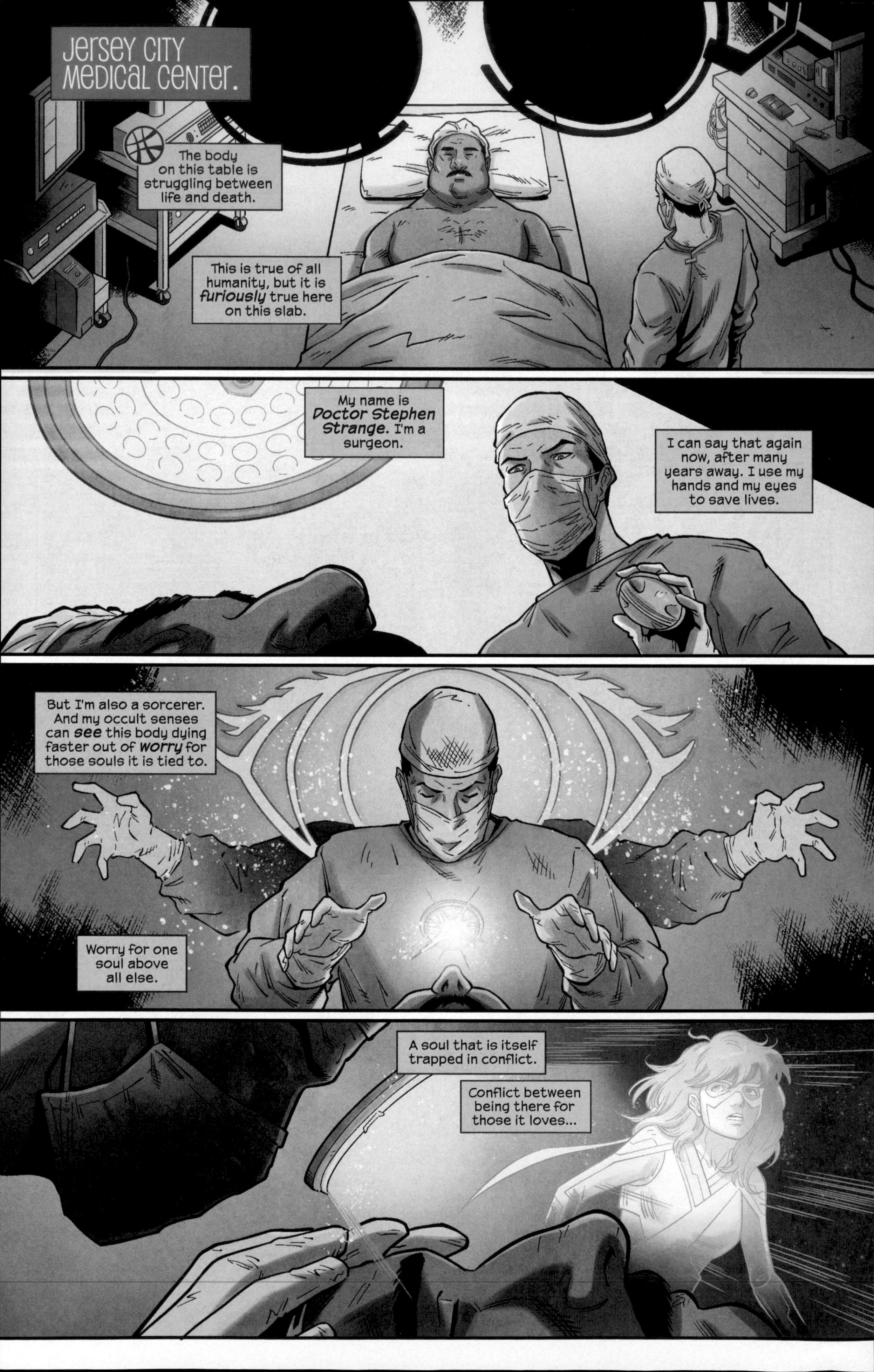

Jersey City Medical Center.
The body on this table is struggling between life and death.
This is true of all humanity, but it is furiously true here on this slab.
My name is Doctor Stephen Strange. I'm a surgeon.
I can say that again now, after many years away. I use my hands and my eyes to save lives.
But I'm also a sorcerer. And my occult senses can see this body dying faster out of worry for those souls it is tied to.
Worry for one soul above all else.
A soul that is itself trapped in conflict.
Conflict between being there for those it loves...

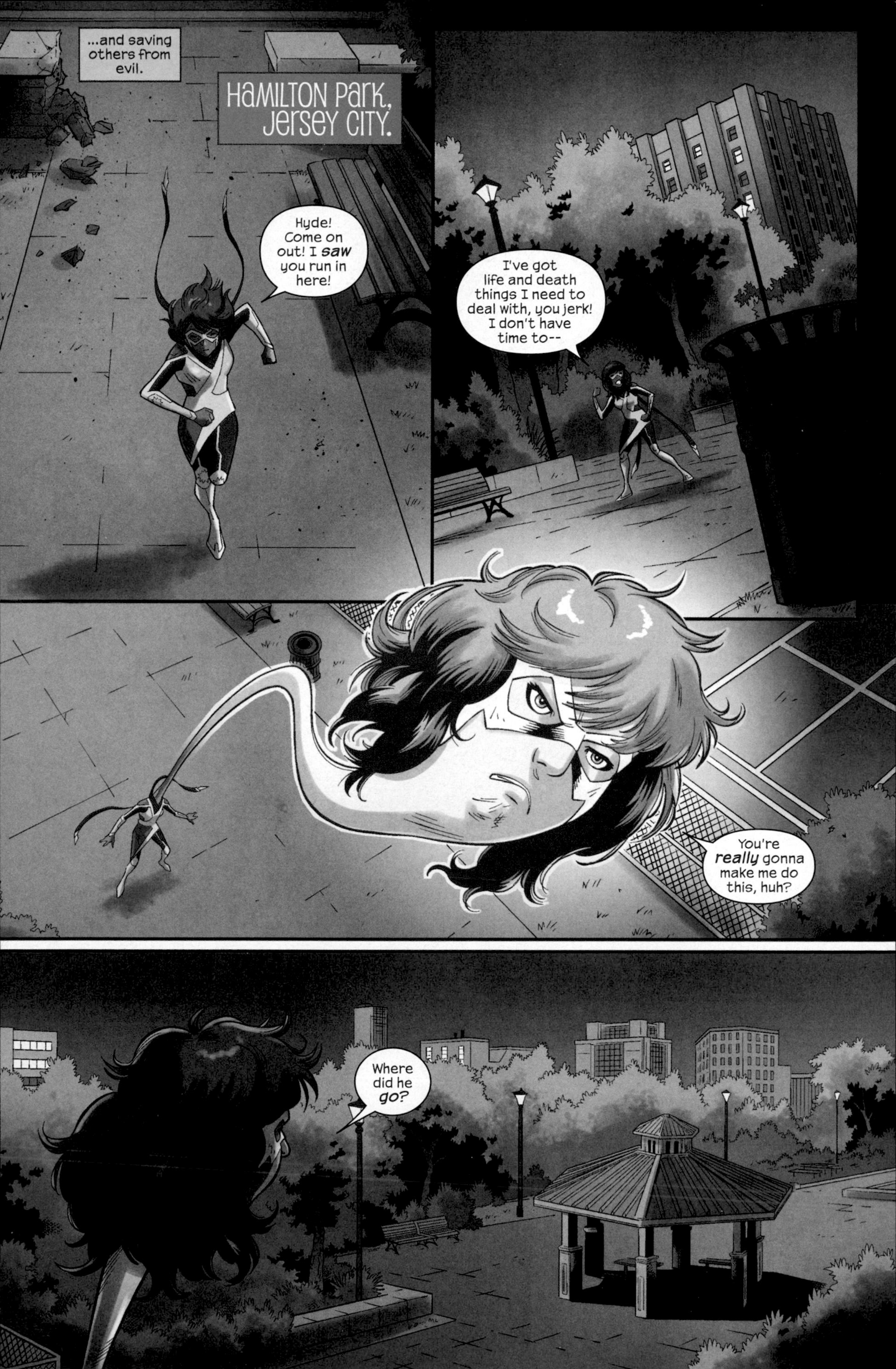
...and saving others from evil.
HAMILTON PARK, JERSEY CITY.
Hyde! Come on out! I *saw* you run in here!
I've got life and death things I need to deal with, you jerk! I don't have time to--
You're *really* gonna make me do this, huh?
Where did he *go*?

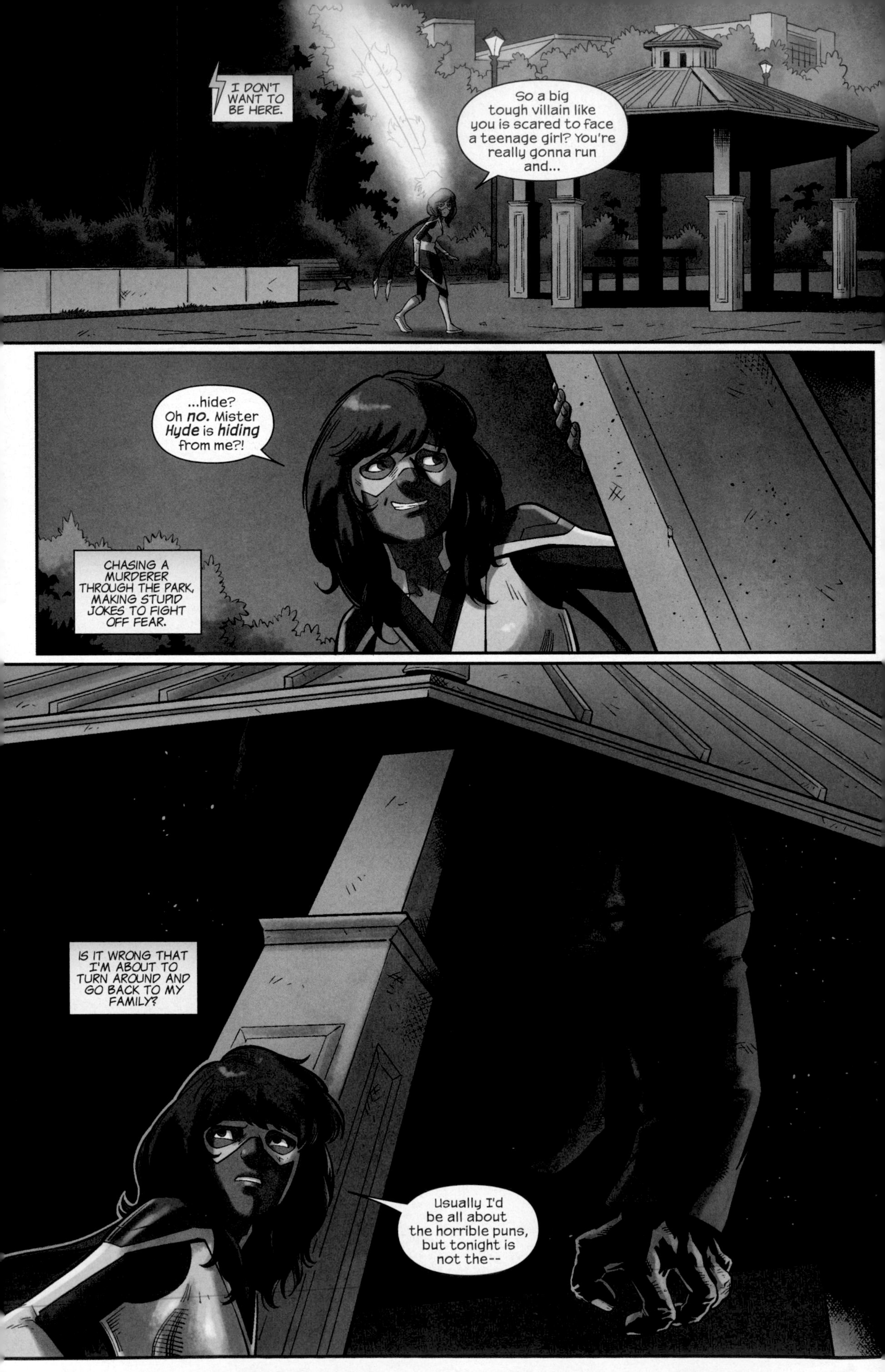
I DON'T WANT TO BE HERE.
So a big tough villain like you is scared to face a teenage girl? You're really gonna run and...
...hide? Oh no. Mister Hyde is hiding from me?!
CHASING A MURDERER THROUGH THE PARK, MAKING STUPID JOKES TO FIGHT OFF FEAR.
IS IT WRONG THAT I'M ABOUT TO TURN AROUND AND GO BACK TO MY FAMILY?
Usually I'd be all about the horrible puns, but tonight is not the--

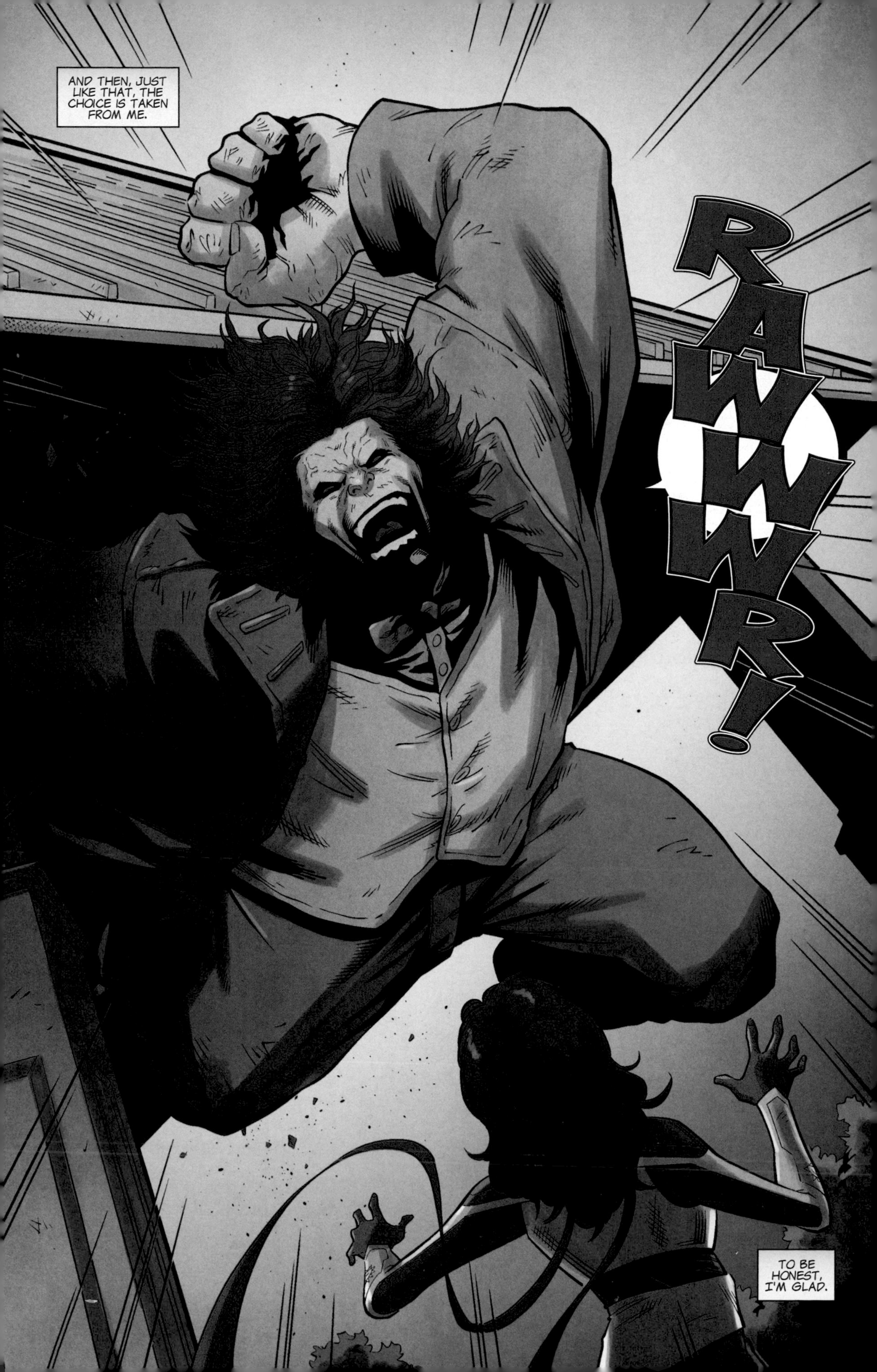
AND THEN, JUST LIKE THAT, THE CHOICE IS TAKEN FROM ME.
RAWWWR!
TO BE HONEST, I'M GLAD.

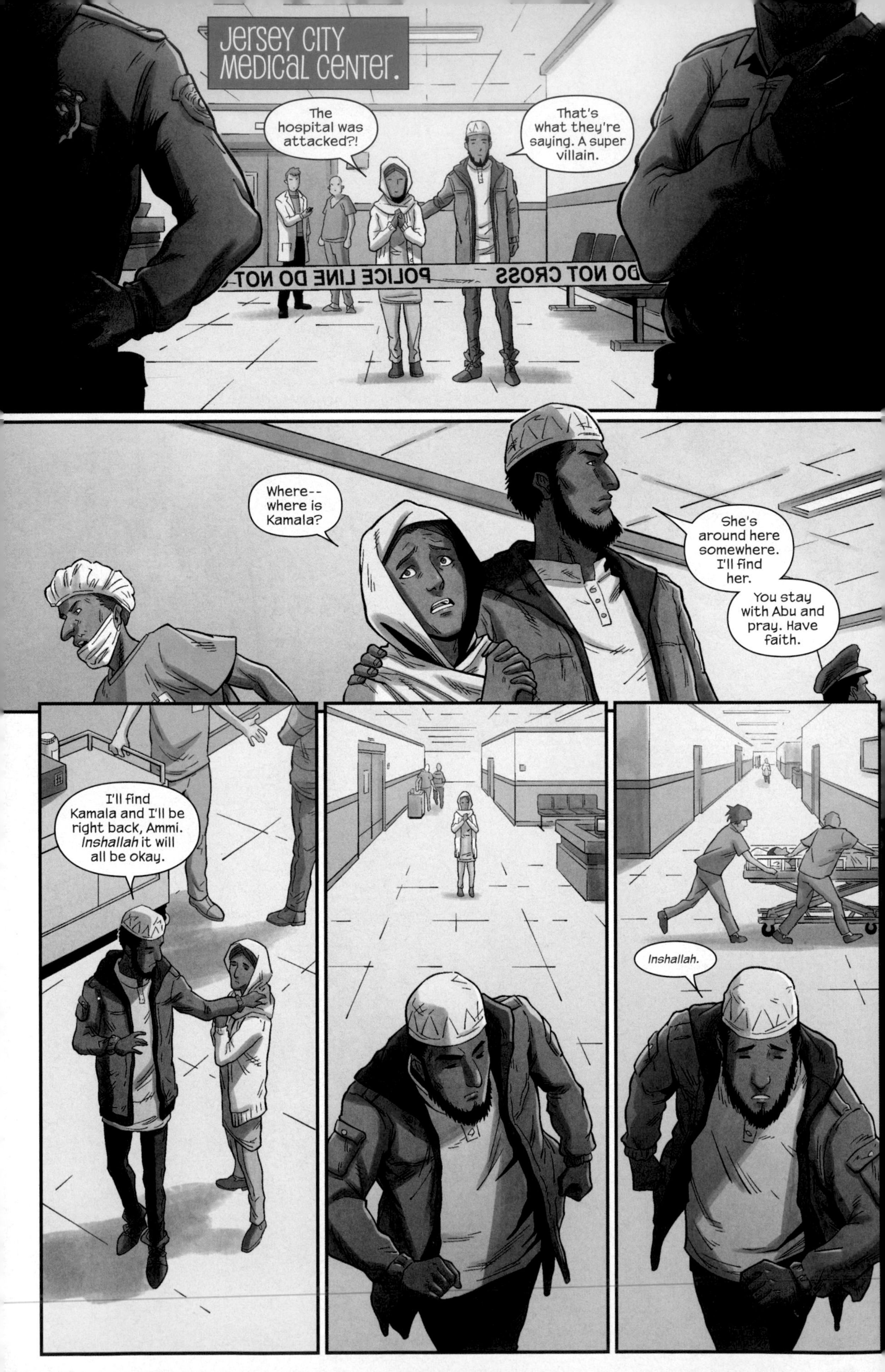
Jersey City Medical Center.
The hospital was attacked?!
That's what they're saying. A super villain.
POLICE LINE DO NOT CROSS
DO NOT CROSS
Where--where is Kamala?
She's around here somewhere. I'll find her.
You stay with Abu and pray. Have faith.
I'll find Kamala and I'll be right back, Ammi. *Inshallah* it will all be okay.
Inshallah.

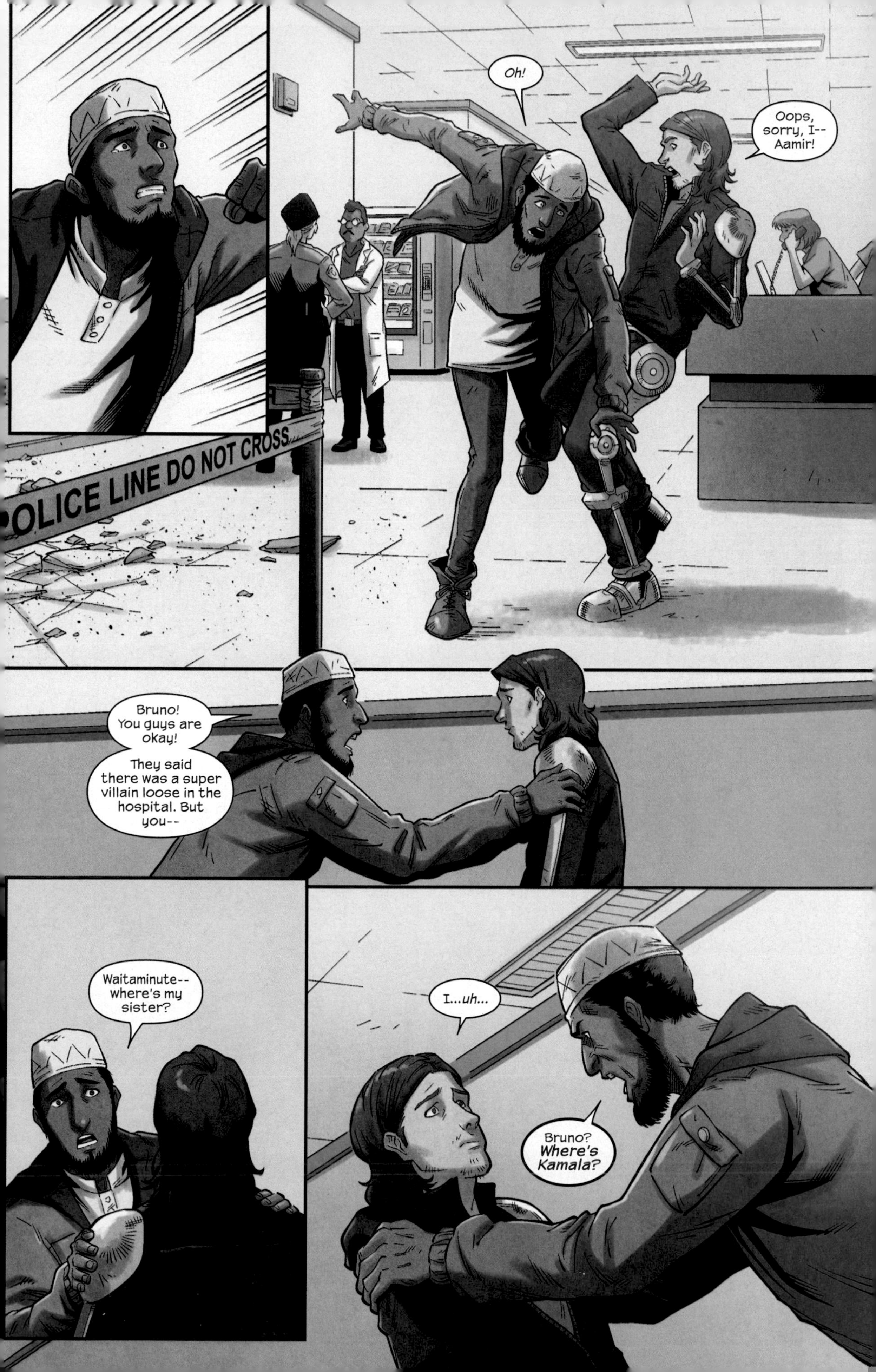
Oh!
Oops, sorry, I-- Aamir!
POLICE LINE DO NOT CROSS
Bruno! You guys are okay!
They said there was a super villain loose in the hospital. But you--
Waitaminute-- where's my sister?
I...uh...
Bruno? Where's Kamala?

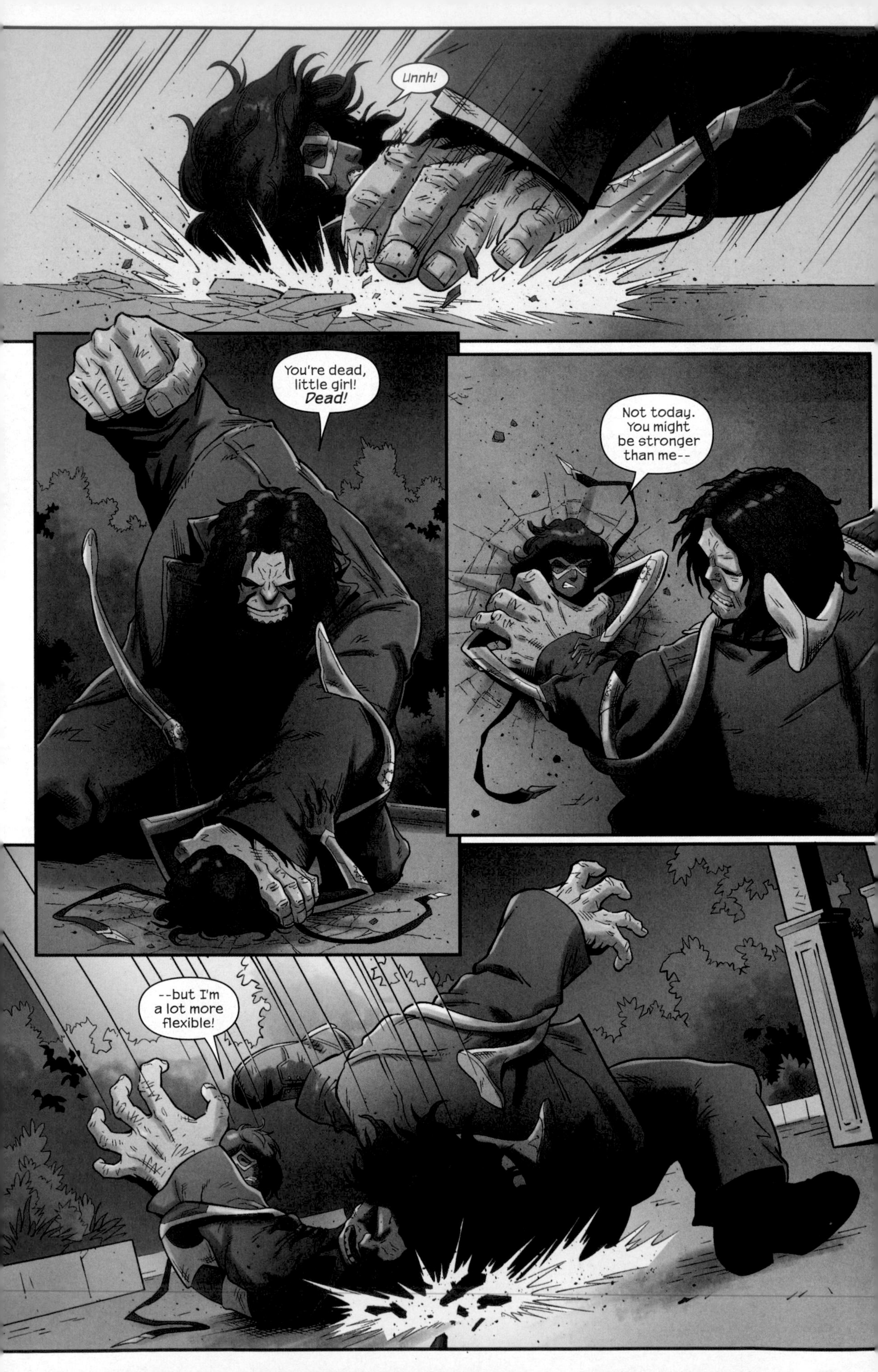
Unnh!
You're dead, little girl! *Dead!*
Not today. You might be stronger than me--
--but I'm a lot more flexible!

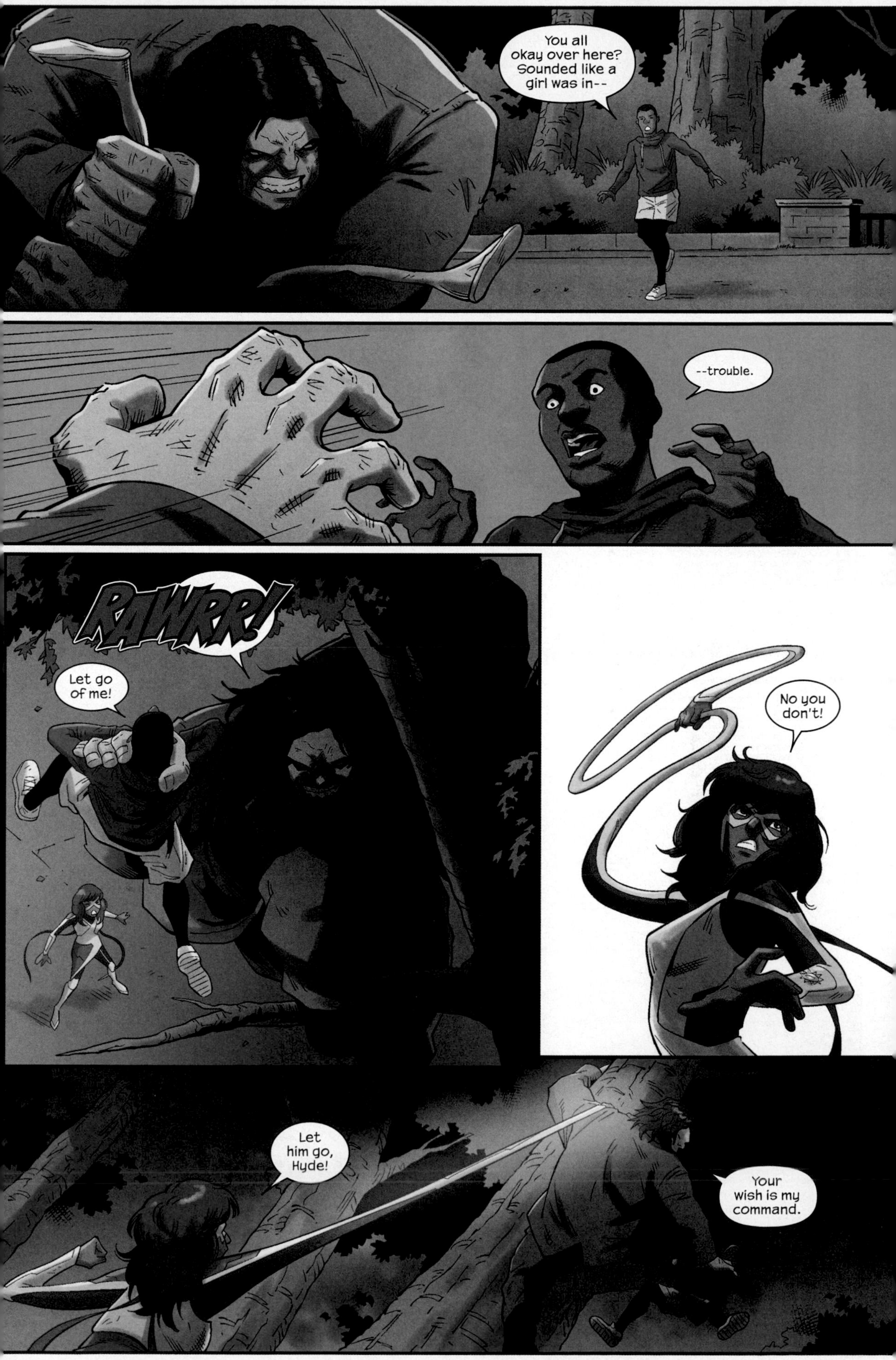
You all okay over here? Sounded like a girl was in--
--trouble.
RAWRR!
Let go of me!
No you don't!
Let him go, Hyde!
Your wish is my command.

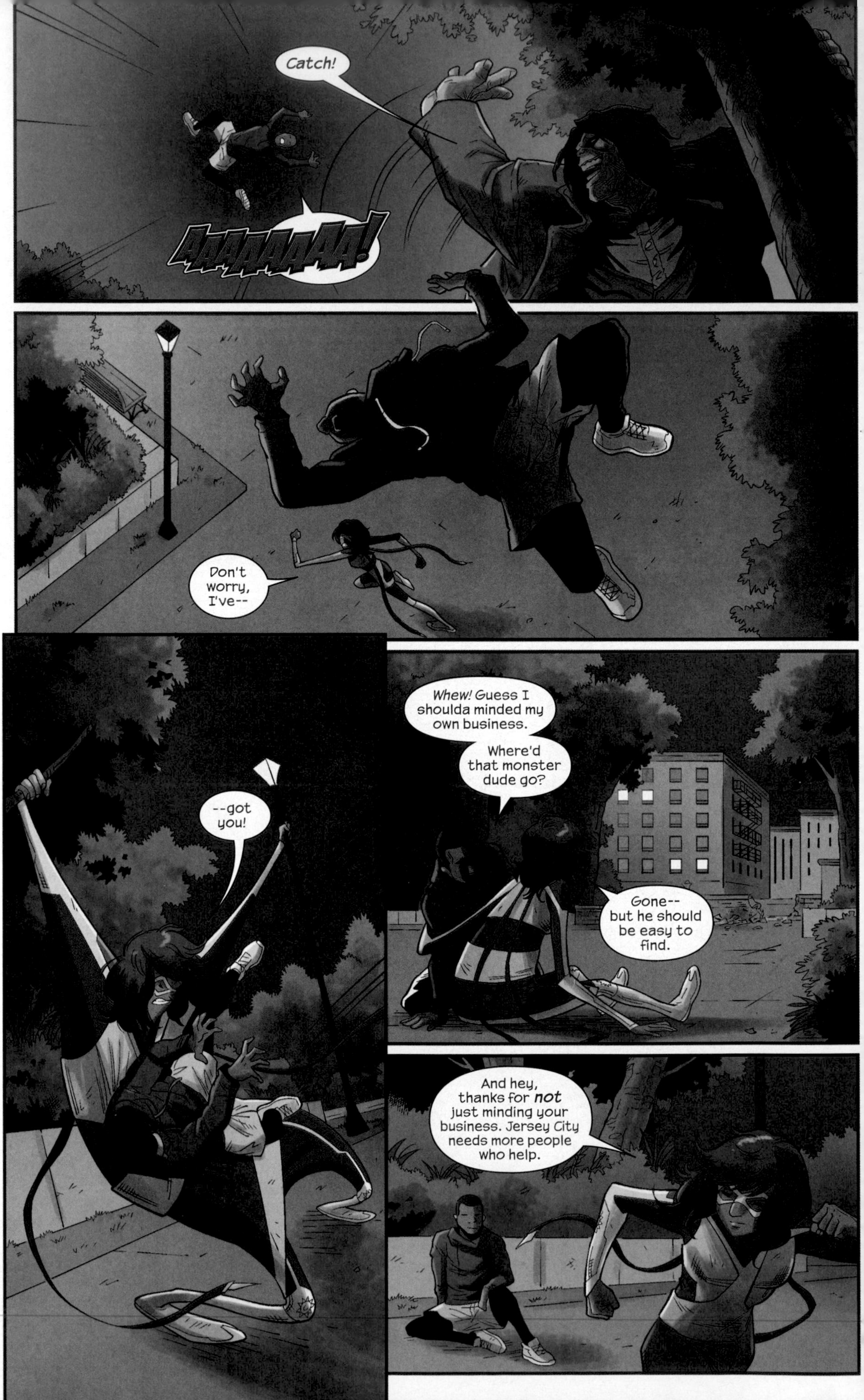
Catch!
AAAAAAAA!
Don't worry, I've--
--got you!
Whew! Guess I shoulda minded my own business.
Where'd that monster dude go?
Gone--but he should be easy to find.
And hey, thanks for **not** just minding your business. Jersey City needs more people who help.

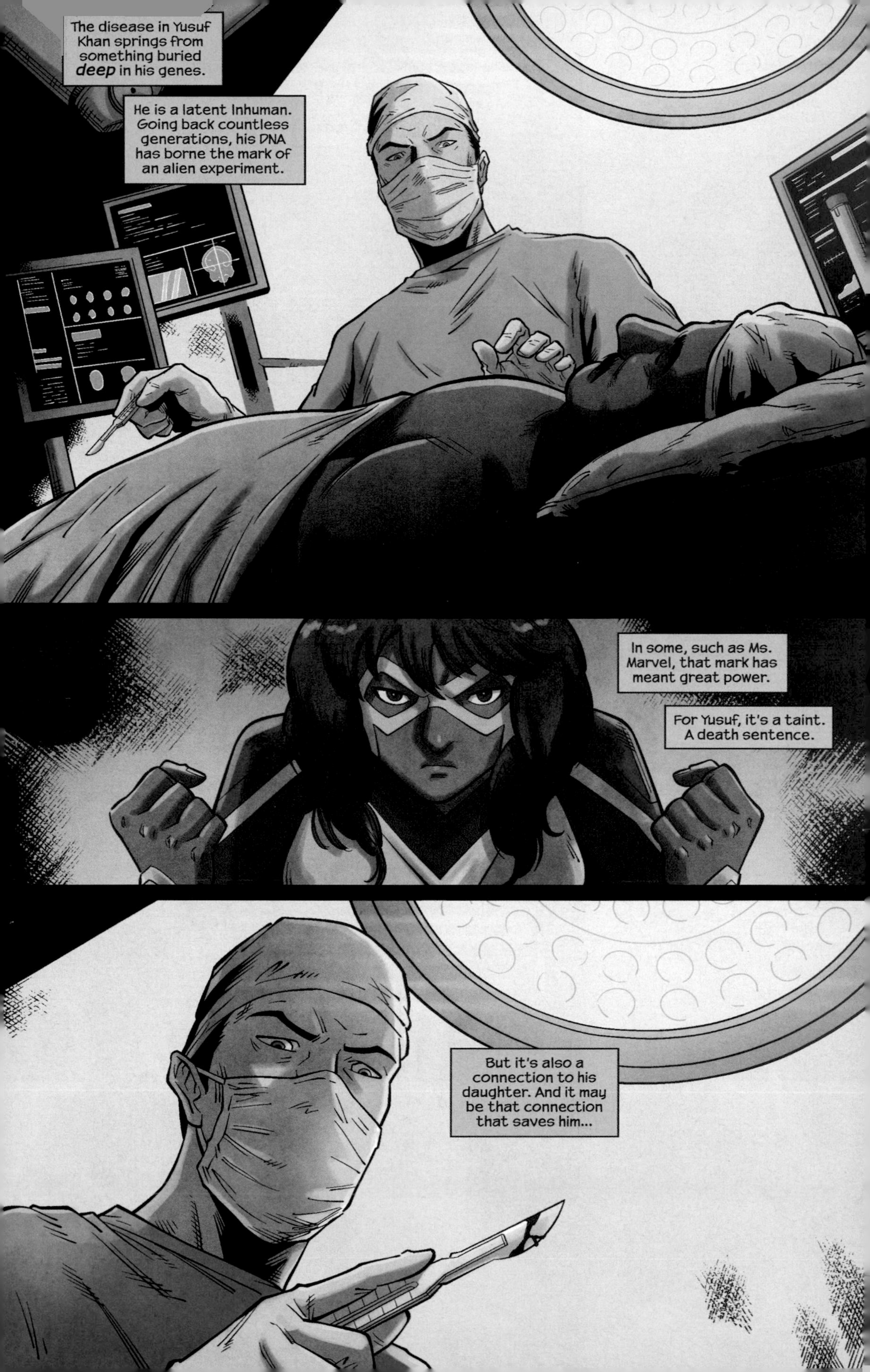
The disease in Yusuf Khan springs from something buried *deep* in his genes.
He is a latent Inhuman. Going back countless generations, his DNA has borne the mark of an alien experiment.
In some, such as Ms. Marvel, that mark has meant great power.
For Yusuf, it's a taint. A death sentence.
But it's also a connection to his daughter. And it may be that connection that saves him...

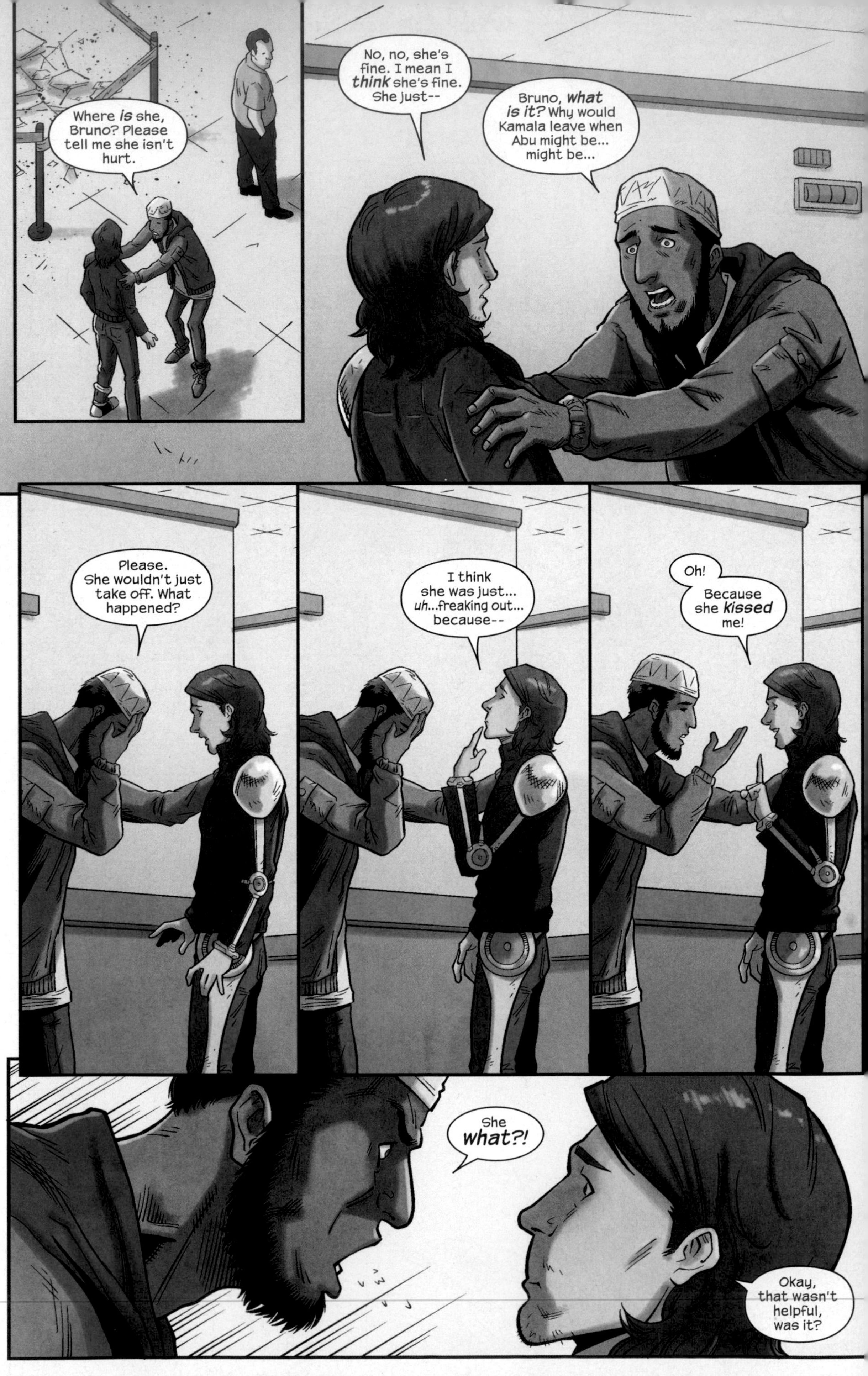
Where *is* she, Bruno? Please tell me she isn't hurt.
No, no, she's fine. I mean I *think* she's fine. She just--
Bruno, *what is it?* Why would Kamala leave when Abu might be... might be...
Please. She wouldn't just take off. What happened?
I think she was just... *uh*...freaking out... because--
Oh!
Because she *kissed* me!
She *what?!*
Okay, that wasn't helpful, was it?

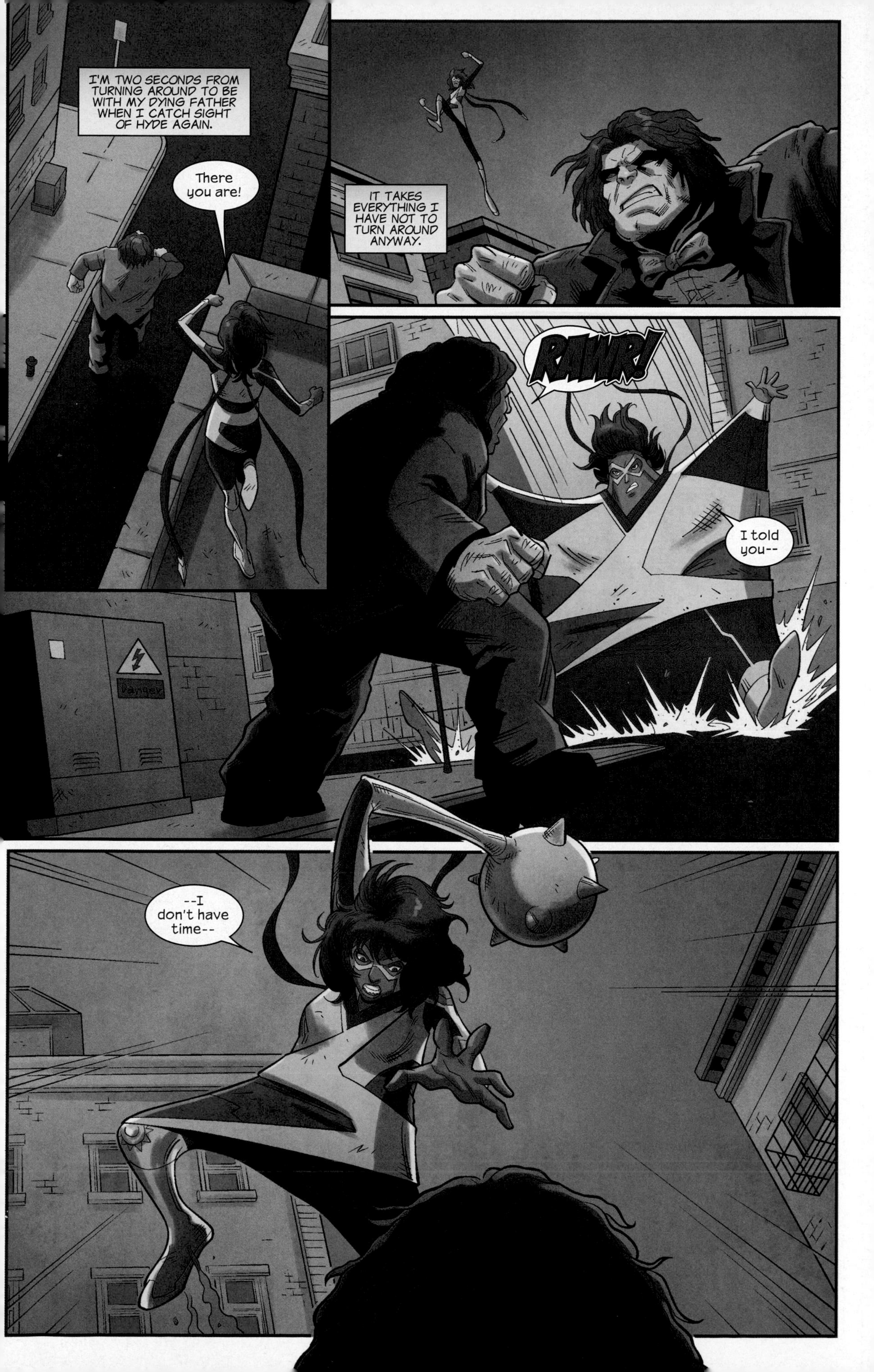
I'M TWO SECONDS FROM TURNING AROUND TO BE WITH MY DYING FATHER WHEN I CATCH SIGHT OF HYDE AGAIN.
There you are!
IT TAKES EVERYTHING I HAVE NOT TO TURN AROUND ANYWAY.
RAWR!
I told you--
--I don't have time--
Danger

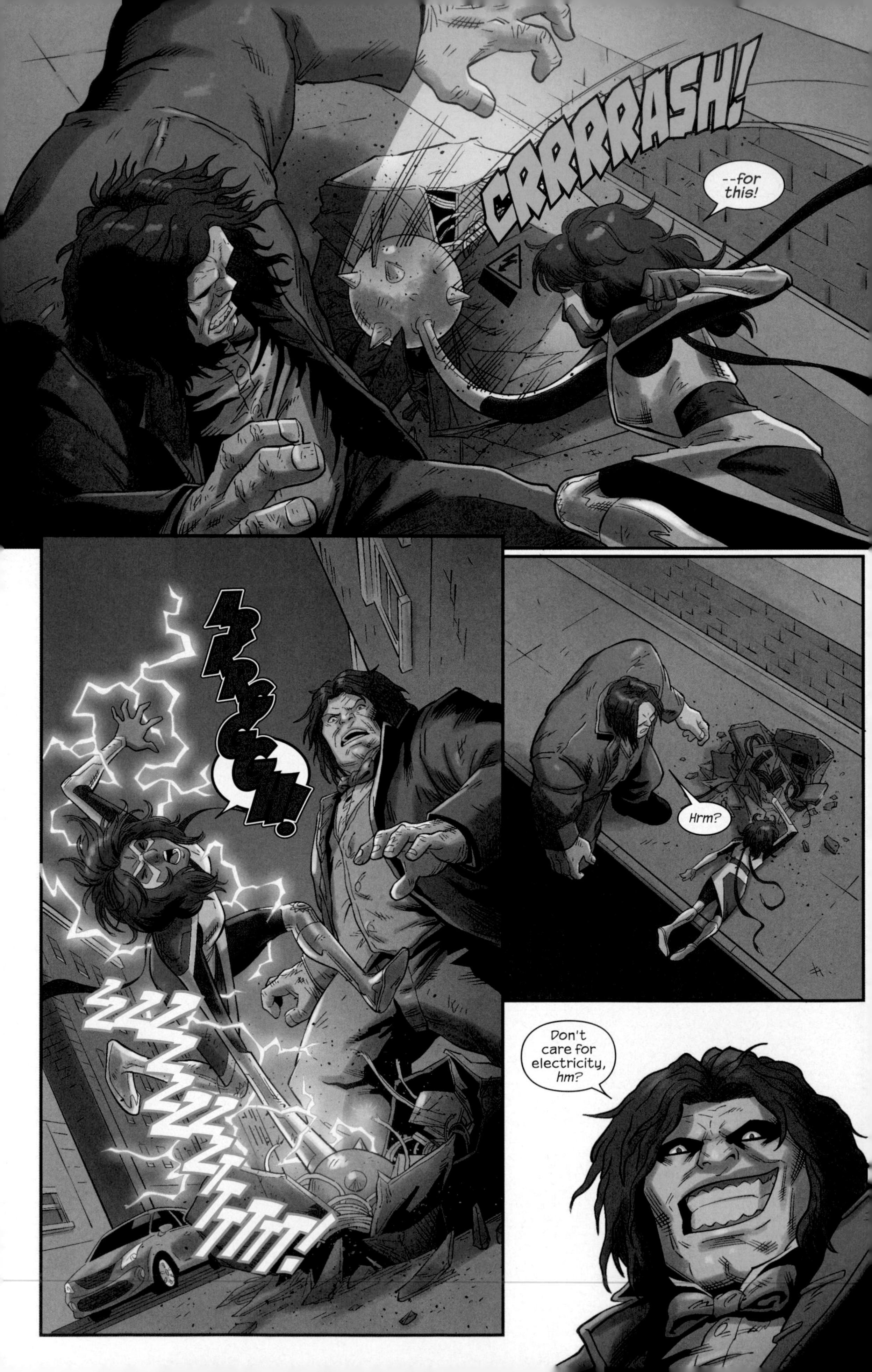

CRRRASH!
--for this!
Hrm?
Don't care for electricity, hm?

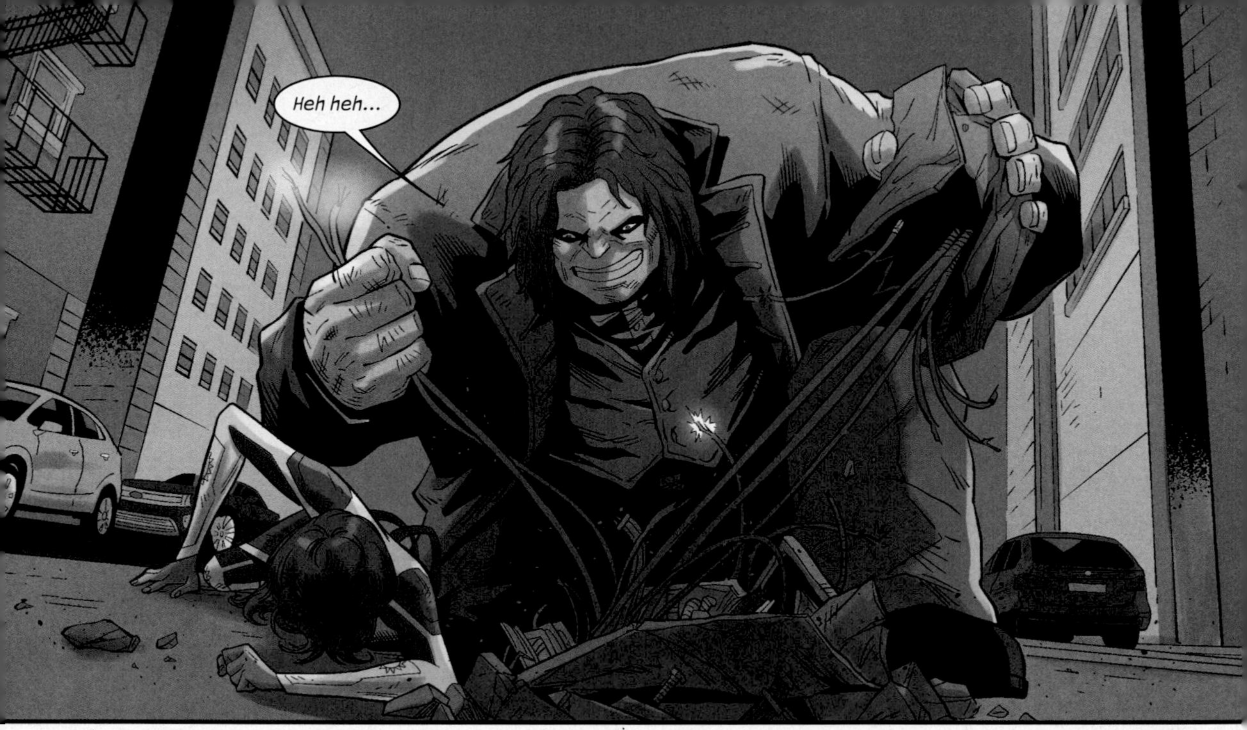
Heh heh...

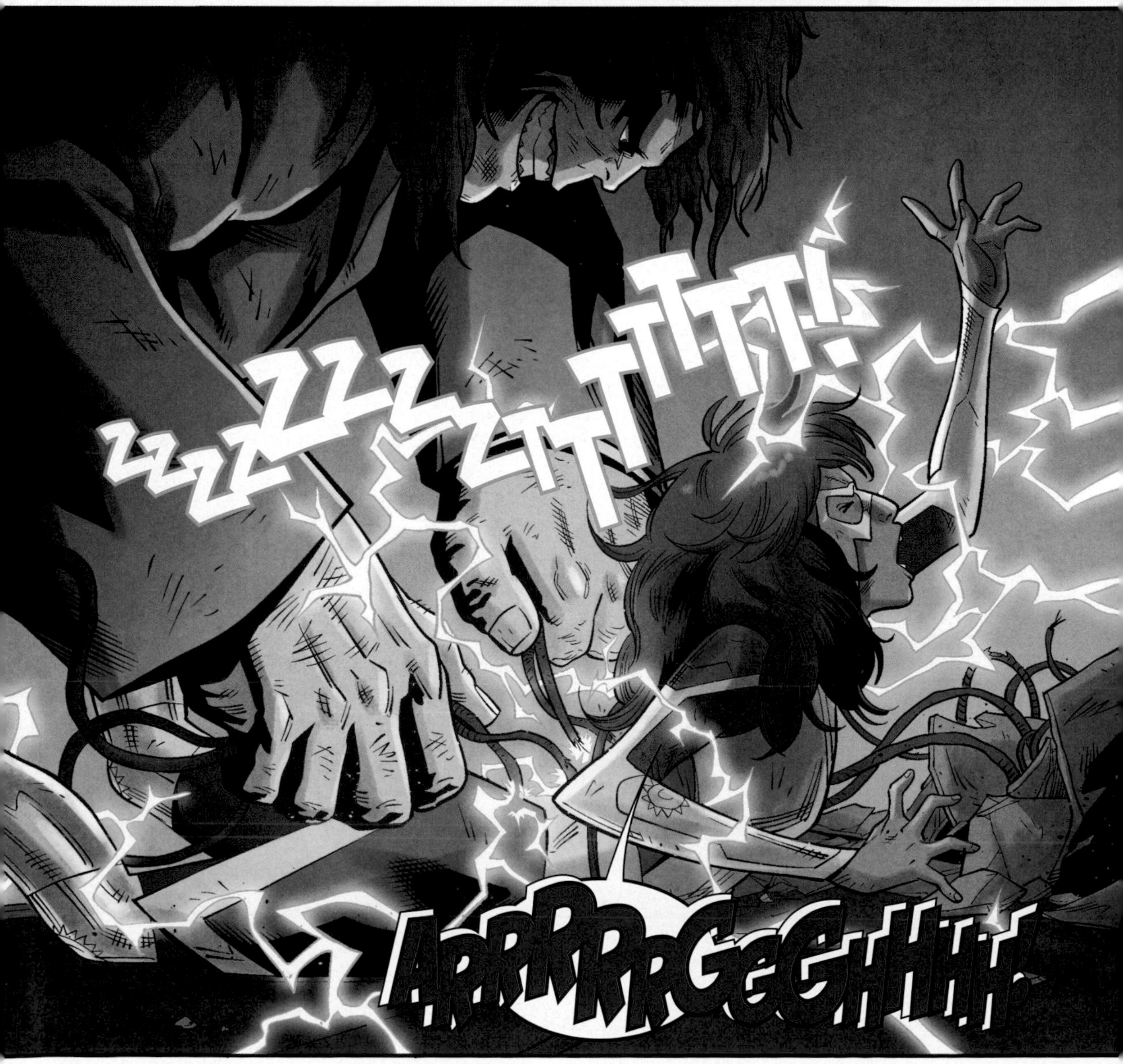
ZZZZZZZZZTTTTTTT!
ARRRRRGGGHHH!

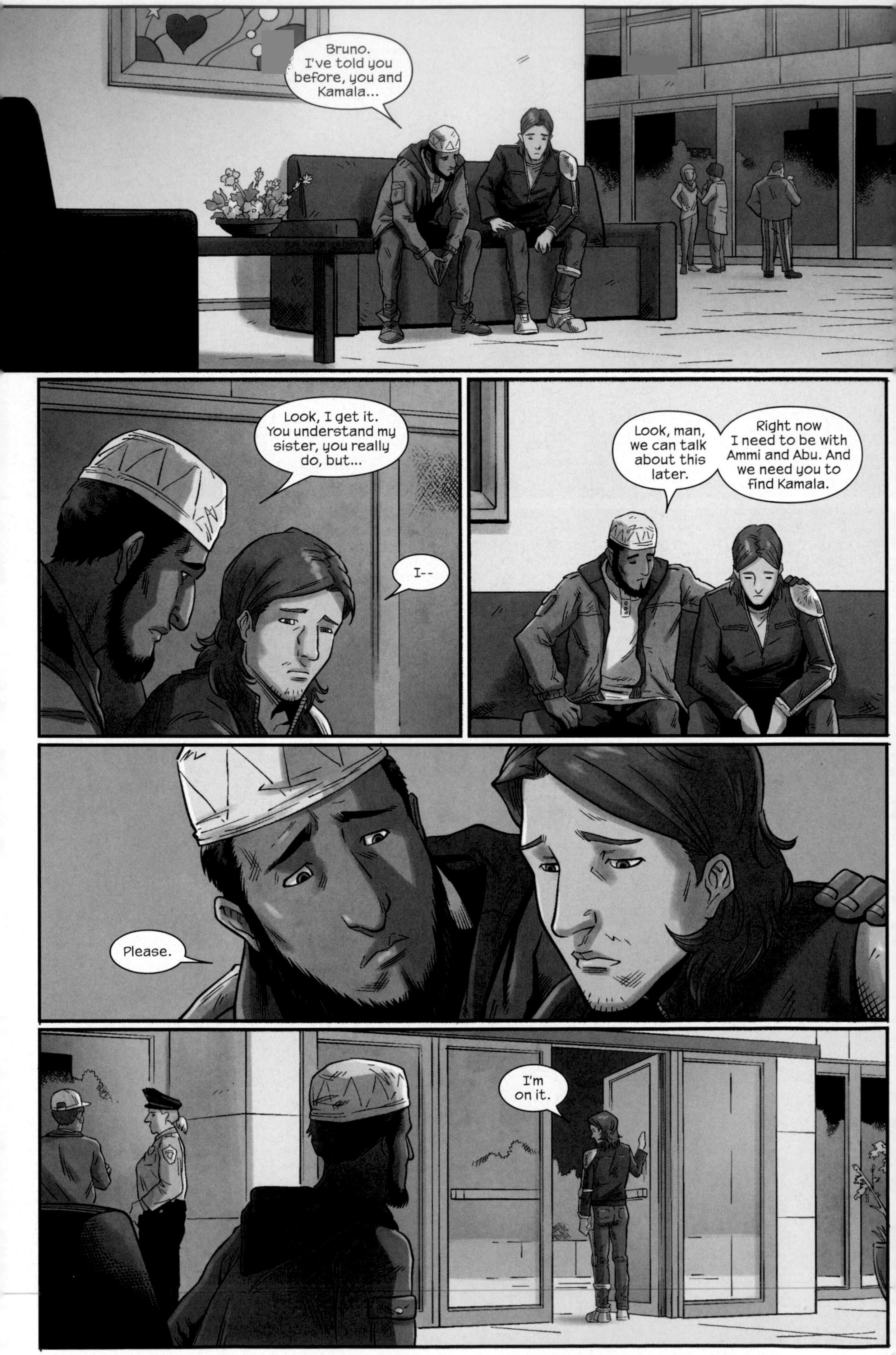
Bruno. I've told you before, you and Kamala...
Look, I get it. You understand my sister, you really do, but...
I--
Look, man, we can talk about this later.
Right now I need to be with Ammi and Abu. And we need you to find Kamala.
Please.
I'm on it.

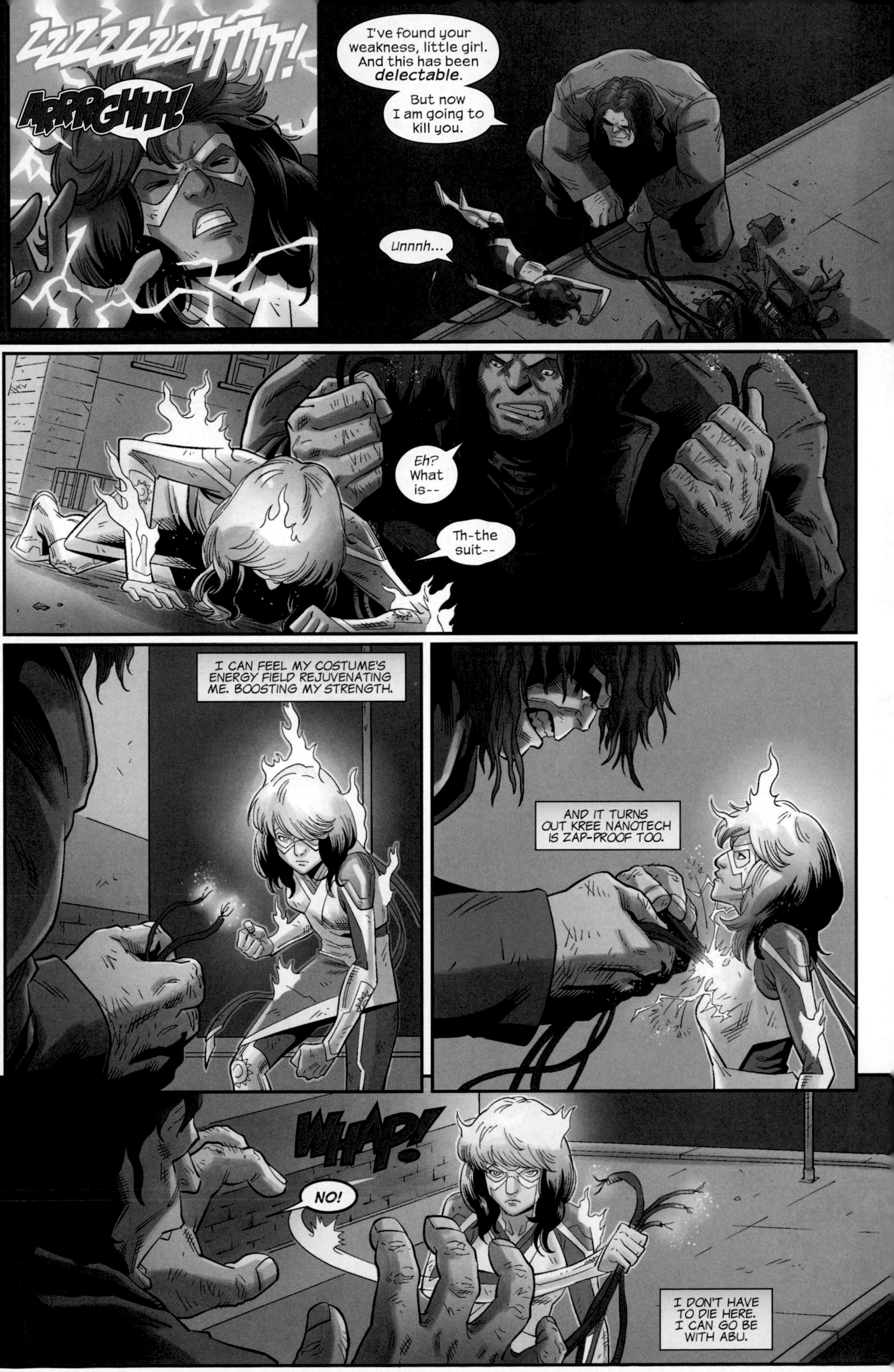
ZZZZZZZZTTTTT!
ARRRGHHH!
I've found your weakness, little girl. And this has been *delectable*.
But now I am going to kill you.
Unnnh...
Eh? What is--
Th-the suit--
I CAN FEEL MY COSTUME'S ENERGY FIELD REJUVENATING ME. BOOSTING MY STRENGTH.
AND IT TURNS OUT KREE NANOTECH IS ZAP-PROOF TOO.
WHAP!
NO!
I DON'T HAVE TO DIE HERE. I CAN GO BE WITH ABU.

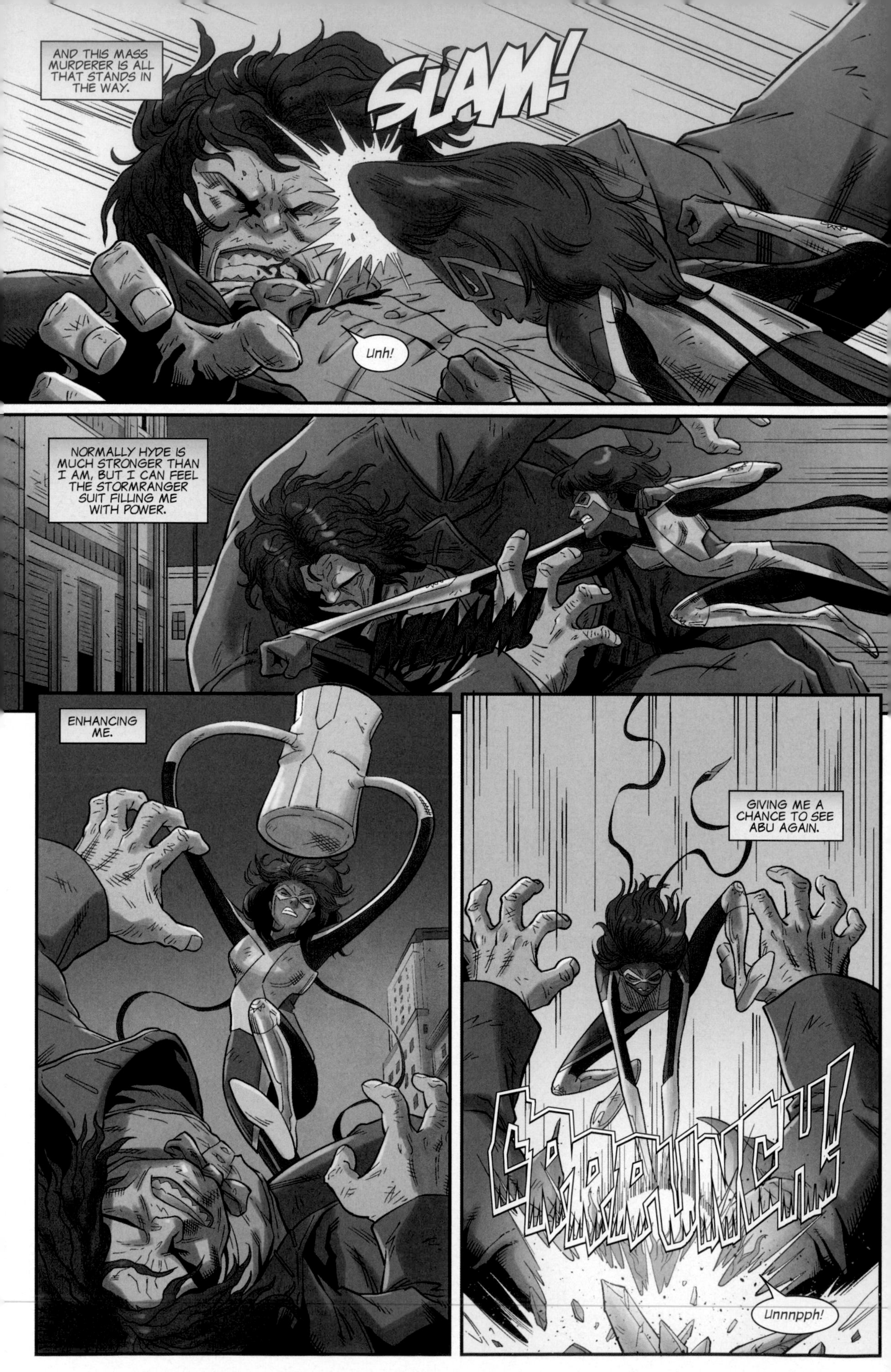
AND THIS MASS MURDERER IS ALL THAT STANDS IN THE WAY.
SLAM!
Unh!
NORMALLY HYDE IS MUCH STRONGER THAN I AM, BUT I CAN FEEL THE STORMRANGER SUIT FILLING ME WITH POWER.
ENHANCING ME.
GIVING ME A CHANCE TO SEE ABU AGAIN.
Unnnpph!

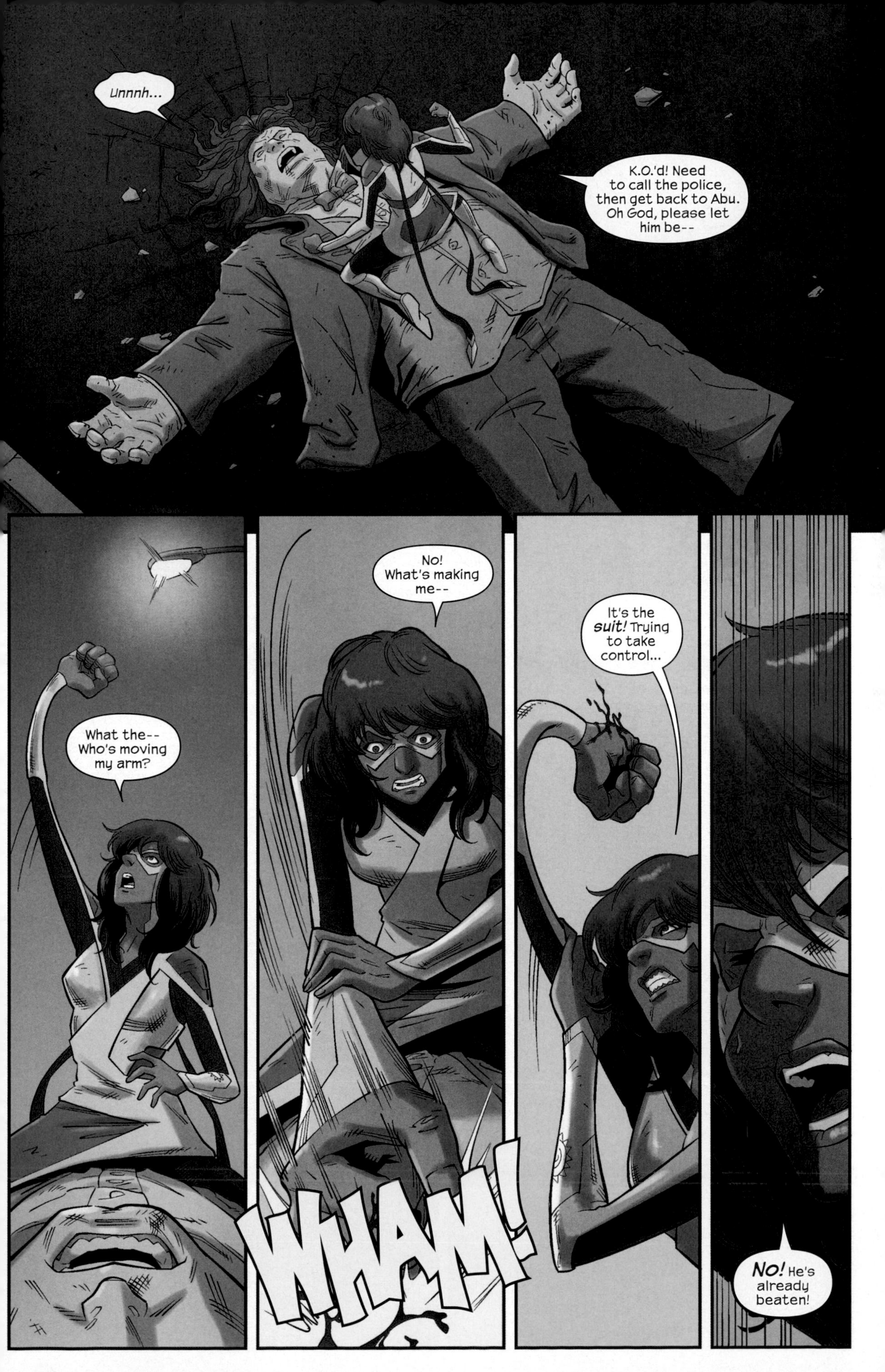
Unnnh...
K.O.'d! Need to call the police, then get back to Abu. Oh God, please let him be--
What the-- Who's moving my arm?
No! What's making me--
WHAM!
It's the *suit!* Trying to take control...
NO! He's already beaten!

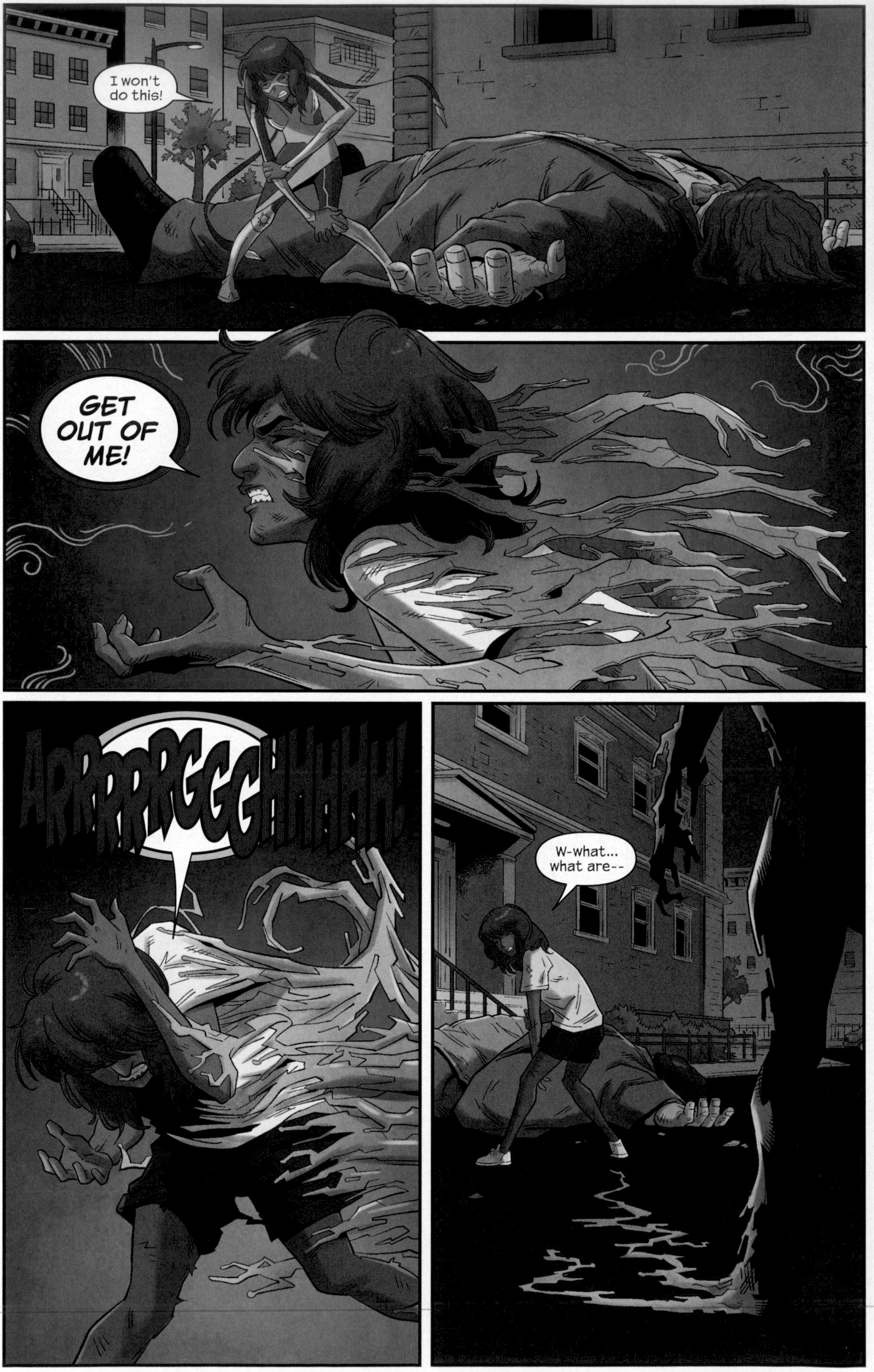
I won't do this!
GET OUT OF ME!
ARRRRRGGGHHHHH!
W-what... what are--

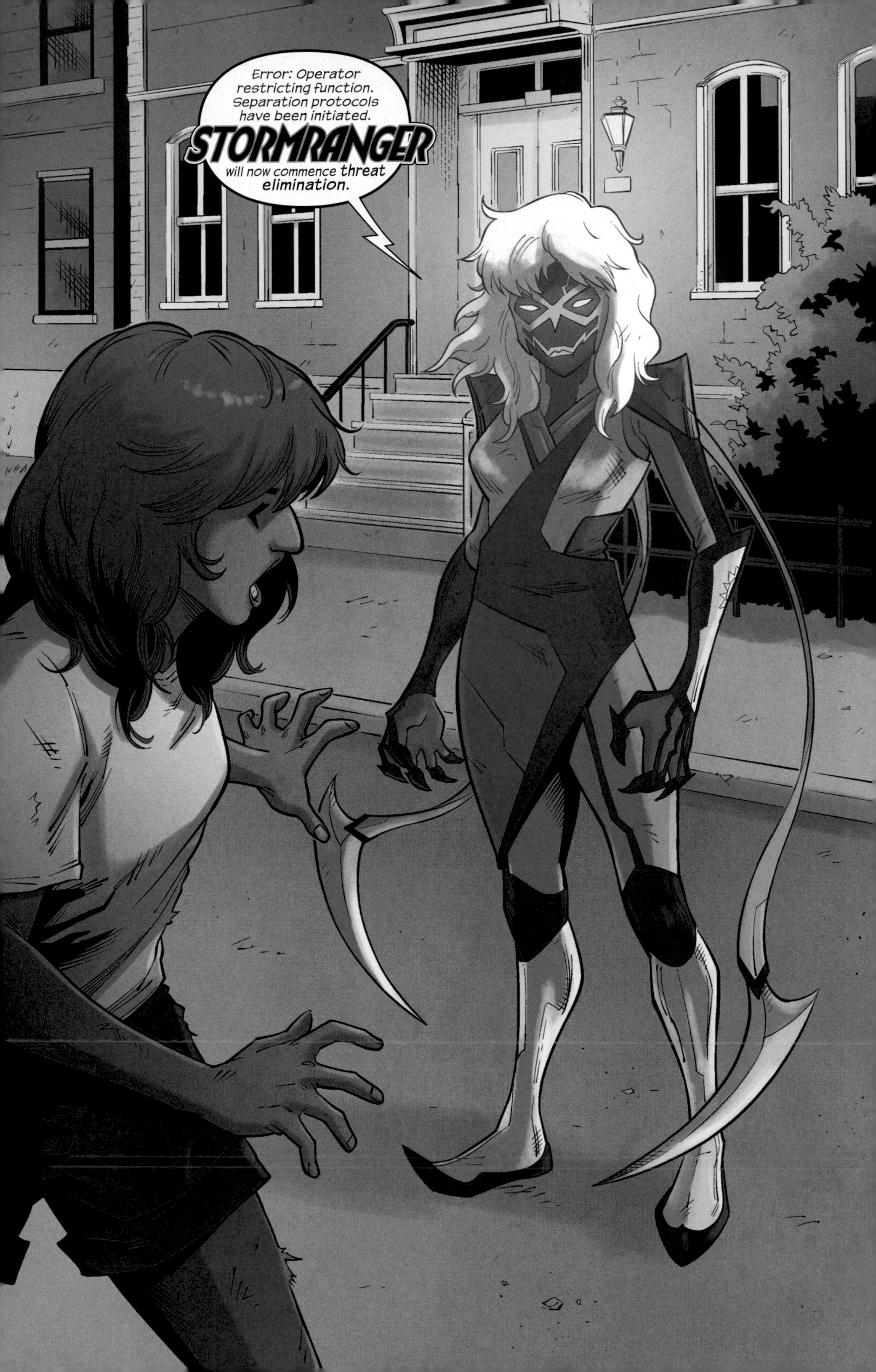
Error: Operator restricting function. Separation protocols have been initiated. STORMRANGER will now commence threat elimination.

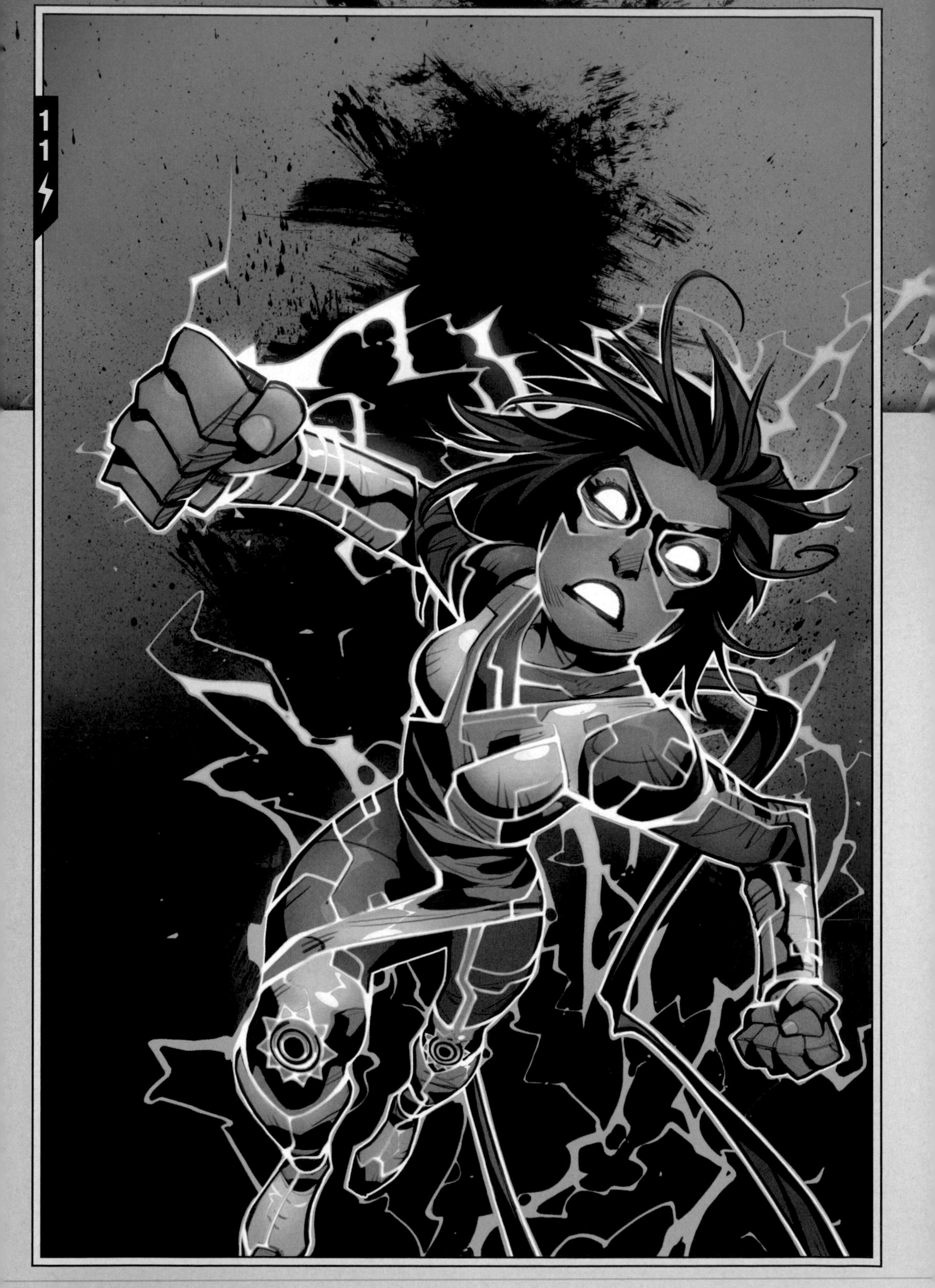
11

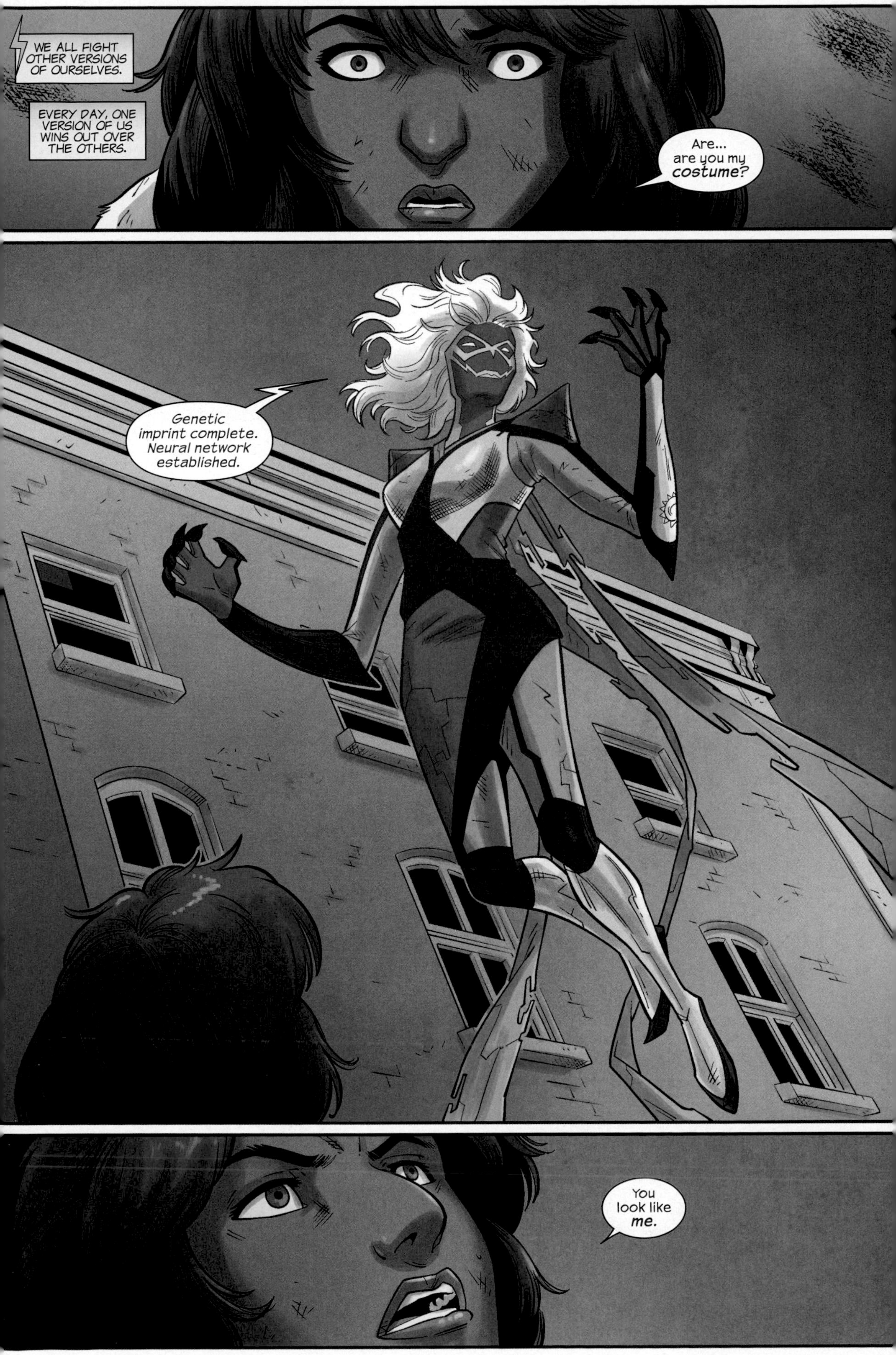
WE ALL FIGHT OTHER VERSIONS OF OURSELVES.
EVERY DAY, ONE VERSION OF US WINS OUT OVER THE OTHERS.
Are... are you my costume?
Genetic imprint complete. Neural network established.
You look like me.

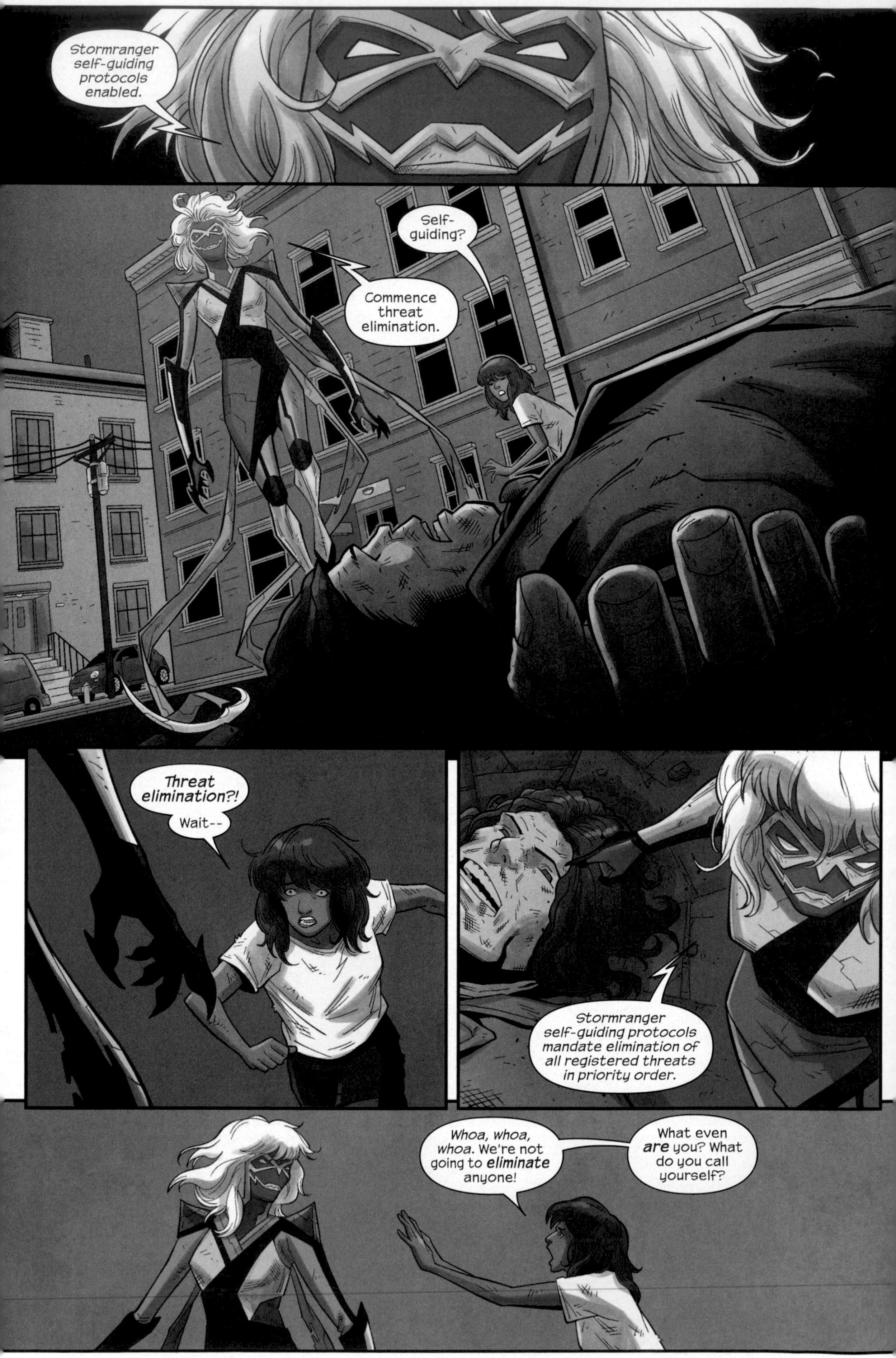
Stormranger self-guiding protocols enabled.
Commence threat elimination.
Self-guiding?
Threat elimination?!
Wait--
Stormranger self-guiding protocols mandate elimination of all registered threats in priority order.
Whoa, whoa, whoa. We're not going to eliminate anyone!
What even are you? What do you call yourself?

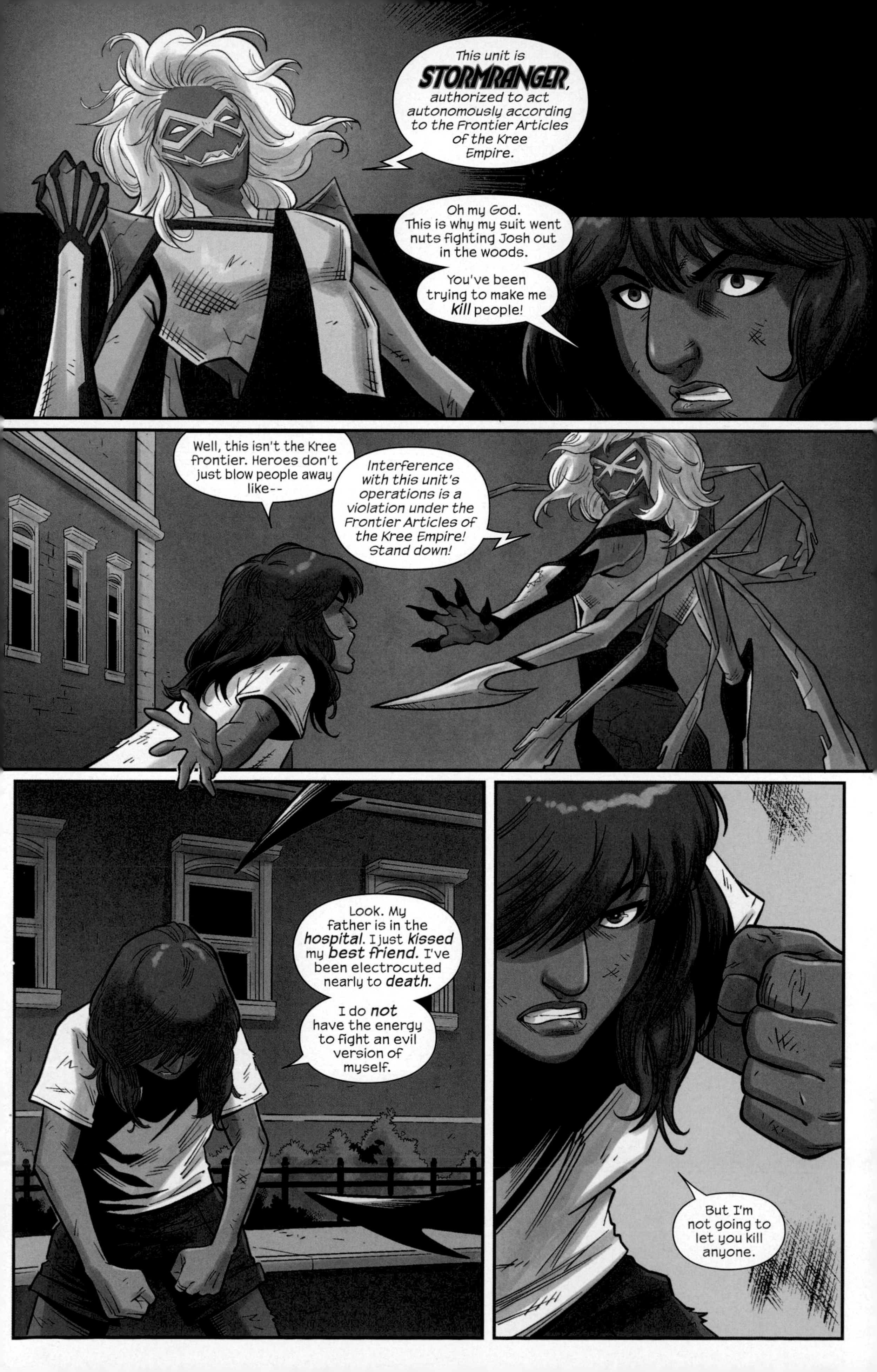
This unit is STORMRANGER, authorized to act autonomously according to the Frontier Articles of the Kree Empire.
Oh my God. This is why my suit went nuts fighting Josh out in the woods.
You've been trying to make me *kill* people!
Well, this isn't the Kree frontier. Heroes don't just blow people away like--
Interference with this unit's operations is a violation under the Frontier Articles of the Kree Empire! Stand down!
Look. My father is in the *hospital*. I just *kissed* my *best friend*. I've been electrocuted nearly to *death*.
I do *not* have the energy to fight an evil version of myself.
But I'm not going to let you kill anyone.

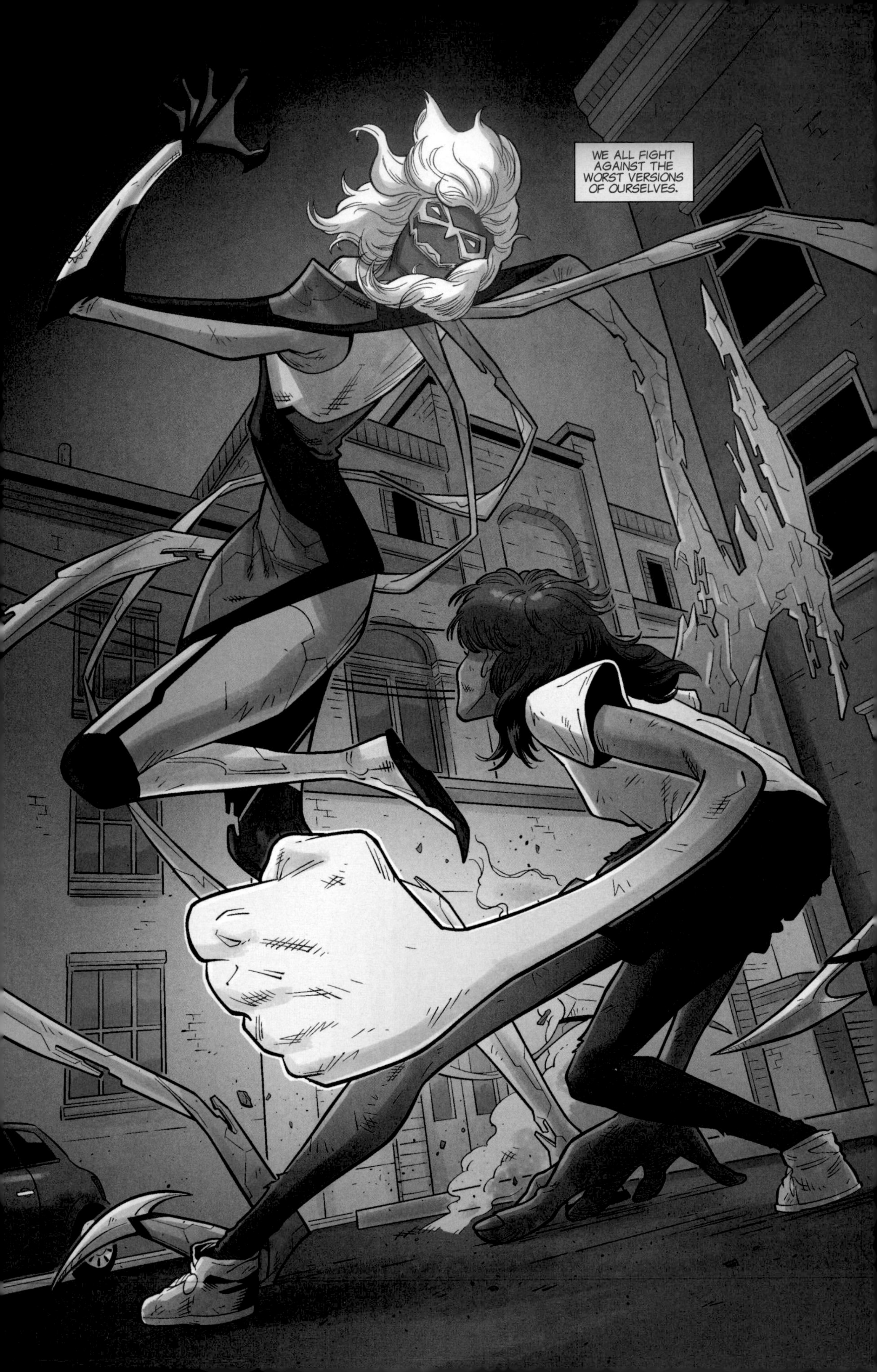
WE ALL FIGHT AGAINST THE WORST VERSIONS OF OURSELVES.

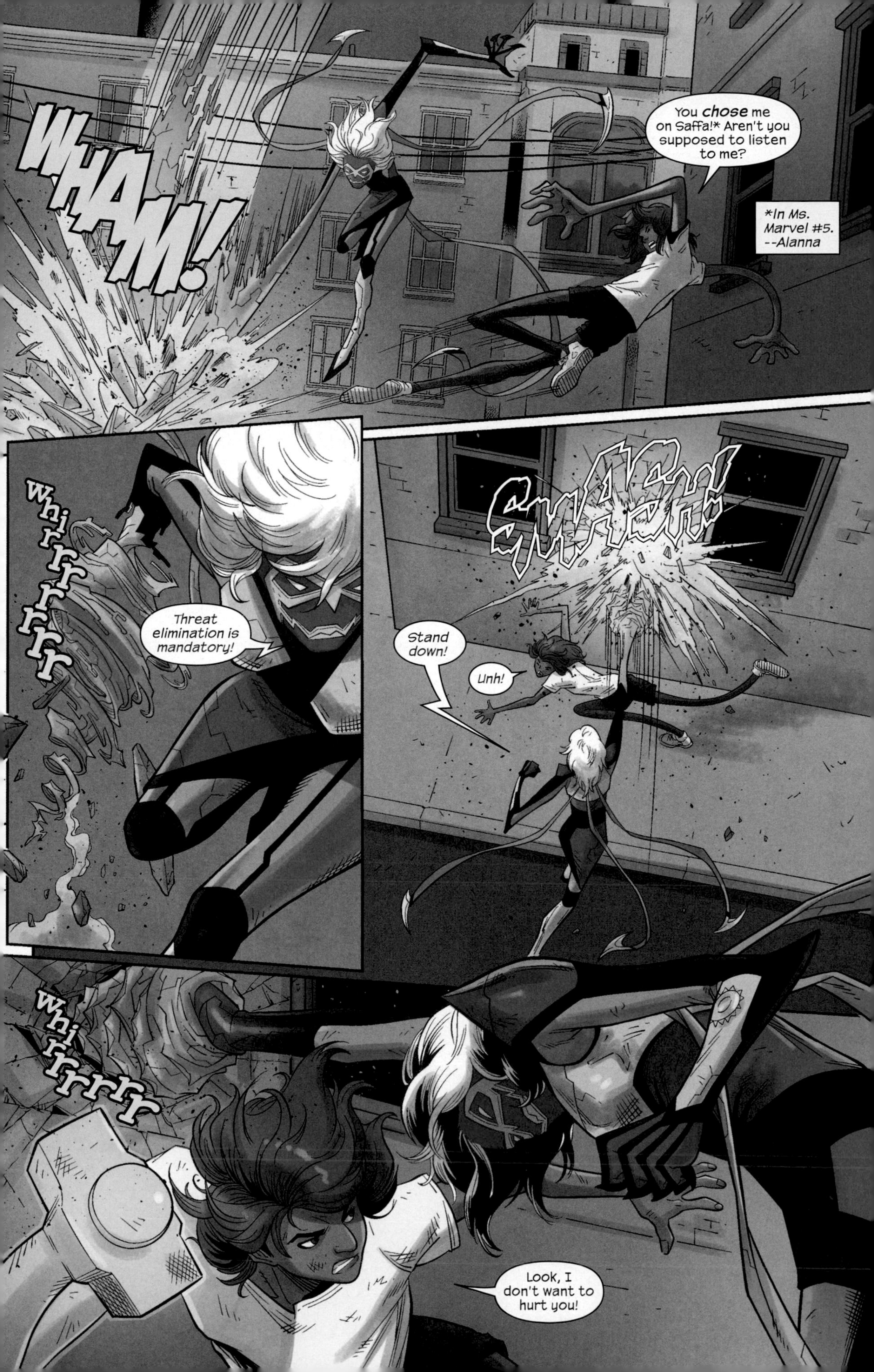
WHAM!
You chose me on Saffa!* Aren't you supposed to listen to me?
*In Ms. Marvel #5. --Alanna
Whirrrrrrrr
Threat elimination is mandatory!
SMASH!
Stand down!
Unh!
Whirrrrrr
Look, I don't want to hurt you!

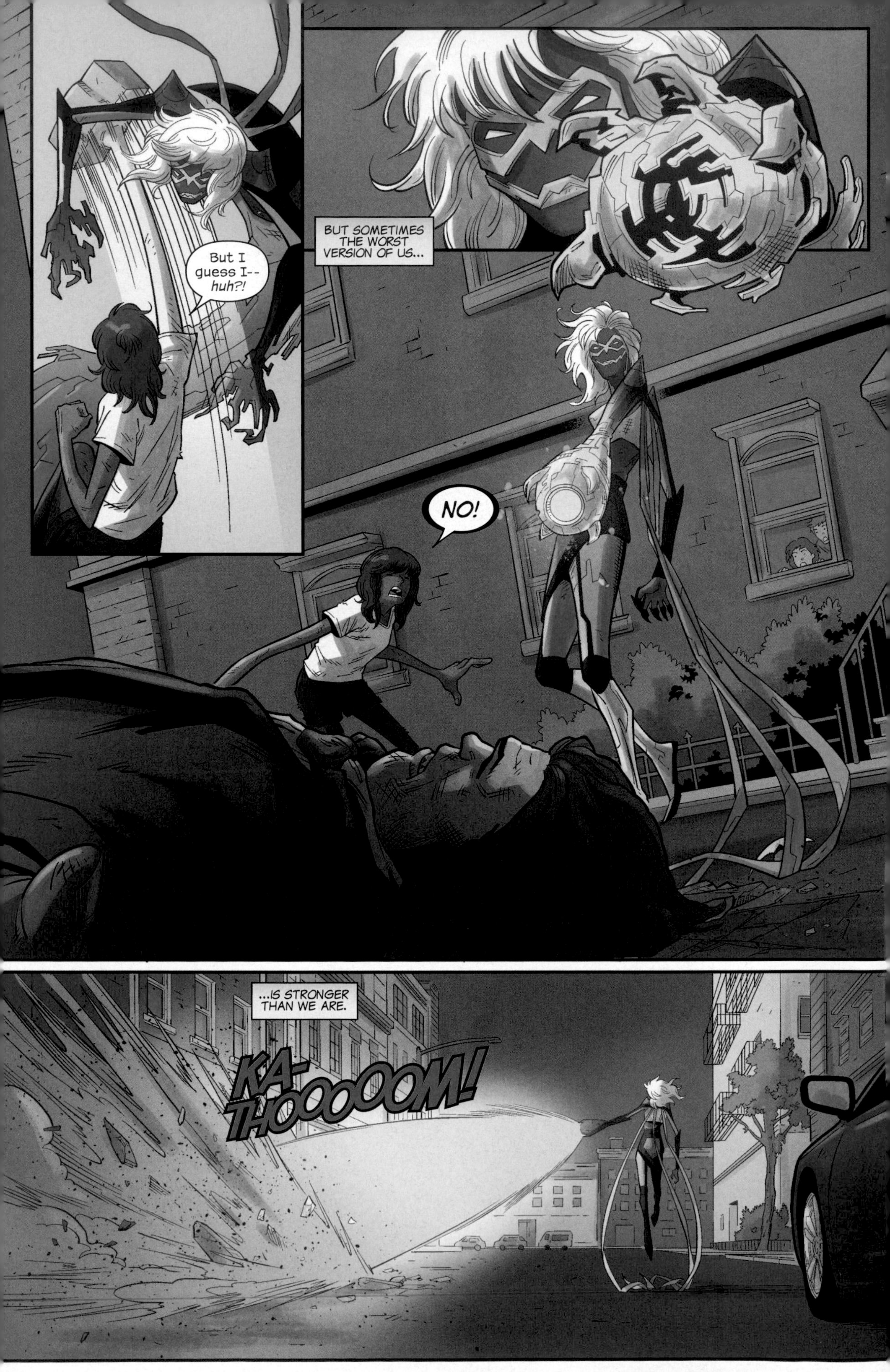
But I guess I-- huh?!
BUT SOMETIMES THE WORST VERSION OF US...
NO!
...IS STRONGER THAN WE ARE.
KA-THOOOOOOM!

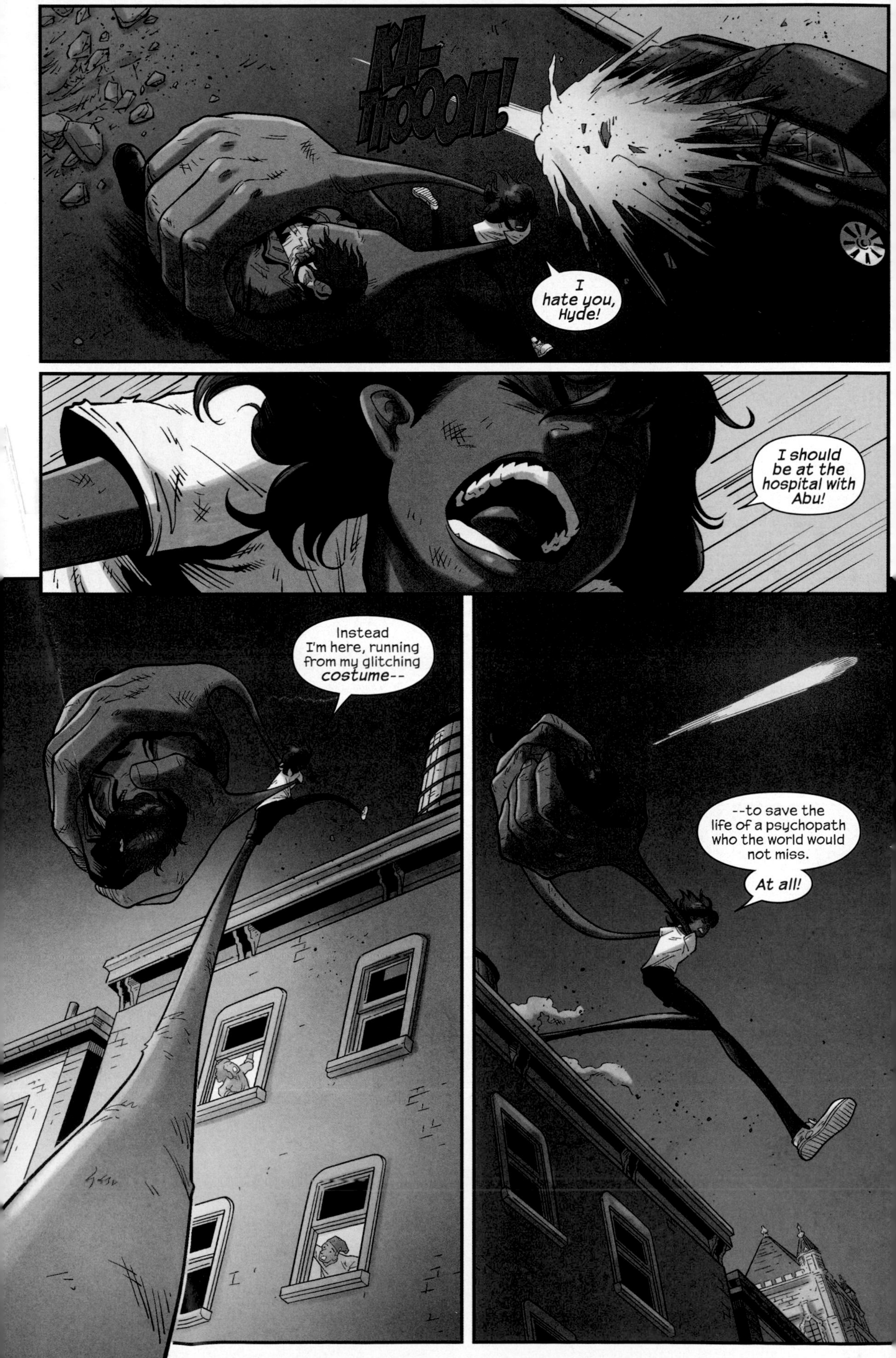
KA-THOOM!
I hate you, Hyde!
I should be at the hospital with Abu!
Instead I'm here, running from my glitching *costume*--
--to save the life of a psychopath who the world would not miss.
At all!

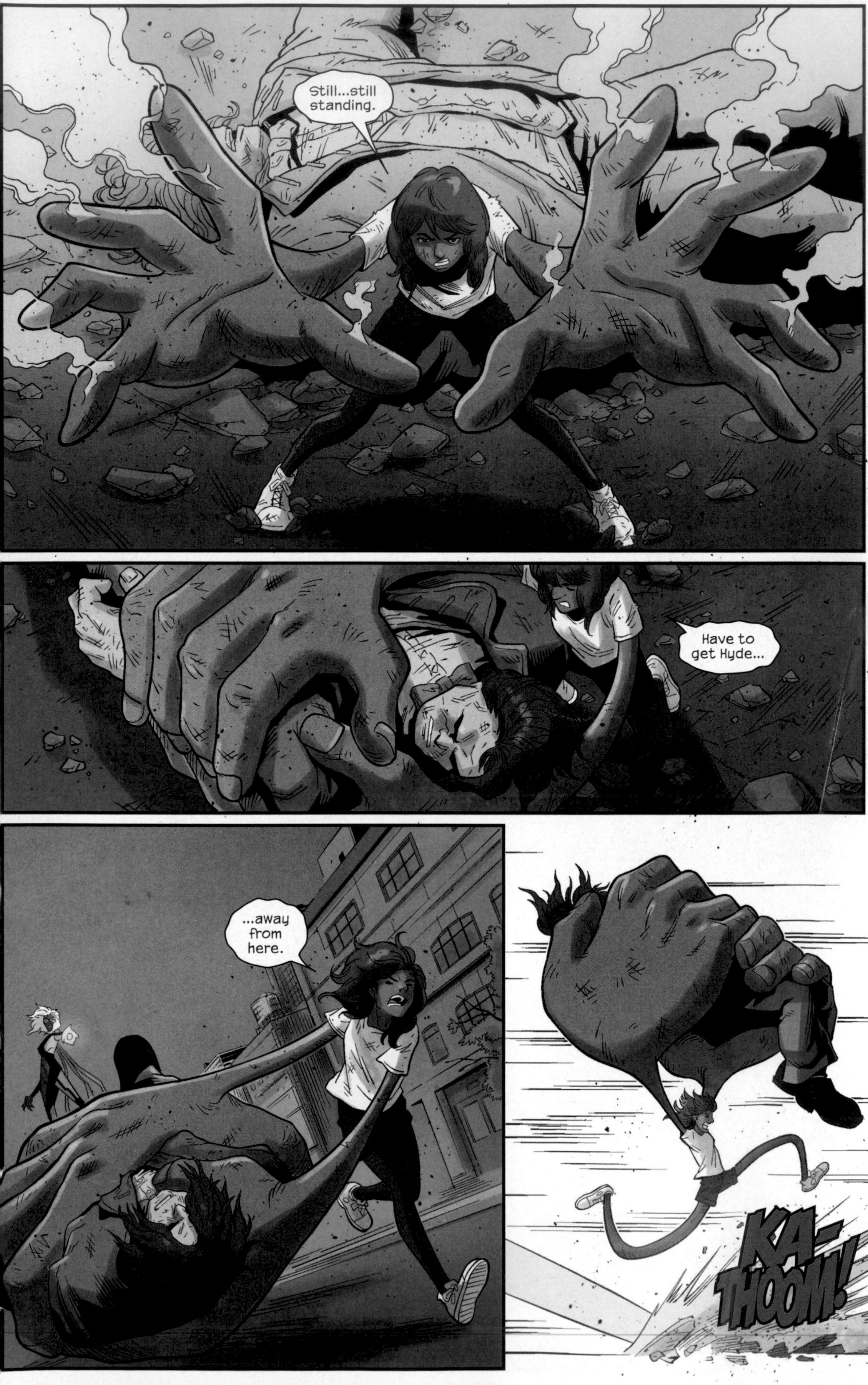
Still...still standing.
Have to get Hyde...
...away from here.
KA-THOOM!

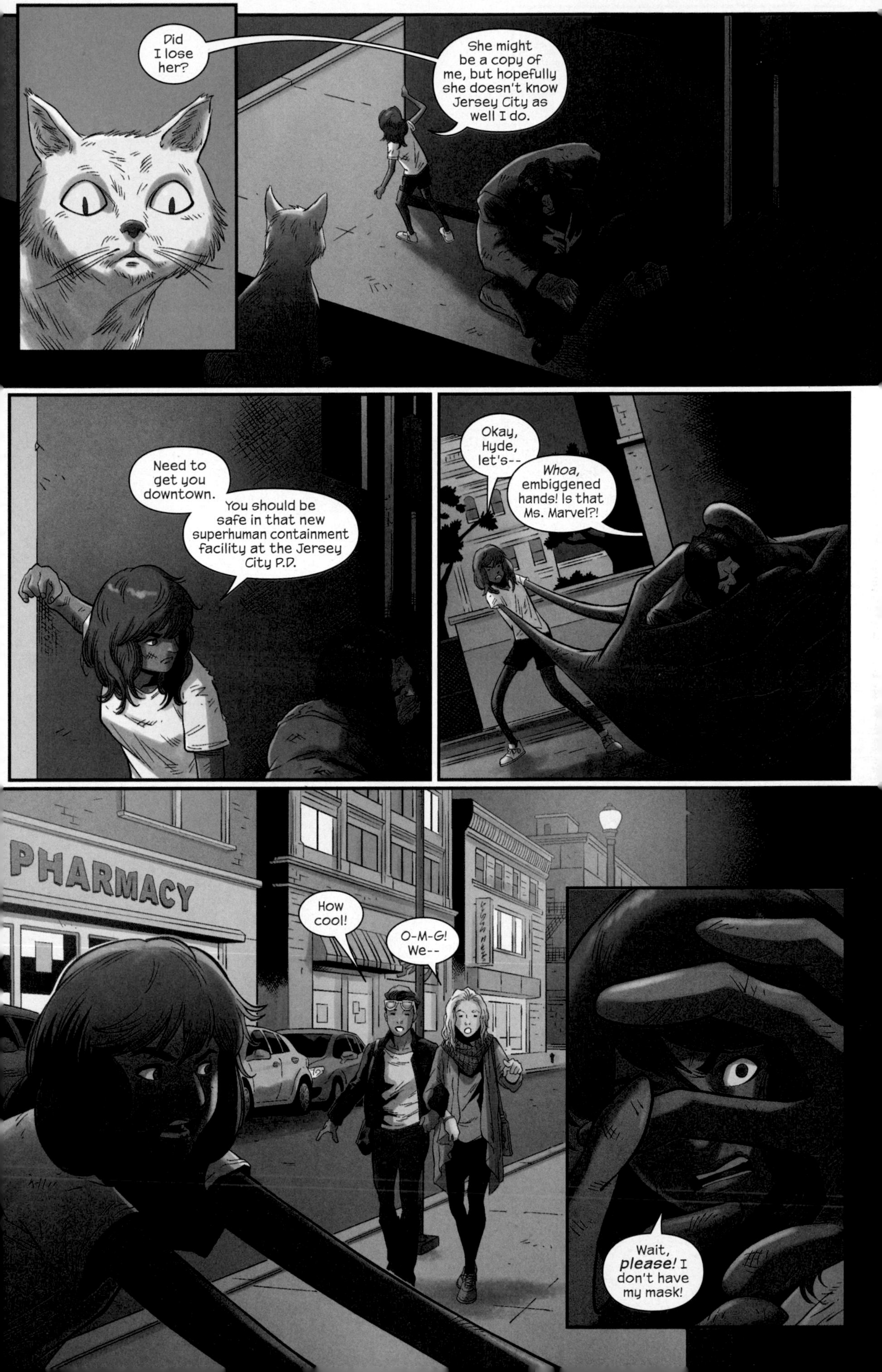
Did I lose her?
She might be a copy of me, but hopefully she doesn't know Jersey City as well I do.
Need to get you downtown.
You should be safe in that new superhuman containment facility at the Jersey City P.D.
Okay, Hyde, let's--
Whoa, embiggened hands! Is that Ms. Marvel?!
PHARMACY
How cool!
O-M-G! We--
Wait, please! I don't have my mask!

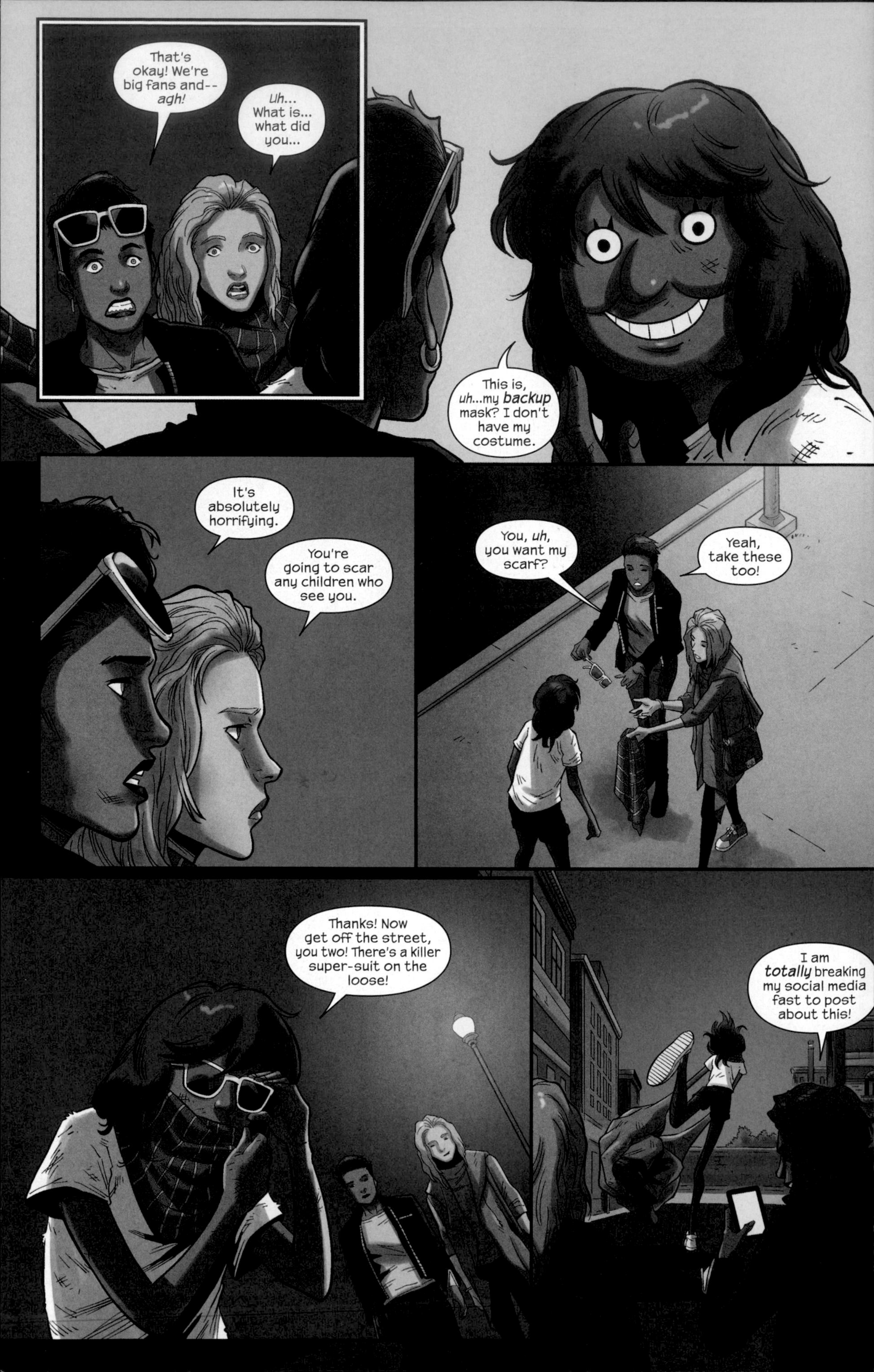
That's okay! We're big fans and-- *agh!*
Uh... What is... what did you...
This is, *uh*...my ***backup*** mask? I don't have my costume.
It's absolutely horrifying.
You're going to scar any children who see you.
You, *uh*, you want my scarf?
Yeah, take these too!
Thanks! Now get off the street, you two! There's a killer super-suit on the loose!
I am ***totally*** breaking my social media fast to post about this!

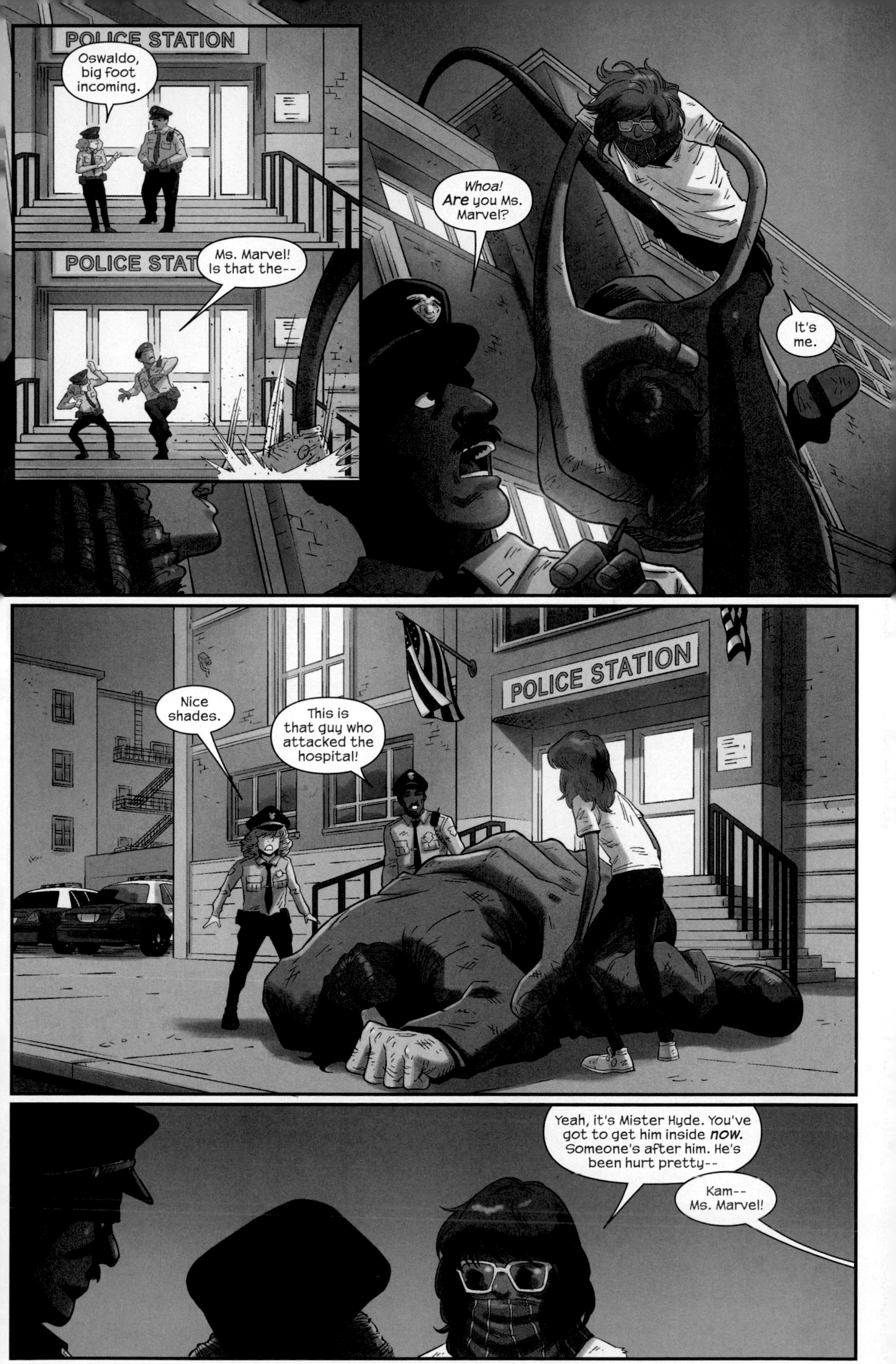
POLICE STATION
Oswaldo, big foot incoming.
POLICE STAT
Ms. Marvel! Is that the--
Whoa! *Are* you Ms. Marvel?
It's me.
POLICE STATION
Nice shades.
This is that guy who attacked the hospital!
Yeah, it's Mister Hyde. You've got to get him inside ***NOW.*** Someone's after him. He's been hurt pretty--
Kam-- Ms. Marvel!

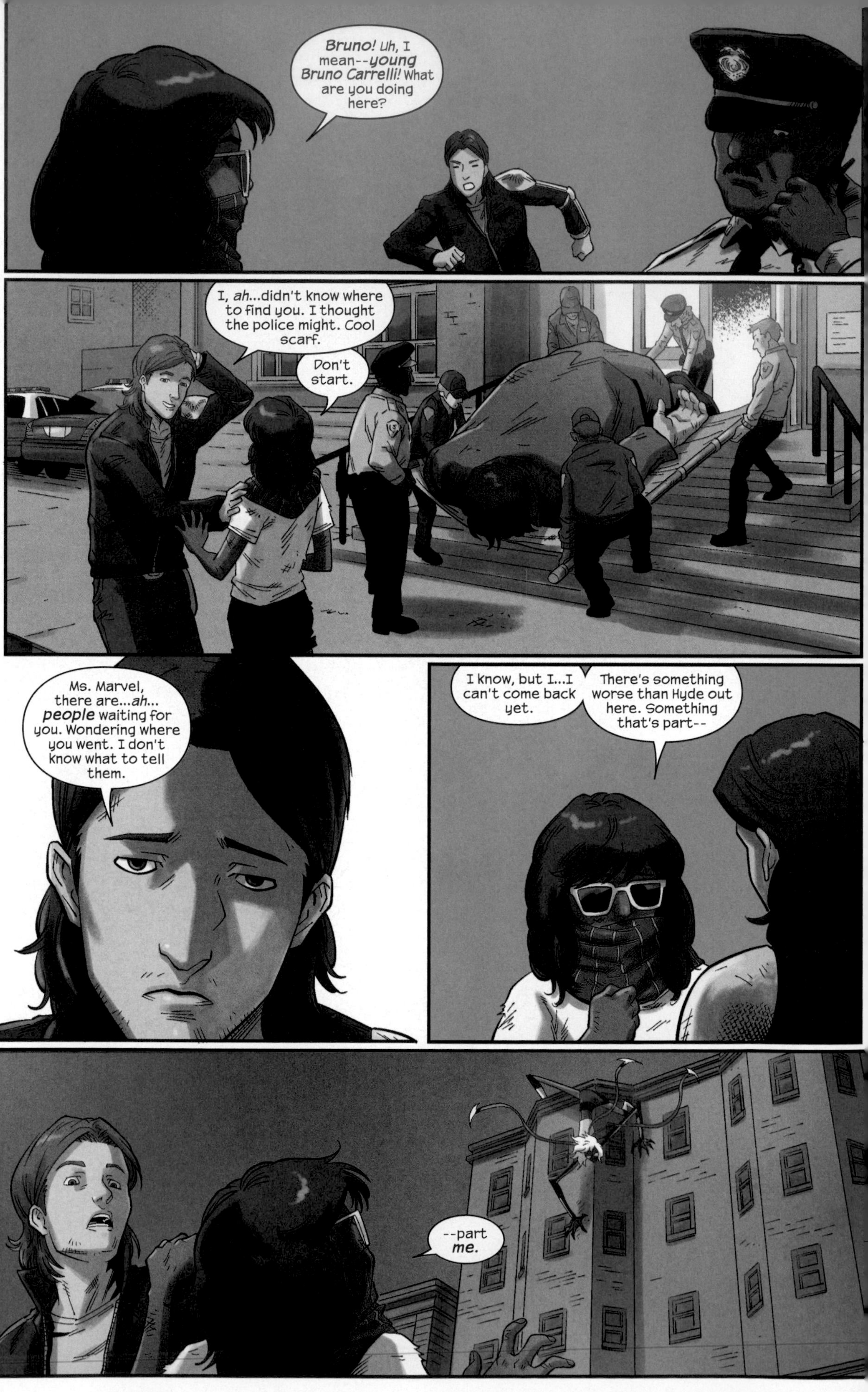
Bruno! Uh, I mean--young Bruno Carrelli! What are you doing here?
I, ah...didn't know where to find you. I thought the police might. Cool scarf.
Don't start.
Ms. Marvel, there are...ah... people waiting for you. Wondering where you went. I don't know what to tell them.
I know, but I...I can't come back yet.
There's something worse than Hyde out here. Something that's part--
--part me.

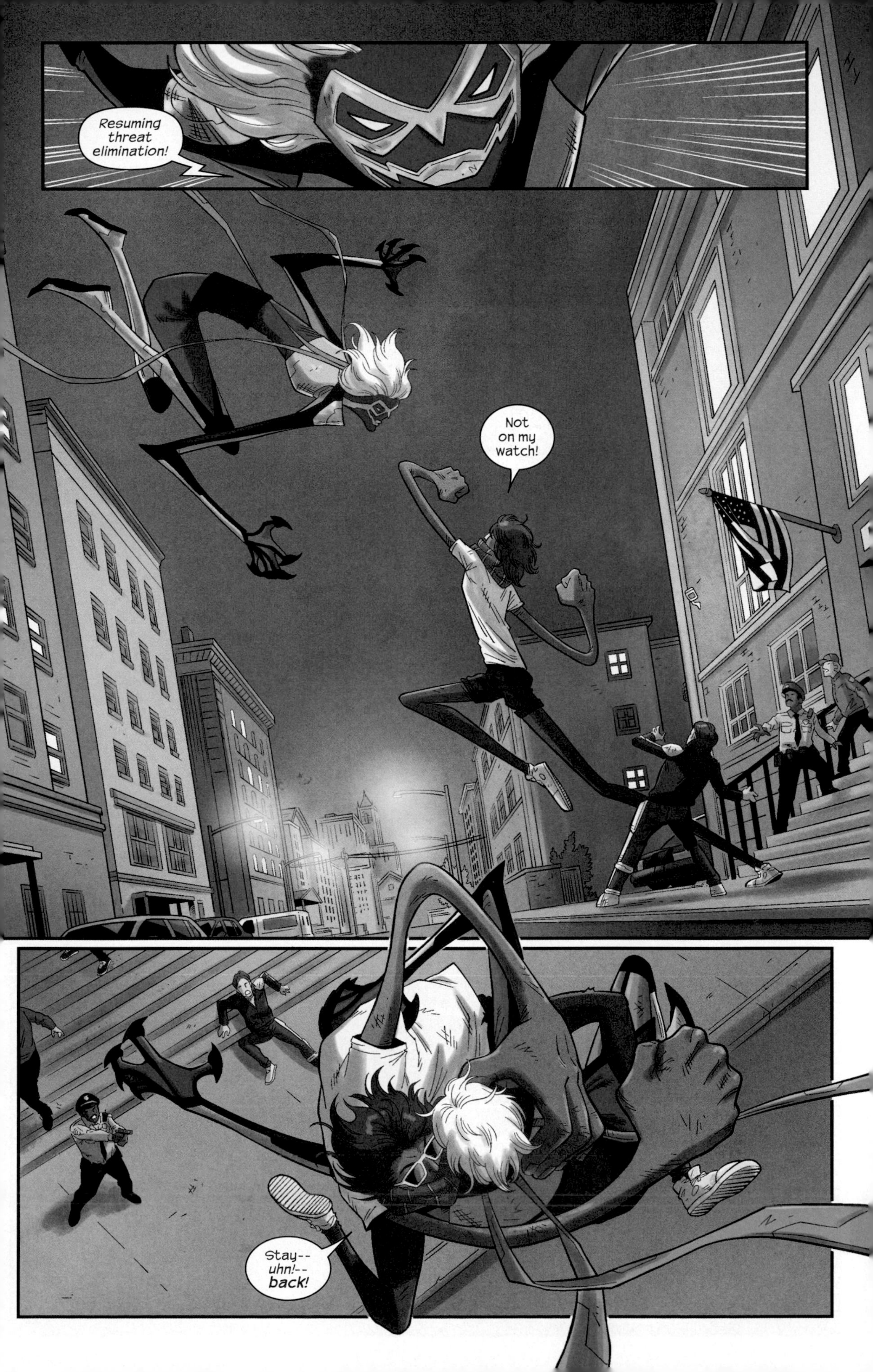
Resuming threat elimination!
Not on my watch!
Stay-- uhn!-- back!

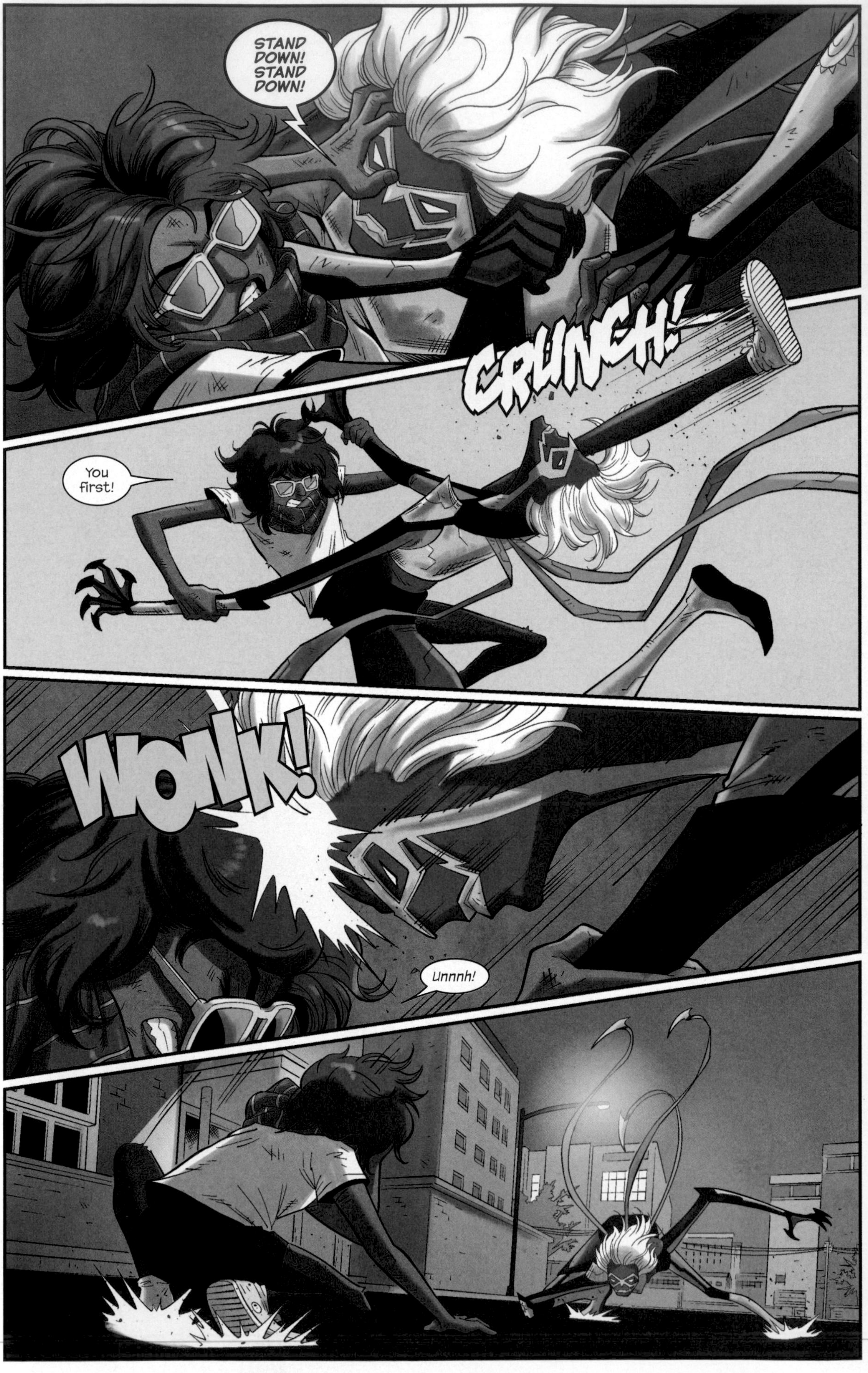
STAND DOWN! STAND DOWN!
CRUNCH!
You first!
WONK!
Unnnh!

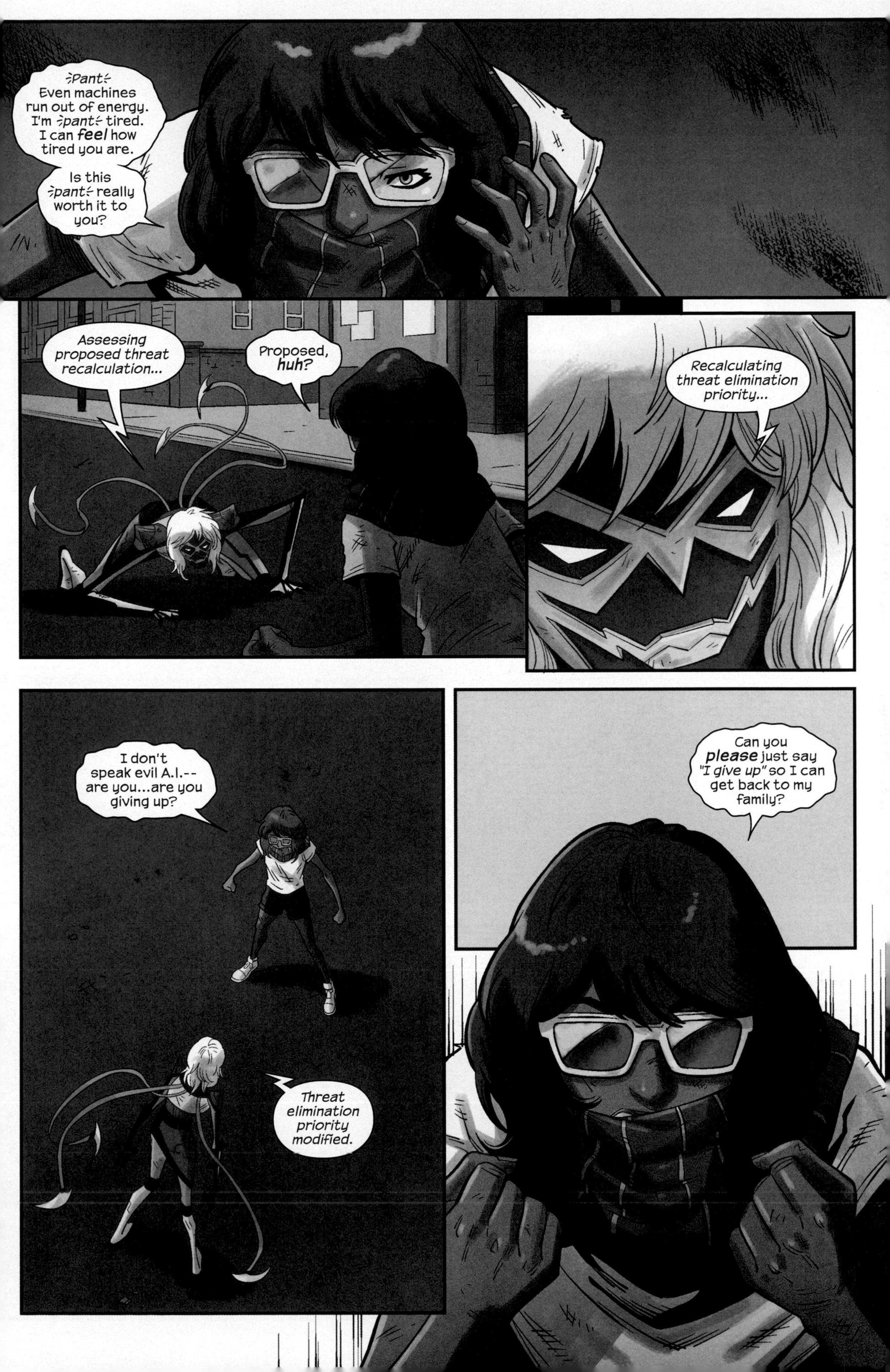

≈Pant≈ Even machines run out of energy. I'm ≈pant≈ tired. I can *feel* how tired you are.
Is this ≈pant≈ really worth it to you?
Assessing proposed threat recalculation...
Proposed, *huh?*
Recalculating threat elimination priority...
I don't speak evil A.I.-- are you...are you giving up?
Threat elimination priority modified.
Can you *please* just say *"I give up"* so I can get back to my family?

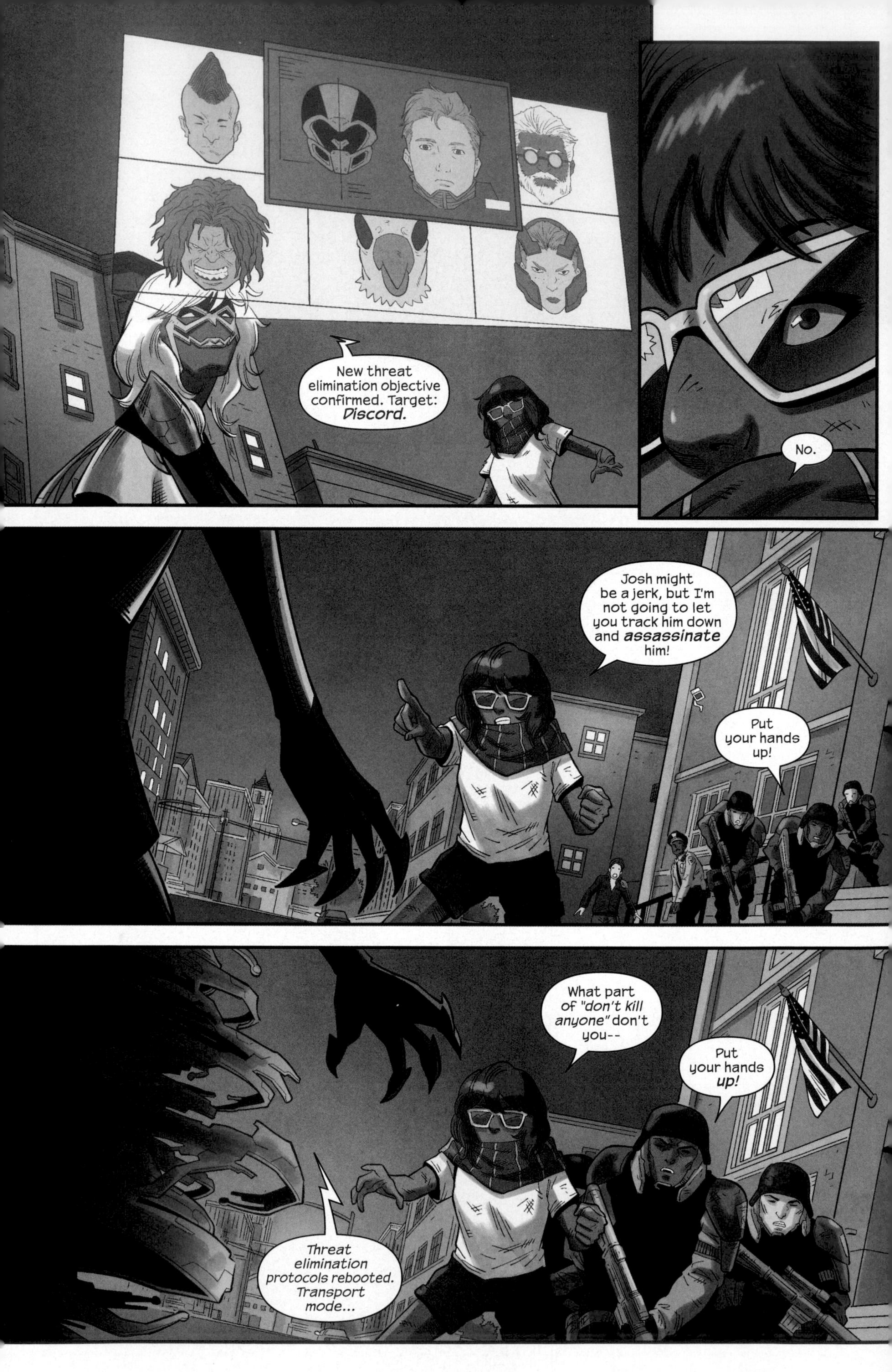
New threat elimination objective confirmed. Target: *Discord*.
No.
Josh might be a jerk, but I'm not going to let you track him down and ***assassinate*** him!
Put your hands up!
What part of *"don't kill anyone"* don't you--
Put your hands ***up!***
Threat elimination protocols rebooted. Transport mode...

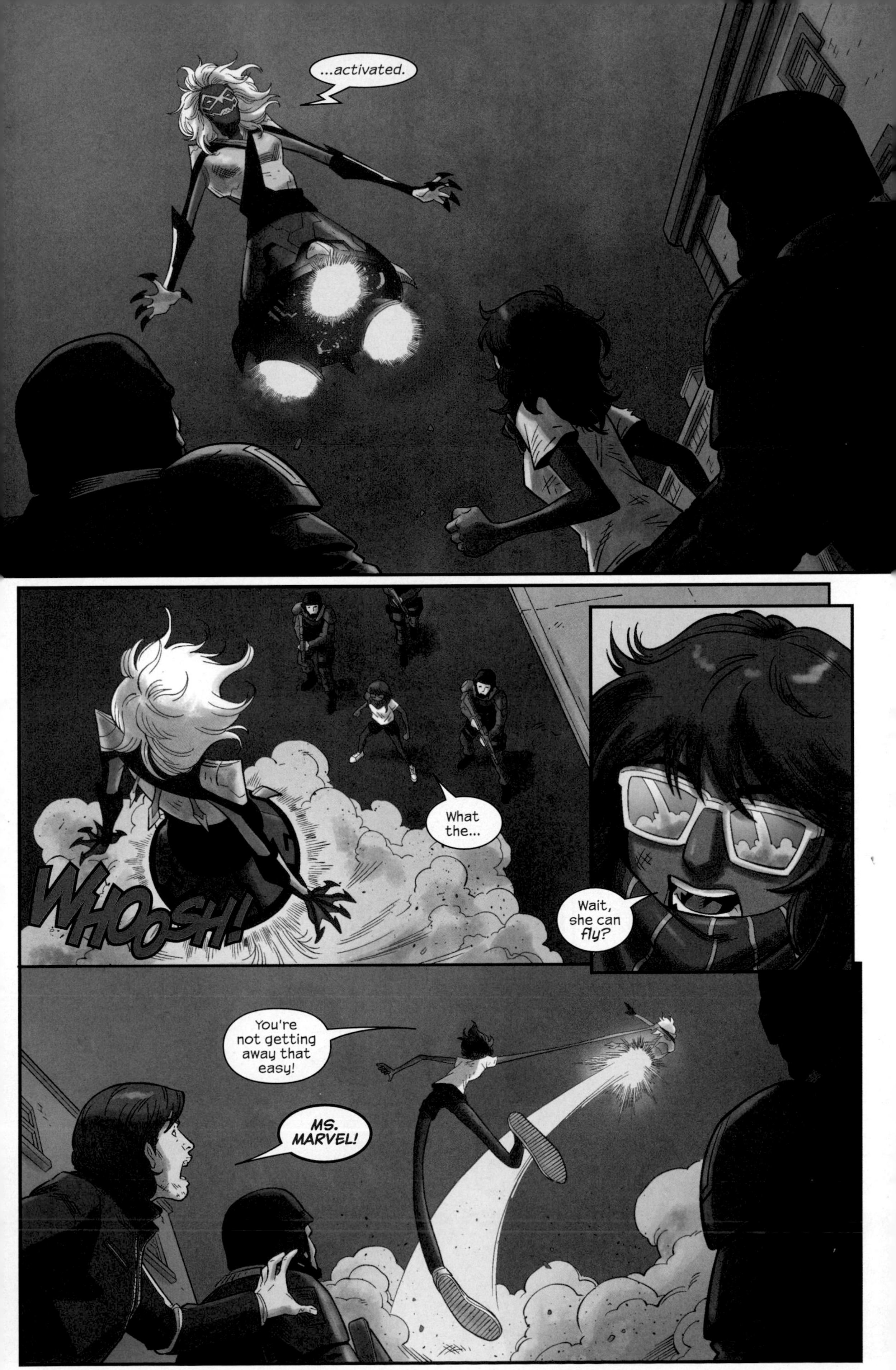
...activated.
What the...
WHOOSH!
Wait, she can fly?
You're not getting away that easy!
MS. MARVEL!

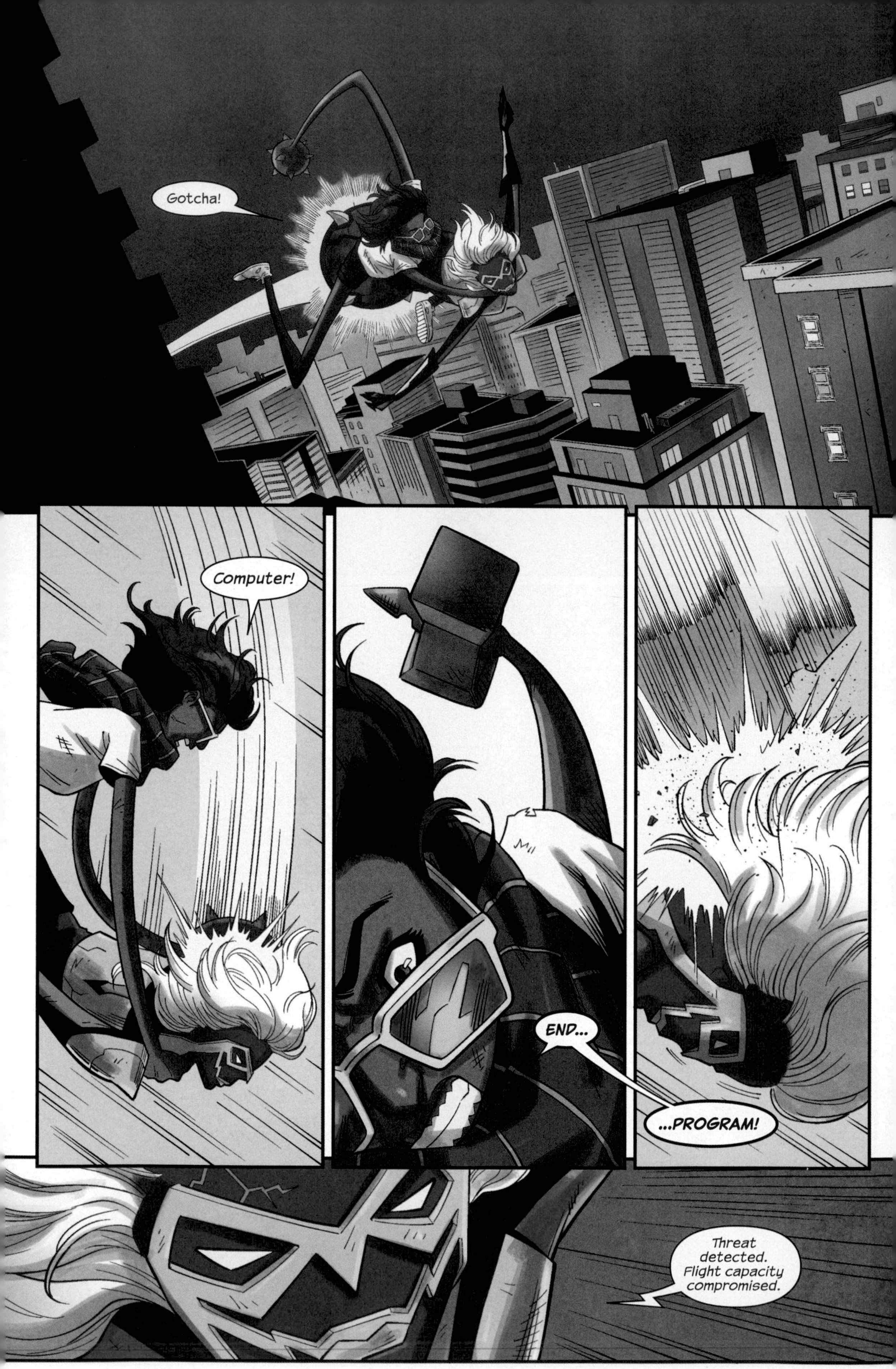
Gotcha!
Computer!
END...
...PROGRAM!
Threat detected. Flight capacity compromised.

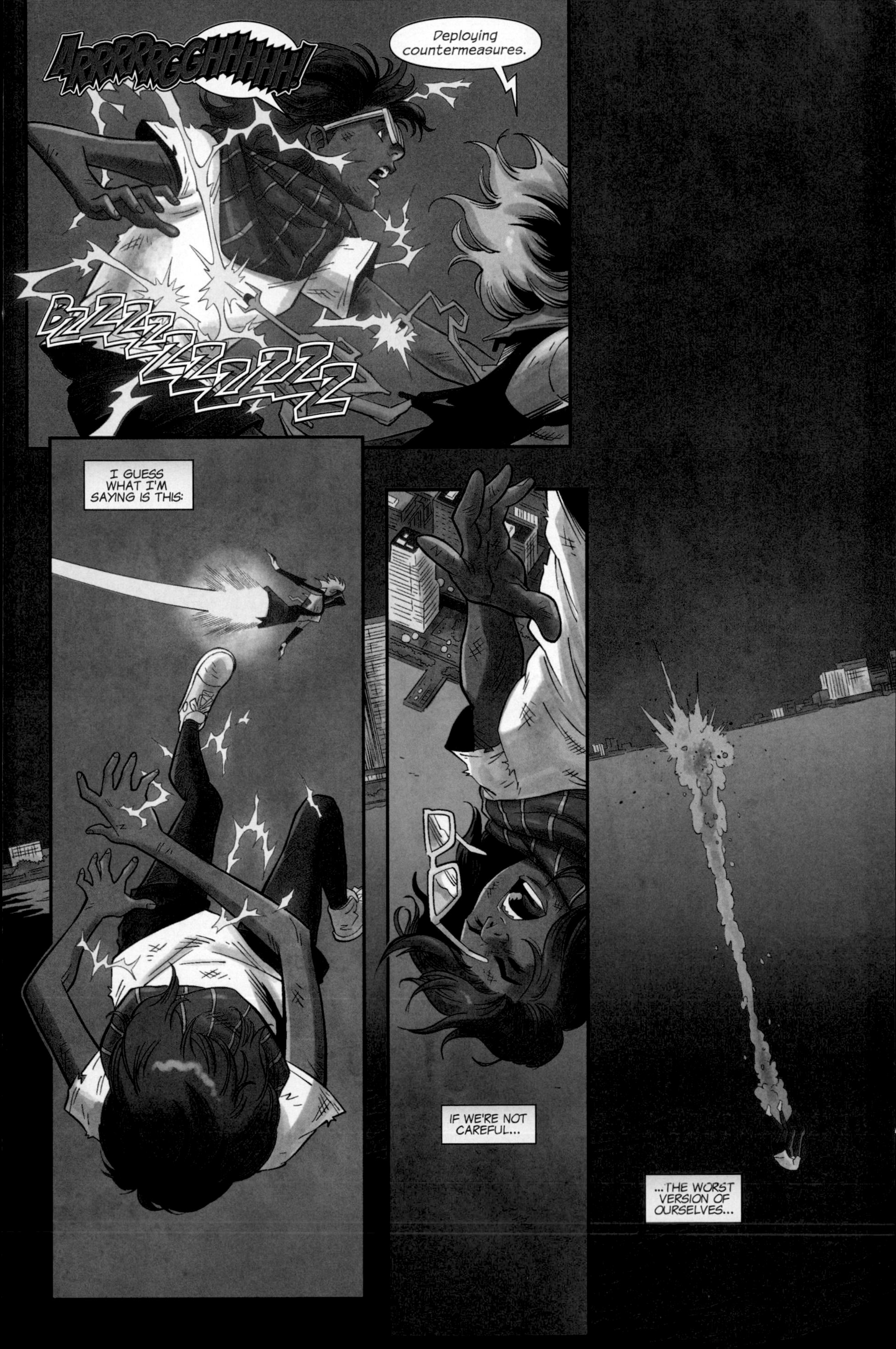
ARRRRRGGHHHHH!
Deploying countermeasures.
BZZZZZZZZZZZZZZ
I GUESS WHAT I'M SAYING IS THIS:
IF WE'RE NOT CAREFUL...
...THE WORST VERSION OF OURSELVES...

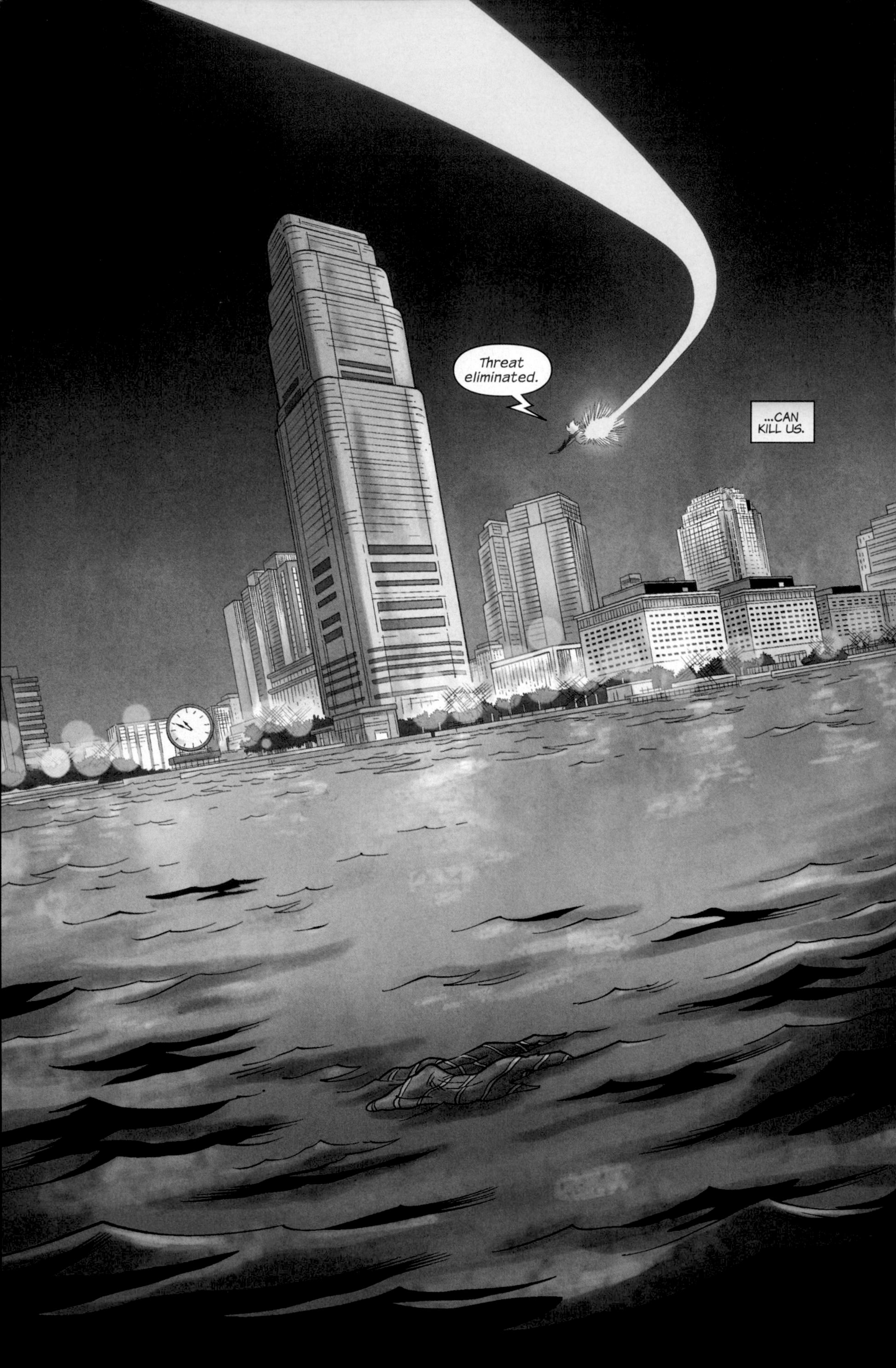
Threat eliminated.
...CAN KILL US.

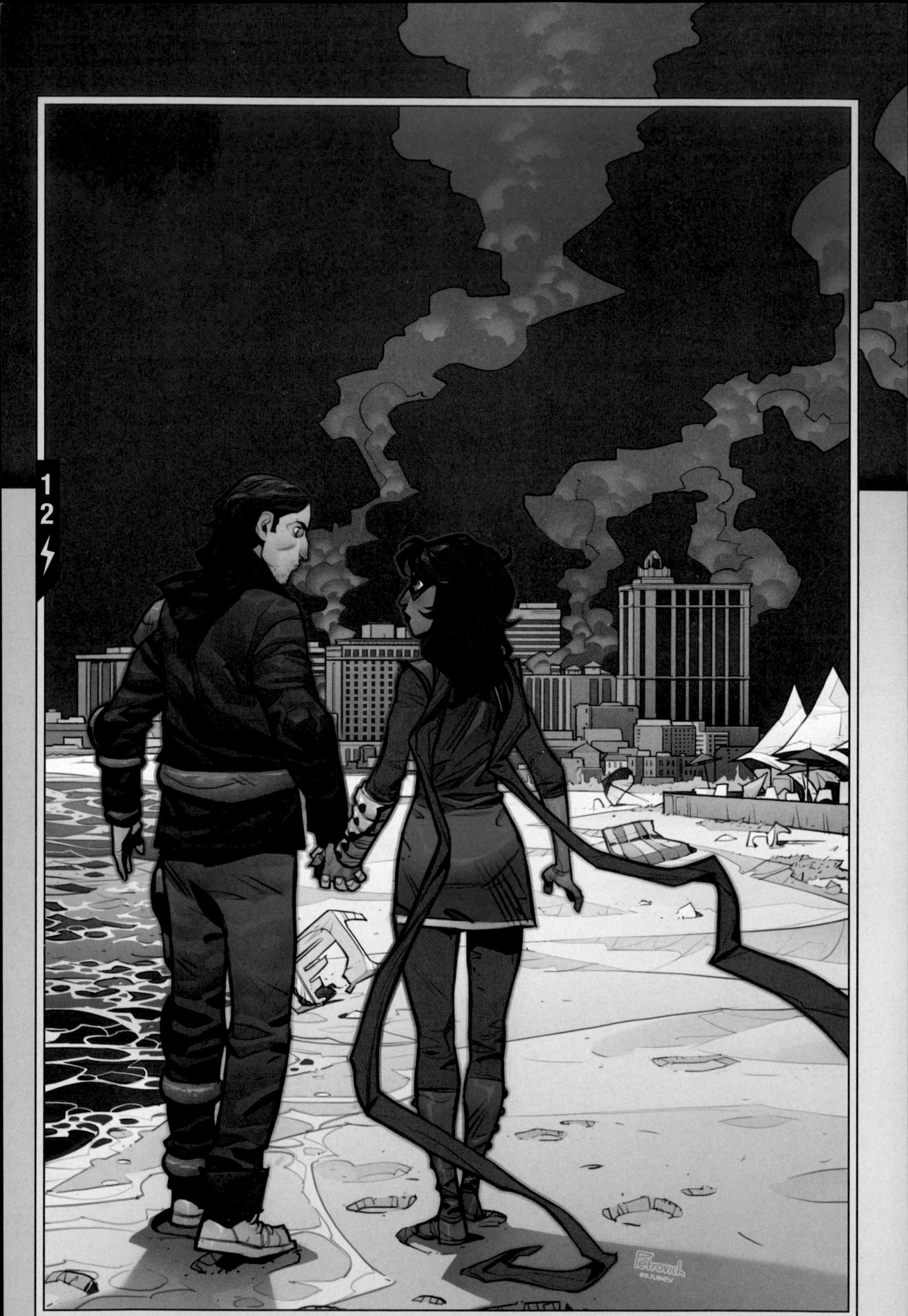
1
2
Petrovich

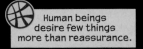

Human beings desire few things more than reassurance.

Is she okay?

We need it to continue on with the unfathomably hard work of living.

She's waking up.

NEW JERSEY MEDICAL CENTER.

Ammi, you fell asleep. Can I get you anything?

Aamir! I-- Tyesha, when did you get here? Where's Malik?

He's with my parents--it's the middle of the night.

This place-- it's so hard to tell time in here. How is your father, Aamir? Any update?

I have seen this as a sorcerer.

Yes, in fact, there is an update.

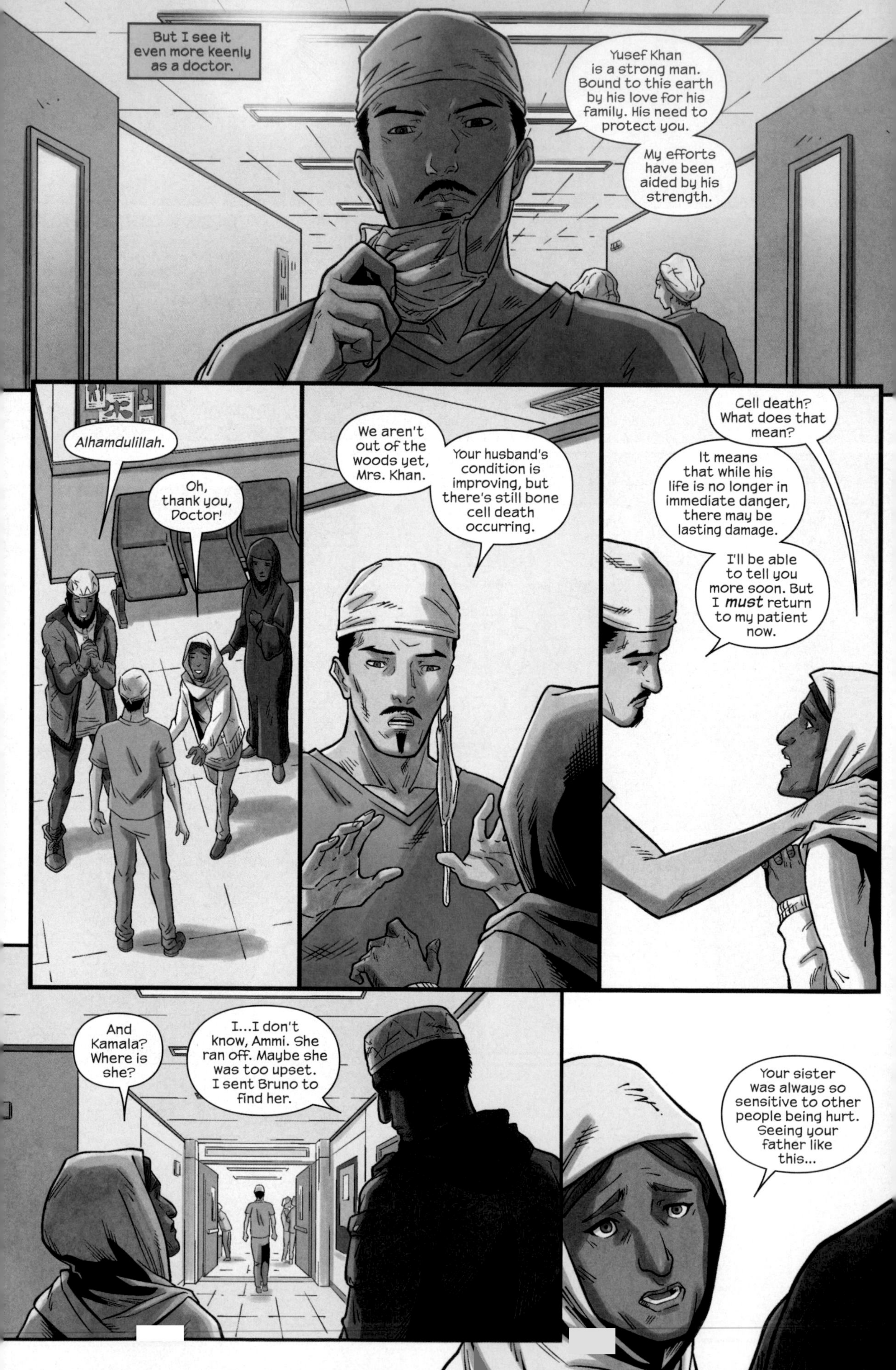

But I see it even more keenly as a doctor.
Yusef Khan is a strong man. Bound to this earth by his love for his family. His need to protect you.
My efforts have been aided by his strength.
Alhamdulillah.
Oh, thank you, Doctor!
We aren't out of the woods yet, Mrs. Khan.
Your husband's condition is improving, but there's still bone cell death occurring.
Cell death? What does that mean?
It means that while his life is no longer in immediate danger, there may be lasting damage.
I'll be able to tell you more soon. But I *must* return to my patient now.
And Kamala? Where is she?
I...I don't know, Ammi. She ran off. Maybe she was too upset. I sent Bruno to find her.
Your sister was always so sensitive to other people being hurt. Seeing your father like this...

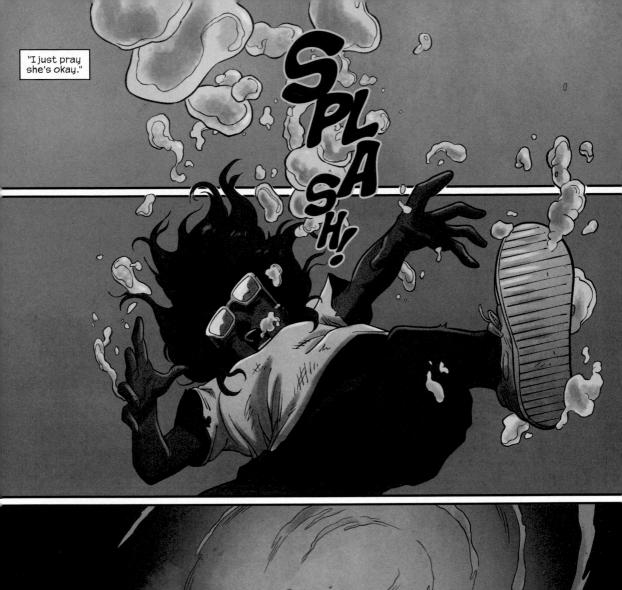

"I just pray she's okay."

SPLASH!

THE HUDSON river.

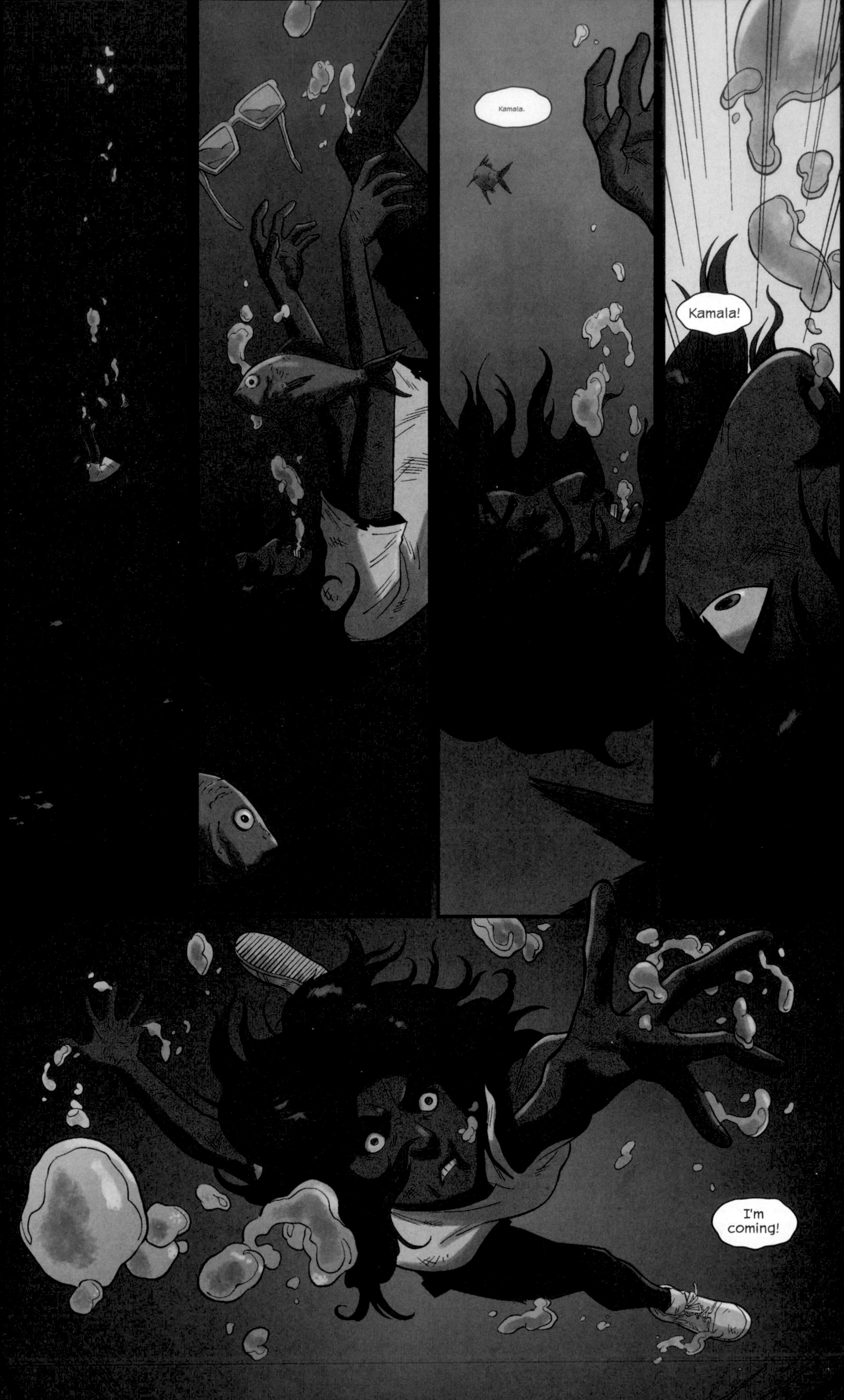
Kamala.
Kamala!
I'm coming!

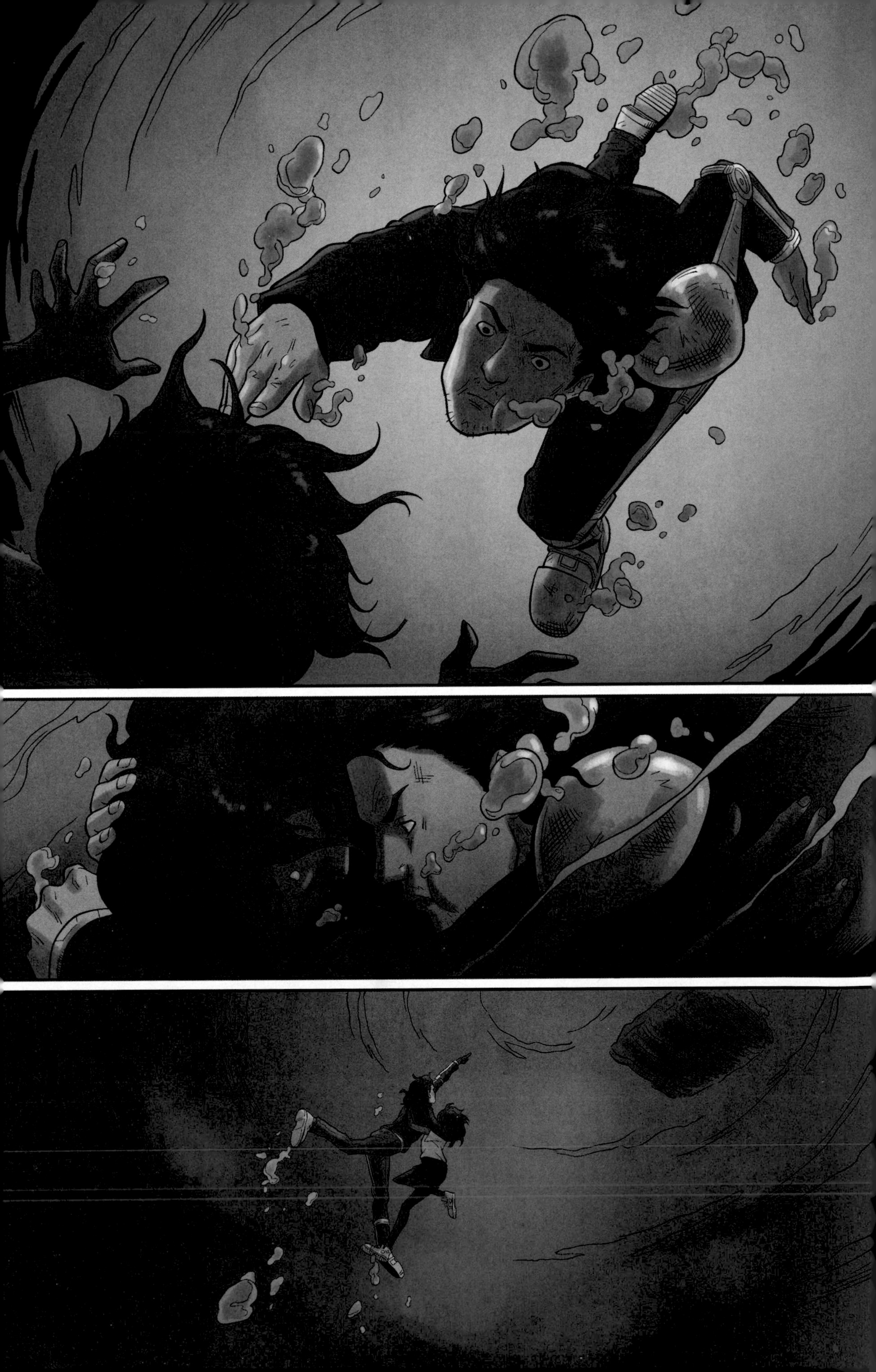

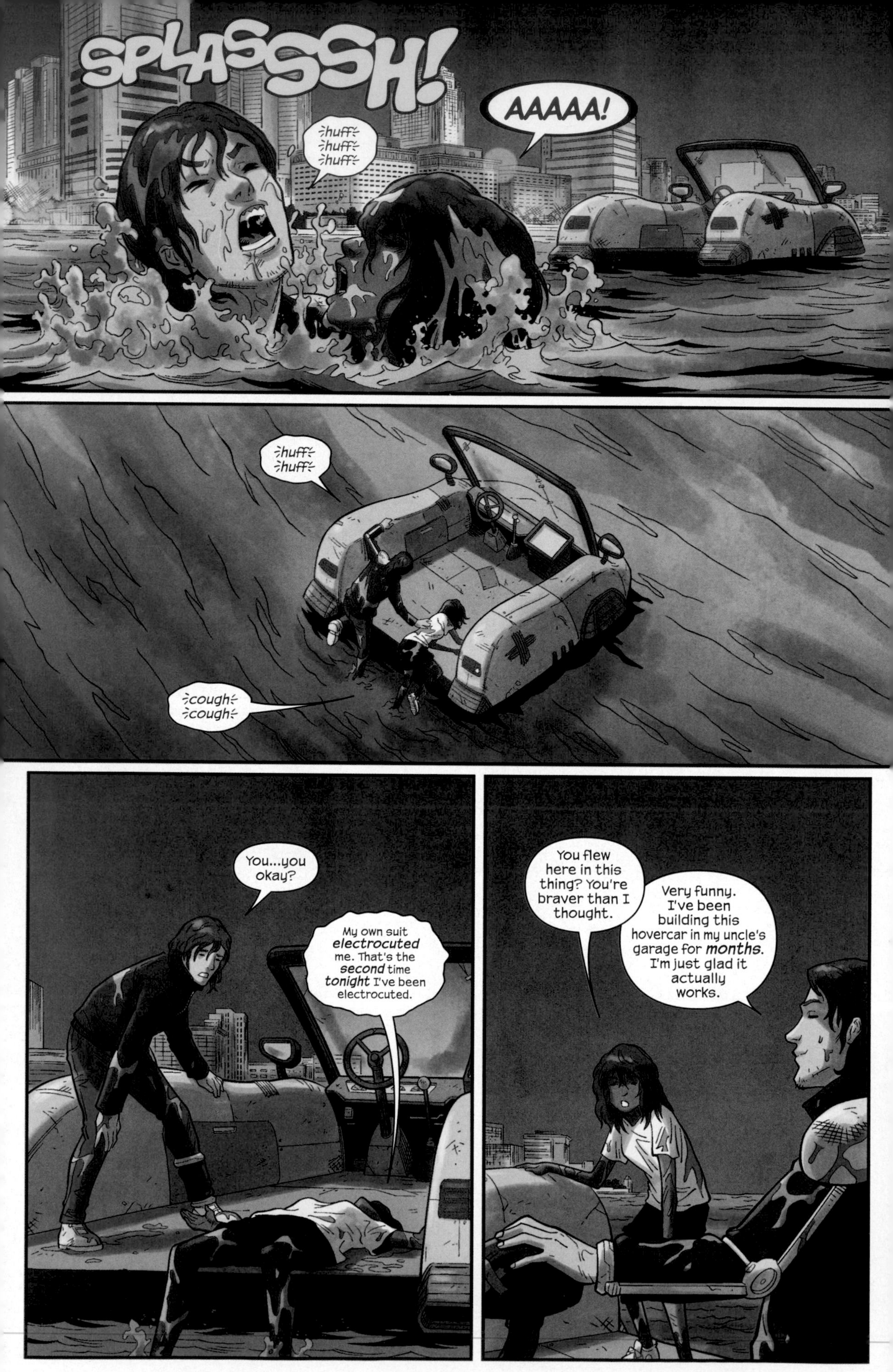
SPLASSSH!
huff huff huff
AAAAA!
huff huff
cough cough
You...you okay?
My own suit electrocuted me. That's the second time tonight I've been electrocuted.
You flew here in this thing? You're braver than I thought.
Very funny. I've been building this hovercar in my uncle's garage for months. I'm just glad it actually works.

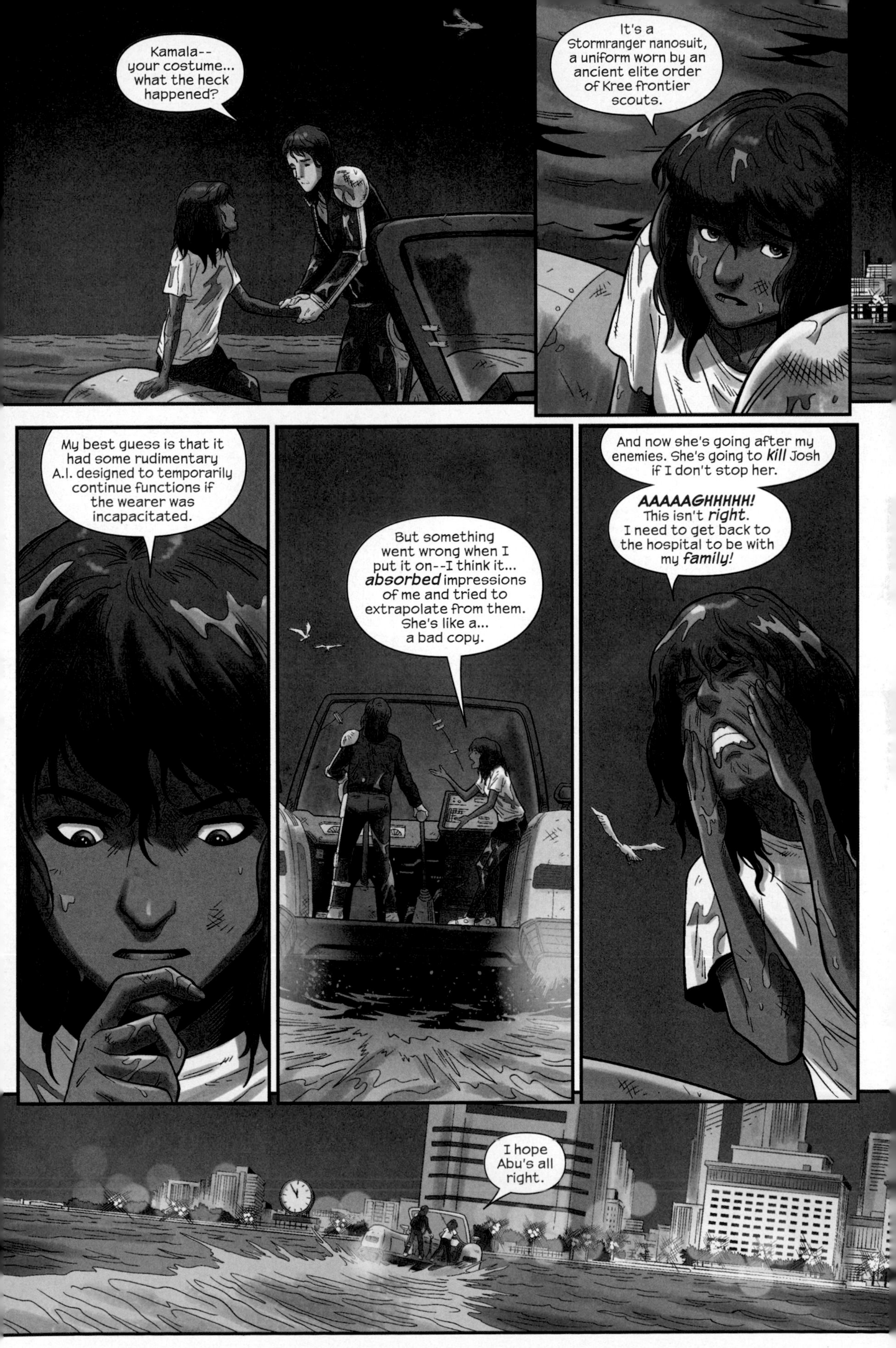
Kamala--
your costume...
what the heck
happened?
It's a
Stormranger nanosuit,
a uniform worn by an
ancient elite order
of Kree frontier
scouts.
My best guess is that it
had some rudimentary
A.I. designed to temporarily
continue functions if
the wearer was
incapacitated.
But something
went wrong when I
put it on--I think it...
absorbed impressions
of me and tried to
extrapolate from them.
She's like a...
a bad copy.
And now she's going after my
enemies. She's going to *kill* Josh
if I don't stop her.
AAAAAGHHHHH!
This isn't *right*.
I need to get back to
the hospital to be with
my *family!*
I hope
Abu's all
right.

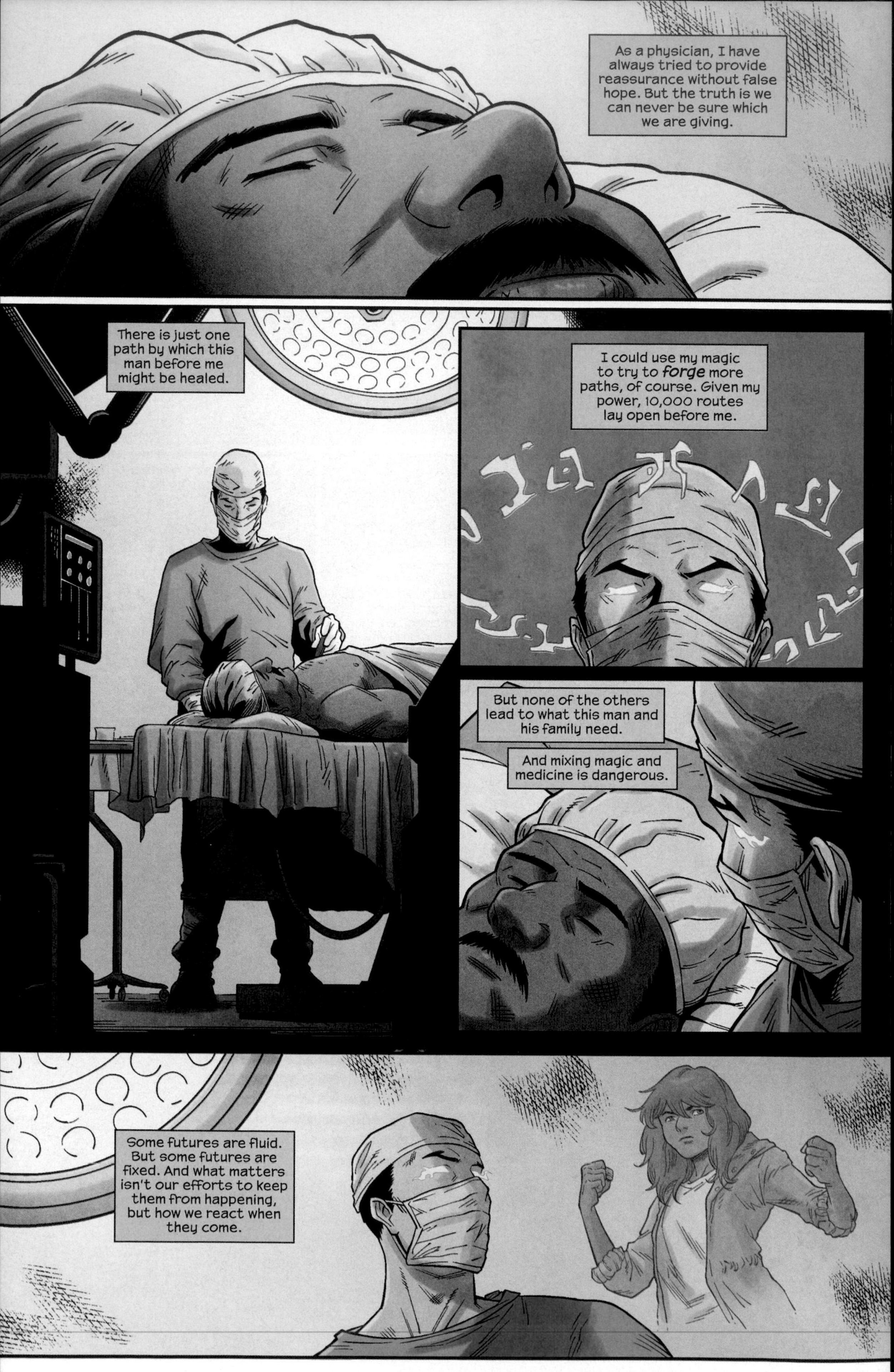

As a physician, I have always tried to provide reassurance without false hope. But the truth is we can never be sure which we are giving.
There is just one path by which this man before me might be healed.
I could use my magic to try to *forge* more paths, of course. Given my power, 10,000 routes lay open before me.
But none of the others lead to what this man and his family need.
And mixing magic and medicine is dangerous.
Some futures are fluid. But some futures are fixed. And what matters isn't our efforts to keep them from happening, but how we react when they come.

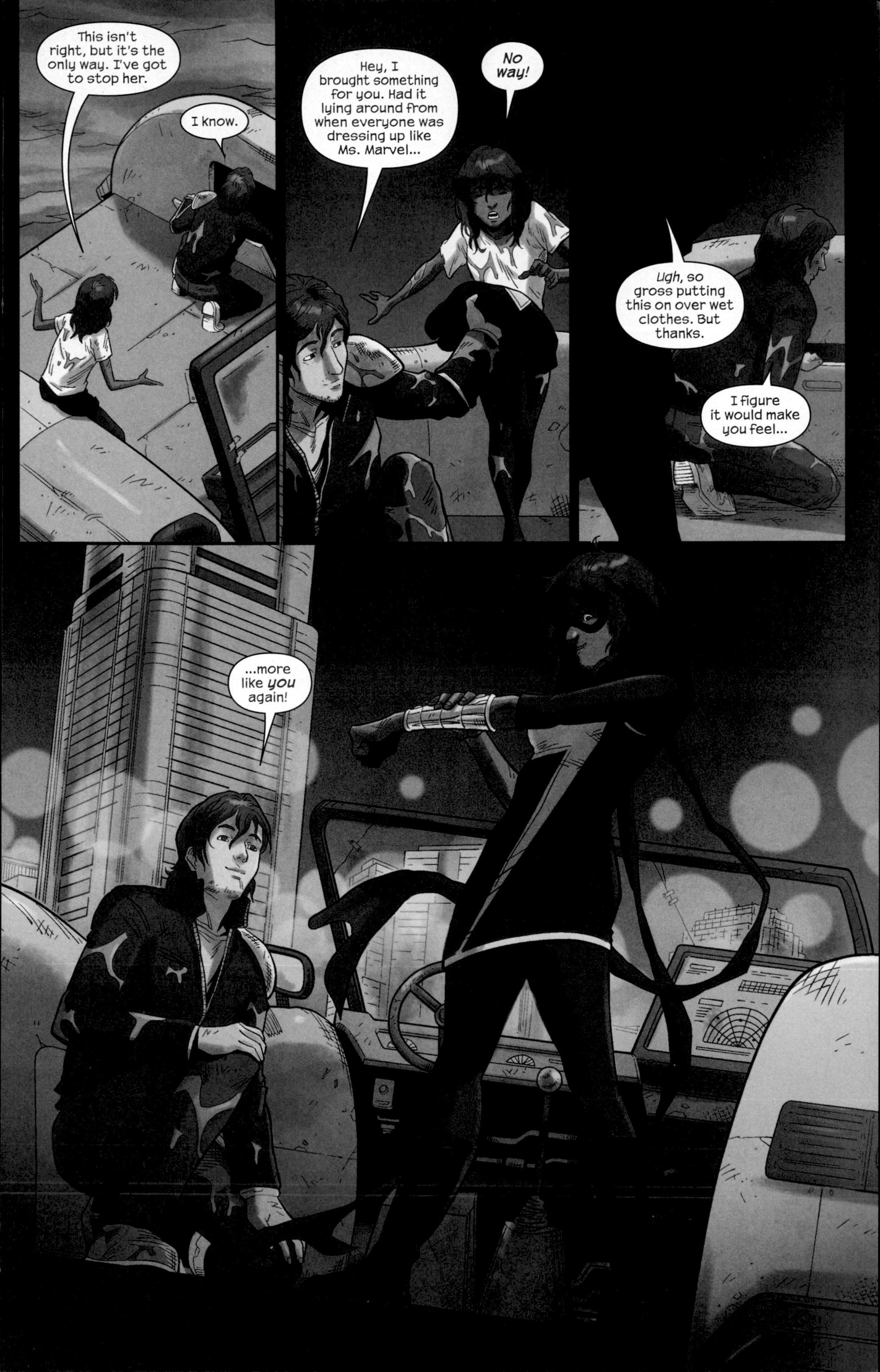
This isn't right, but it's the only way. I've got to stop her.
I know.
Hey, I brought something for you. Had it lying around from when everyone was dressing up like Ms. Marvel...
No way!
Ugh, so gross putting this on over wet clothes. But thanks.
I figure it would make you feel...
...more like ***you*** again!

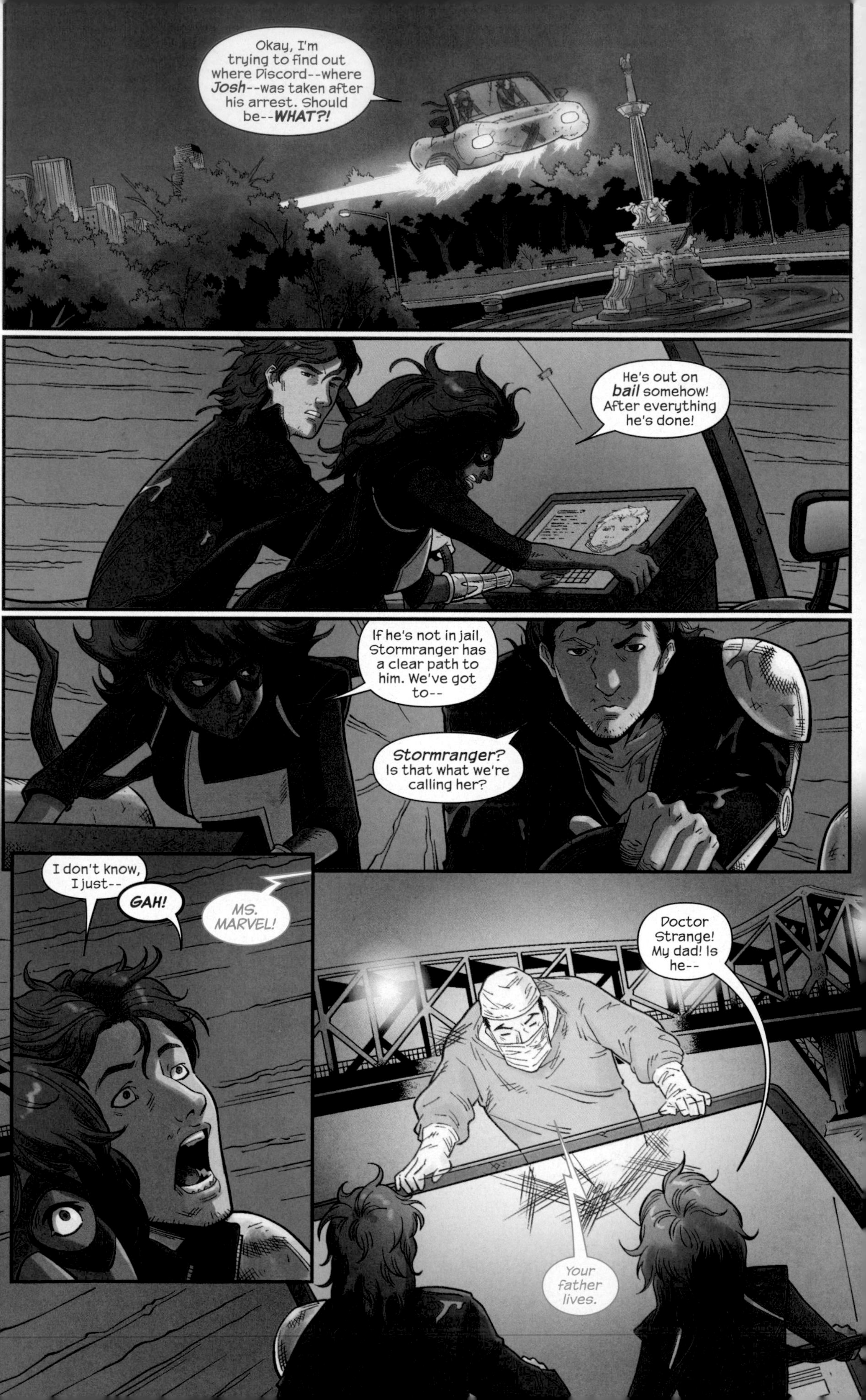

Okay, I'm trying to find out where Discord--where Josh--was taken after his arrest. Should be--WHAT?!
He's out on bail somehow! After everything he's done!
If he's not in jail, Stormranger has a clear path to him. We've got to--
Stormranger? Is that what we're calling her?
I don't know, I just--
GAH!
MS. MARVEL!
Doctor Strange! My dad! Is he--
Your father lives.

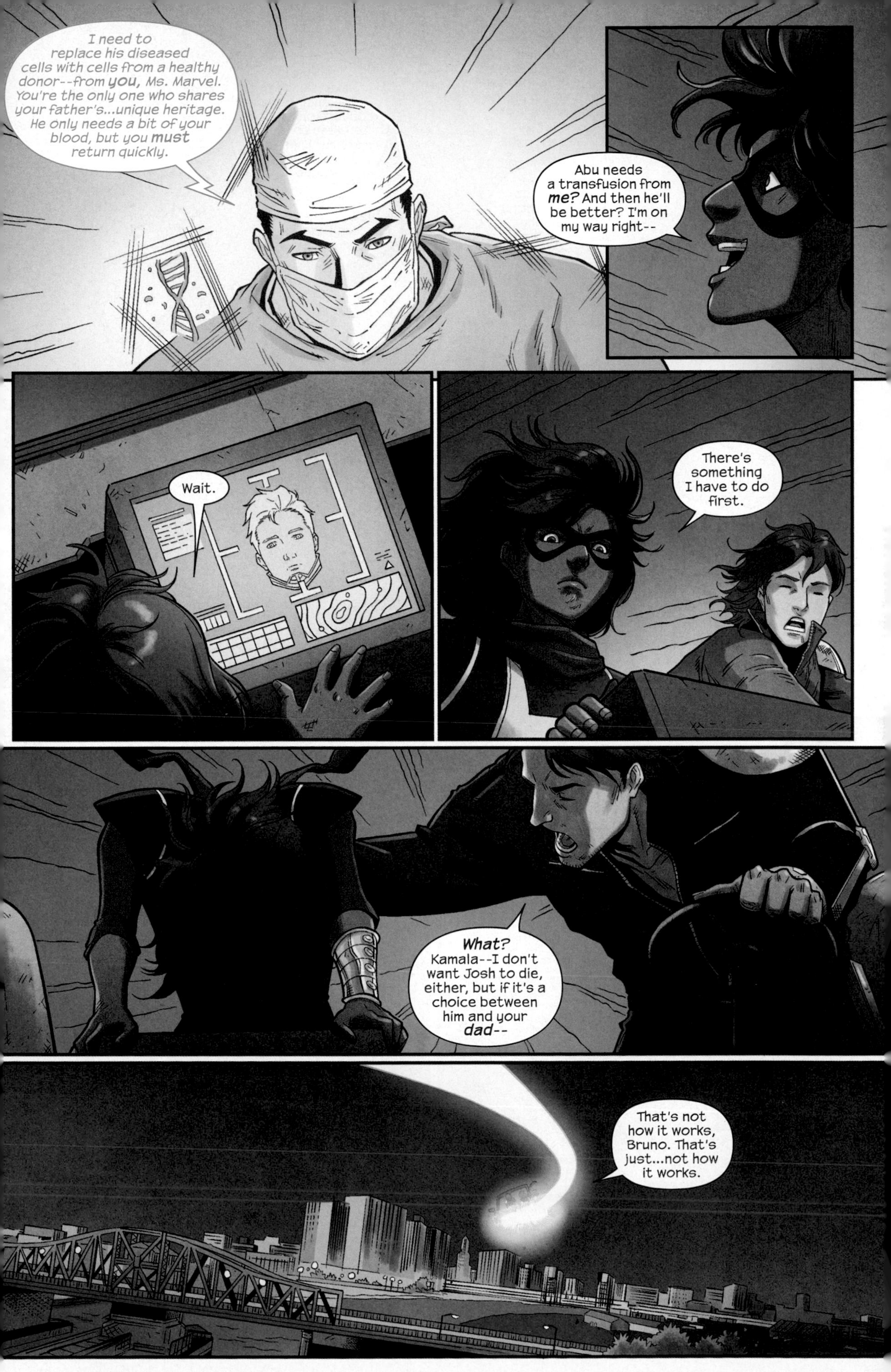

I need to replace his diseased cells with cells from a healthy donor--from **you,** Ms. Marvel. You're the only one who shares your father's...unique heritage. He only needs a bit of your blood, but you **must** return quickly.
Abu needs a transfusion from ***me?*** And then he'll be better? I'm on my way right--
Wait.
There's something I have to do first.
What? Kamala--I don't want Josh to die, either, but if it's a choice between him and your ***dad***--
That's not how it works, Bruno. That's just...not how it works.

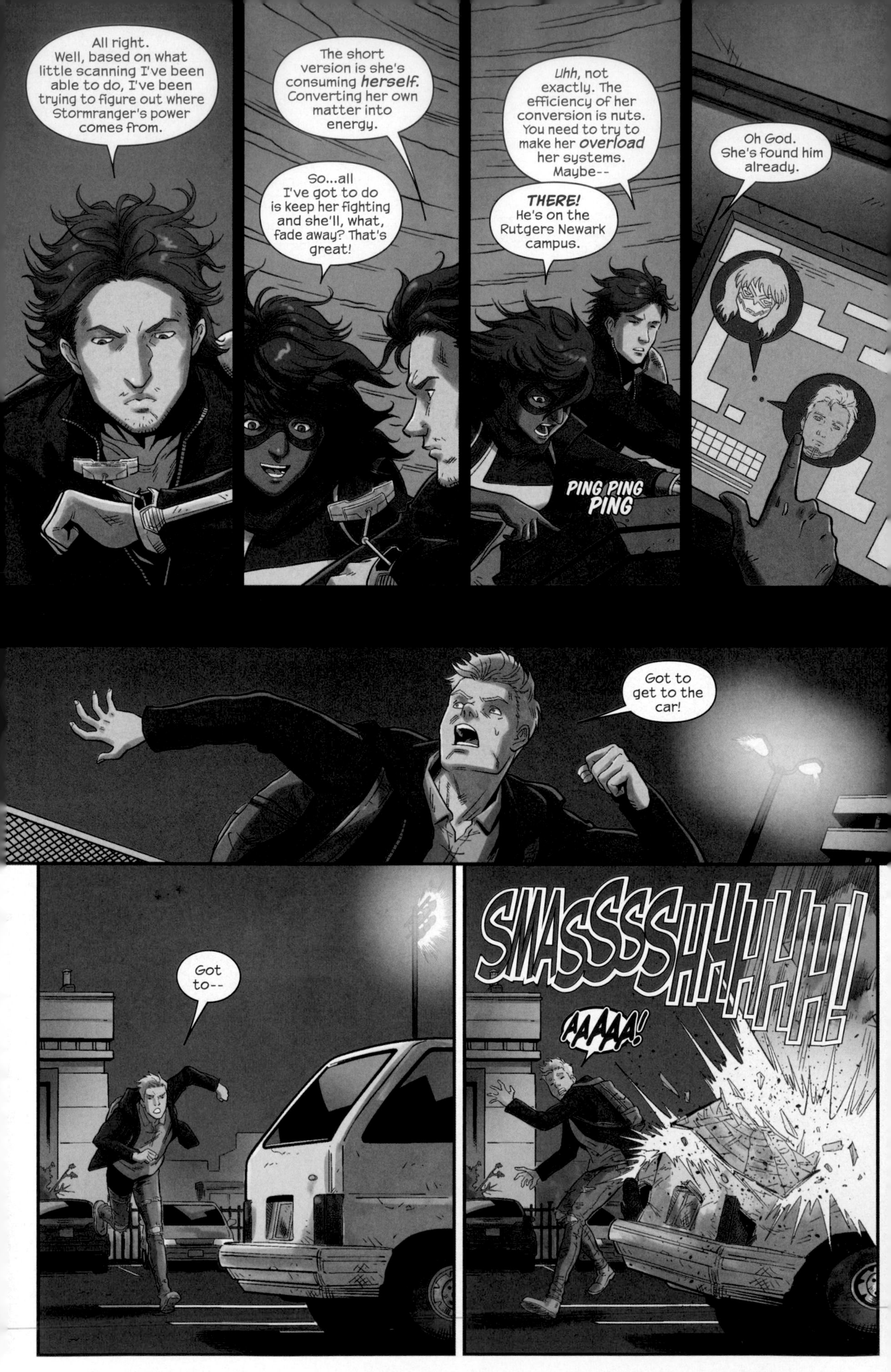
All right. Well, based on what little scanning I've been able to do, I've been trying to figure out where Stormranger's power comes from.
The short version is she's consuming **herself**. Converting her own matter into energy.
So...all I've got to do is keep her fighting and she'll, what, fade away? That's great!
Uhh, not exactly. The efficiency of her conversion is nuts. You need to try to make her **overload** her systems. Maybe--
THERE! He's on the Rutgers Newark campus.
PING PING PING
Oh God. She's found him already.
Got to get to the car!
Got to--
SMASSSSHHHHHH!
AAAAA!

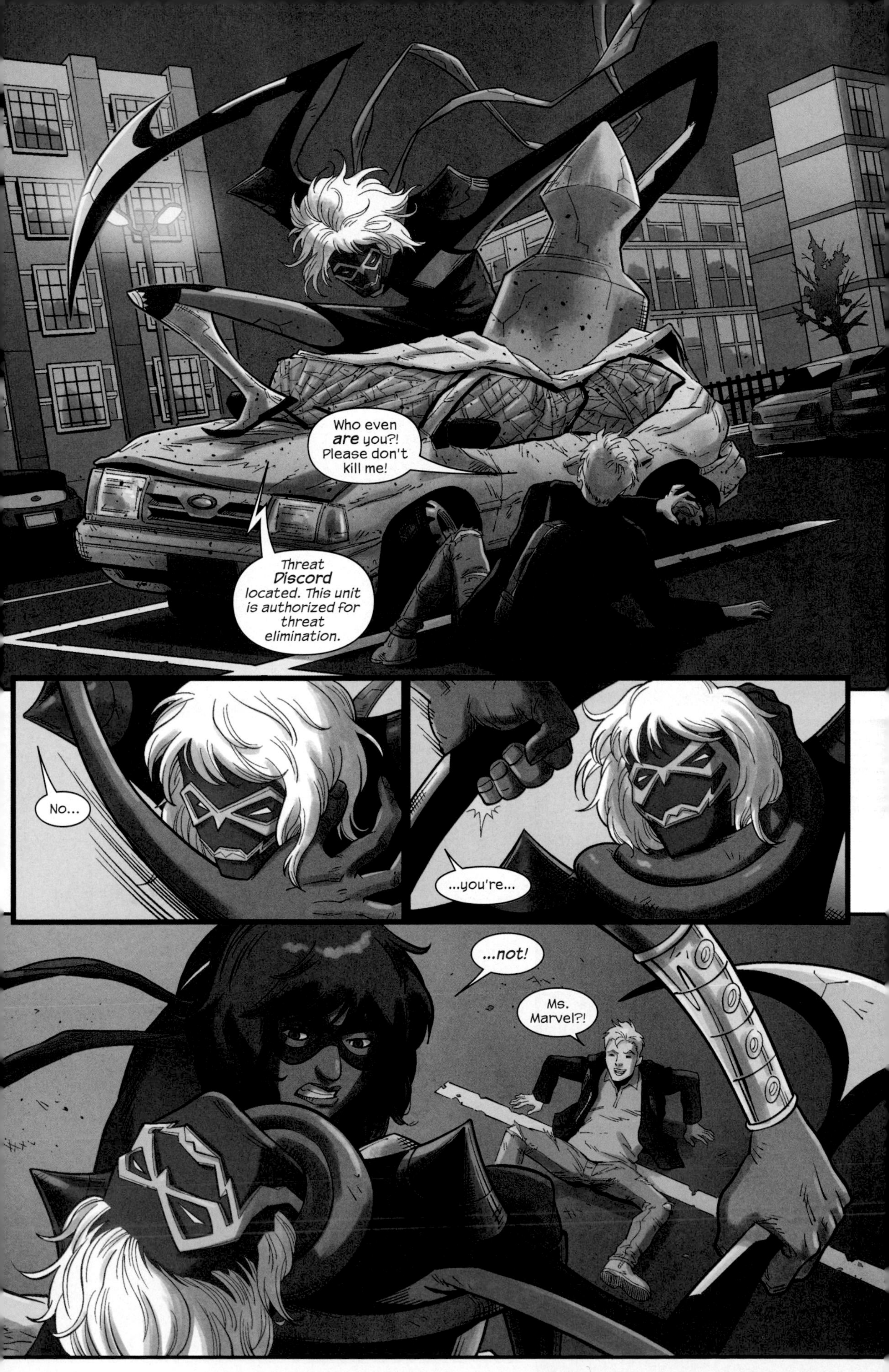
Who even are you?! Please don't kill me!
Threat Discord located. This unit is authorized for threat elimination.
No...
...you're...
...not!
Ms. Marvel?!

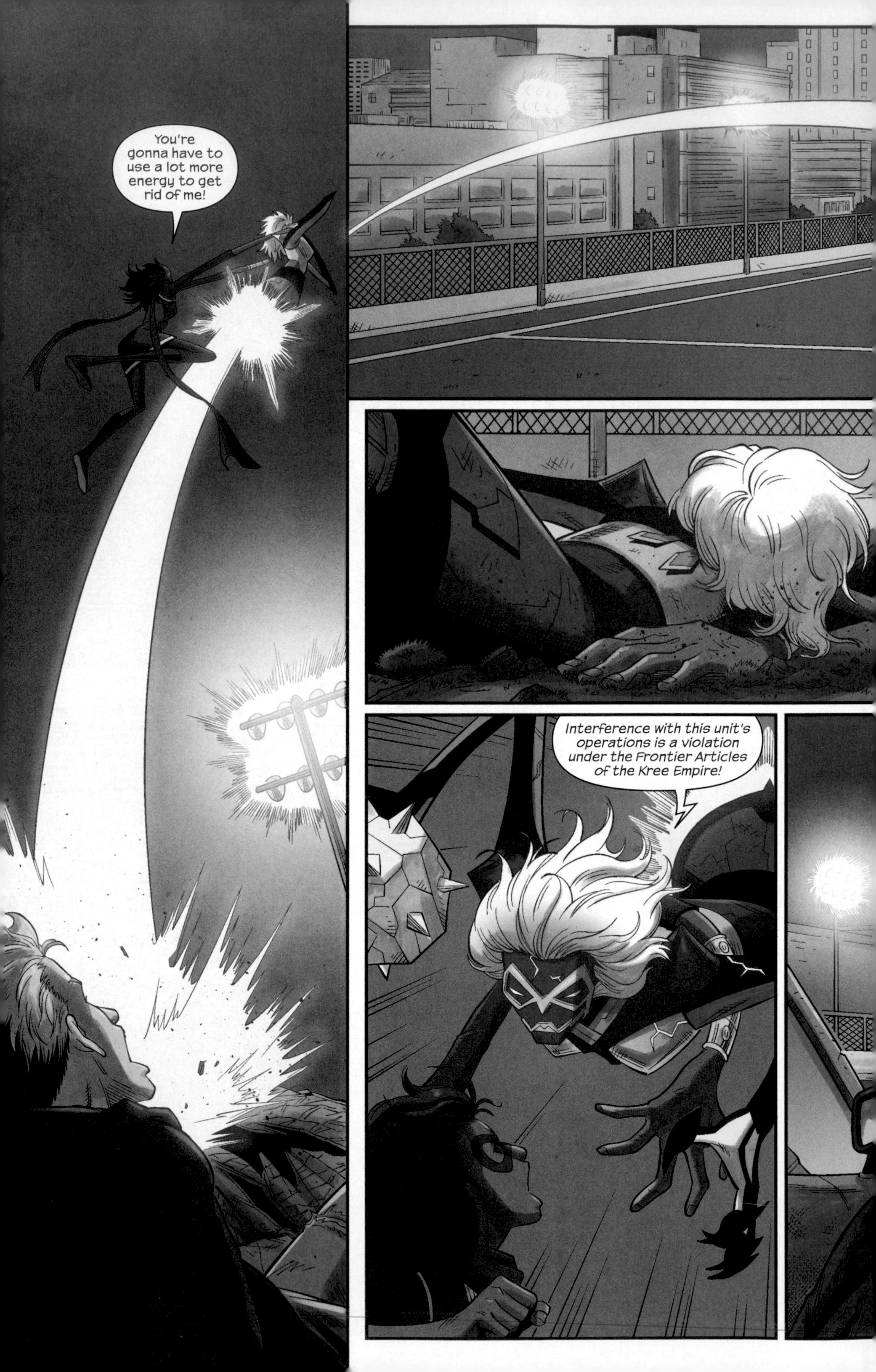
You're gonna have to use a lot more energy to get rid of me!
Interference with this unit's operations is a violation under the Frontier Articles of the Kree Empire!

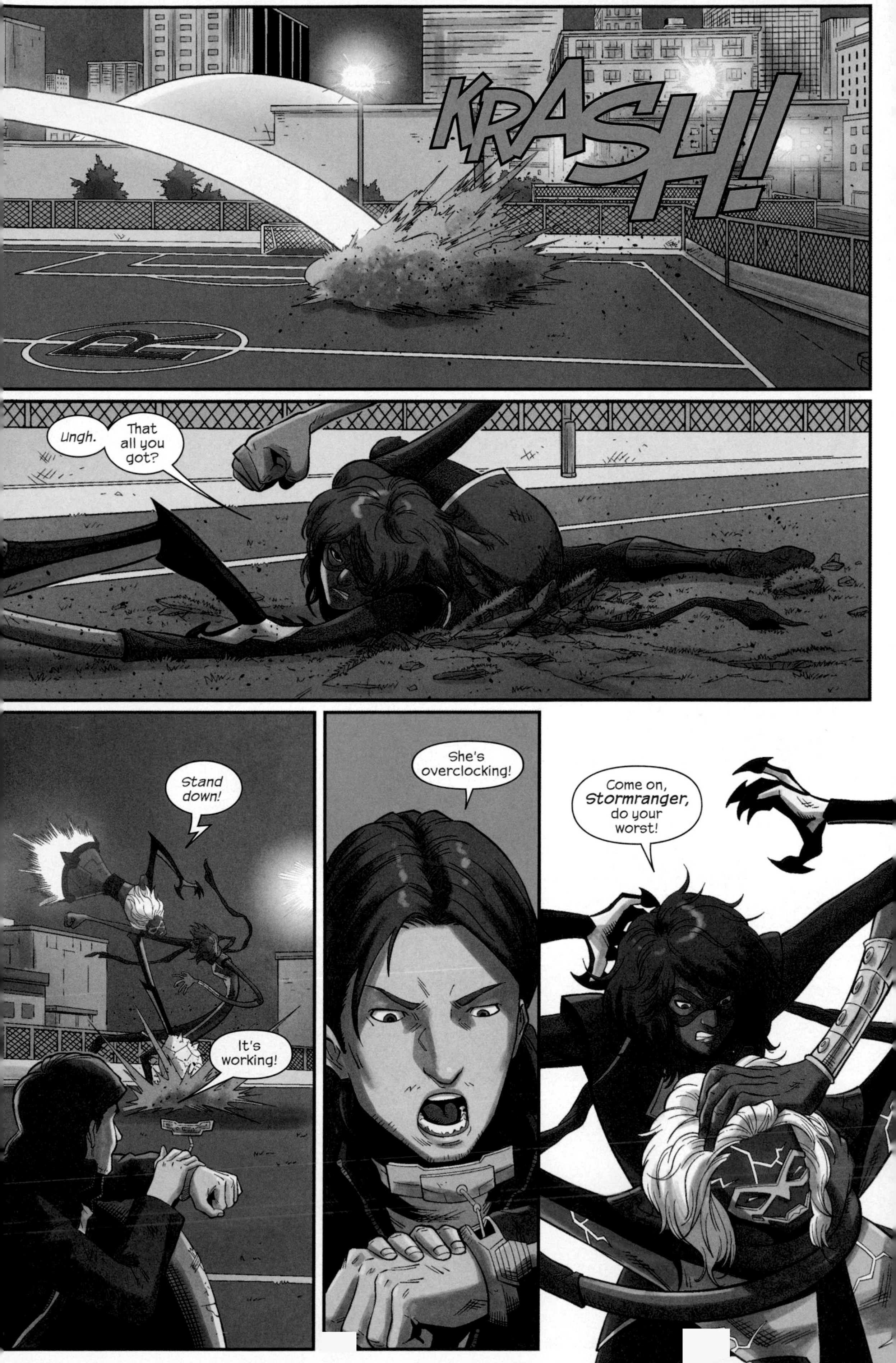
KRASH!!
Ungh.
That all you got?
Stand down!
It's working!
She's overclocking!
Come on, Stormranger, do your worst!

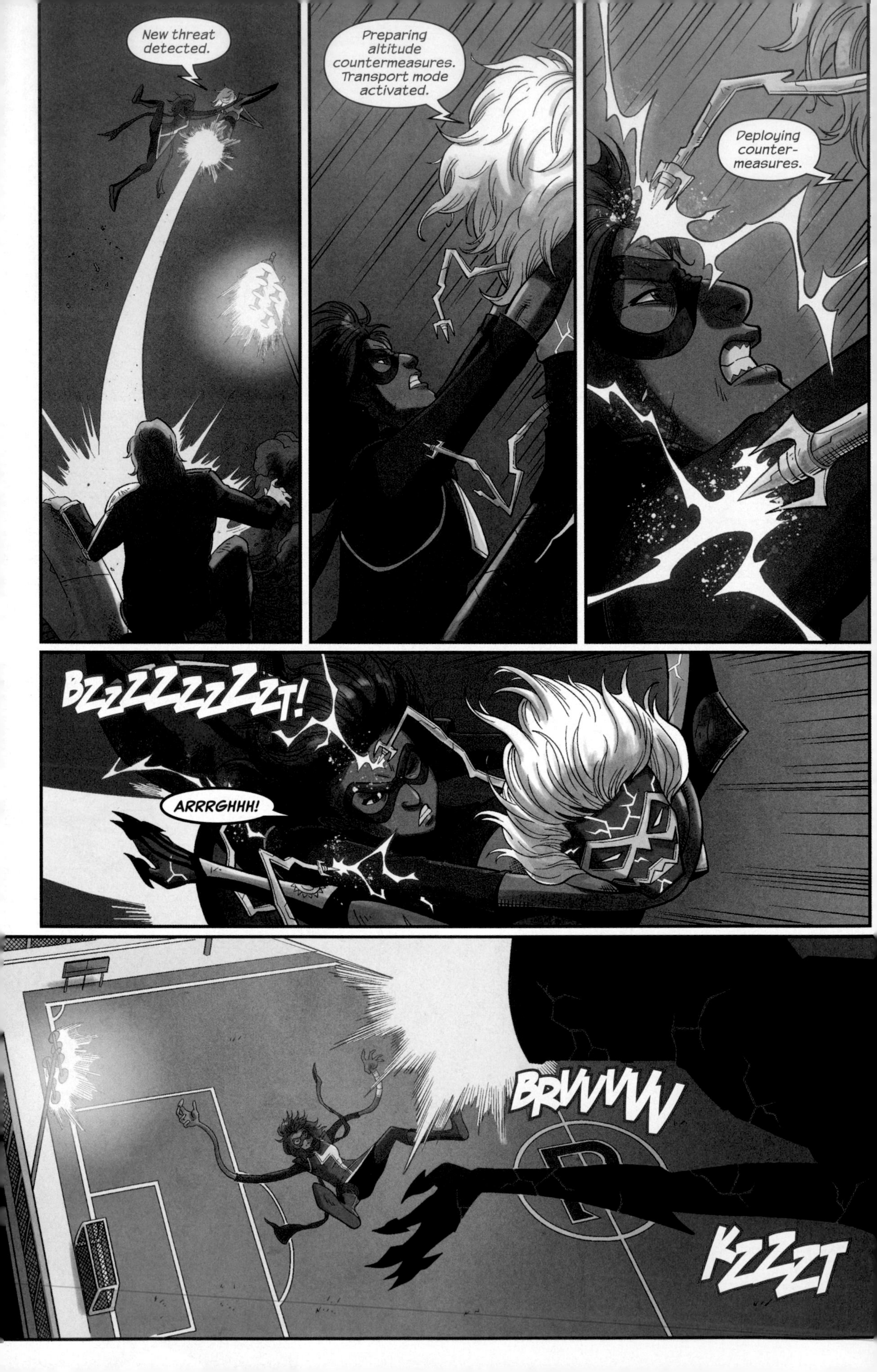
New threat detected.
Preparing altitude countermeasures. Transport mode activated.
Deploying counter-measures.
BZZZZZZZZZZT!
ARRRGHHH!
BRVVVVV
KZZZT

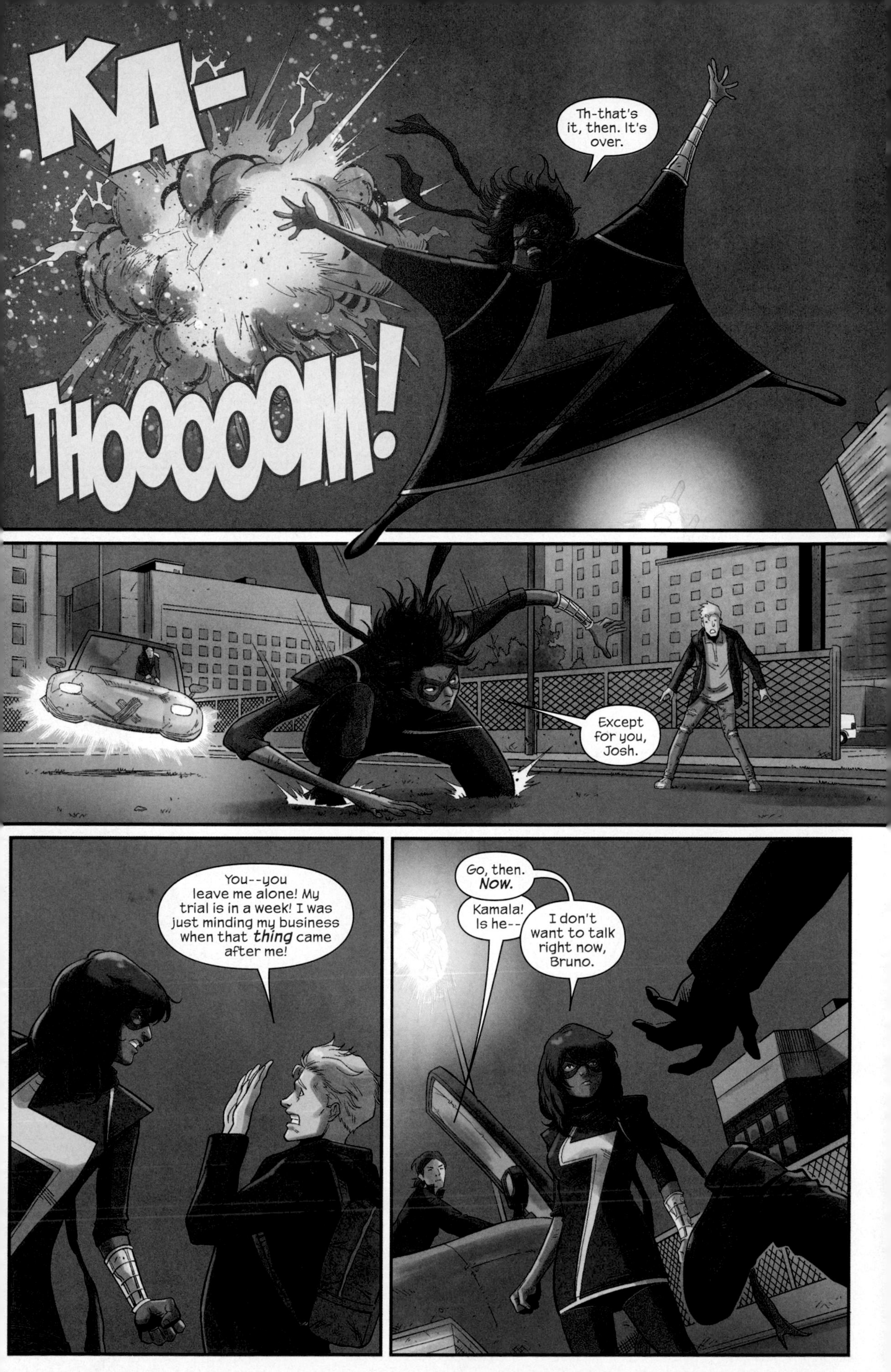
KA-
THOOOOOM!
Th-that's it, then. It's over.
Except for you, Josh.
You--you leave me alone! My trial is in a week! I was just minding my business when that *thing* came after me!
Go, then. **NOW.**
Kamala! Is he--
I don't want to talk right now, Bruno.

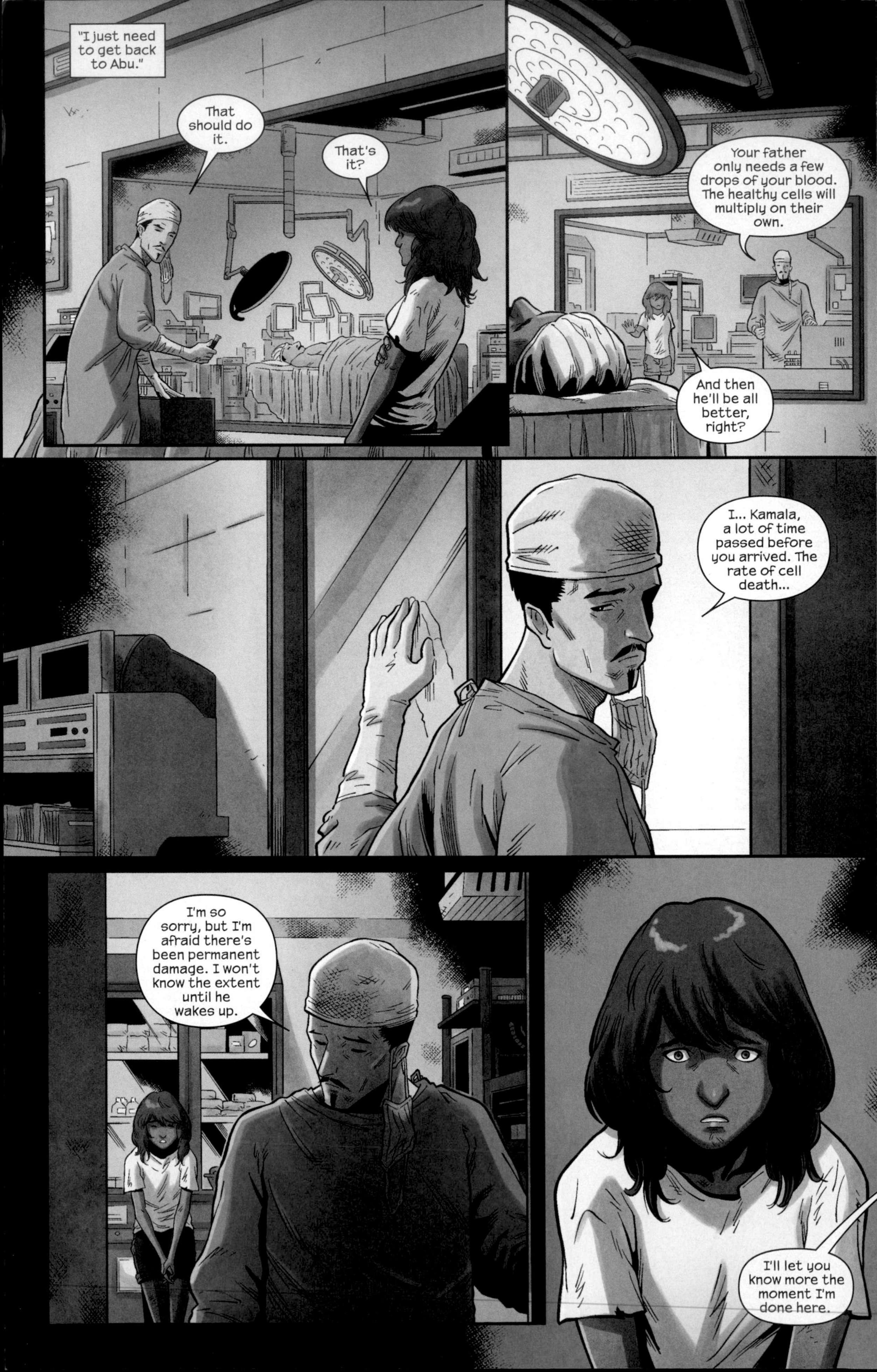
"I just need to get back to Abu."
That should do it.
That's it?
Your father only needs a few drops of your blood. The healthy cells will multiply on their own.
And then he'll be all better, right?
I... Kamala, a lot of time passed before you arrived. The rate of cell death...
I'm so sorry, but I'm afraid there's been permanent damage. I won't know the extent until he wakes up.
I'll let you know more the moment I'm done here.

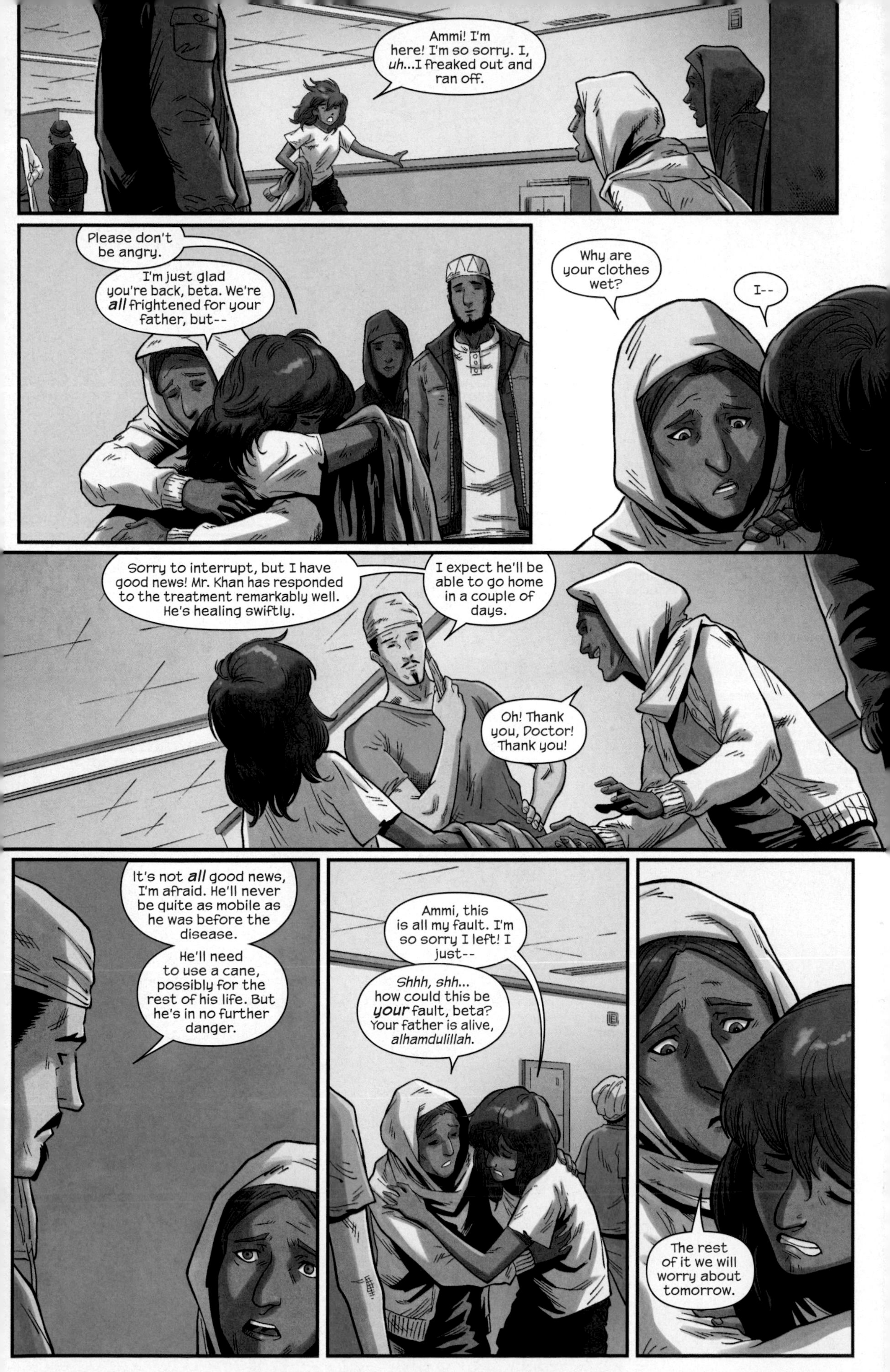

Ammi! I'm here! I'm so sorry. I, *uh*...I freaked out and ran off.
Please don't be angry.
I'm just glad you're back, beta. We're *all* frightened for your father, but--
Why are your clothes wet?
I--
Sorry to interrupt, but I have good news! Mr. Khan has responded to the treatment remarkably well. He's healing swiftly.
I expect he'll be able to go home in a couple of days.
Oh! Thank you, Doctor! Thank you!
It's not *all* good news, I'm afraid. He'll never be quite as mobile as he was before the disease.
He'll need to use a cane, possibly for the rest of his life. But he's in no further danger.
Ammi, this is all my fault. I'm so sorry I left! I just--
Shhh, shh... how could this be *your* fault, beta? Your father is alive, *alhamdulillah*.
The rest of it we will worry about tomorrow.

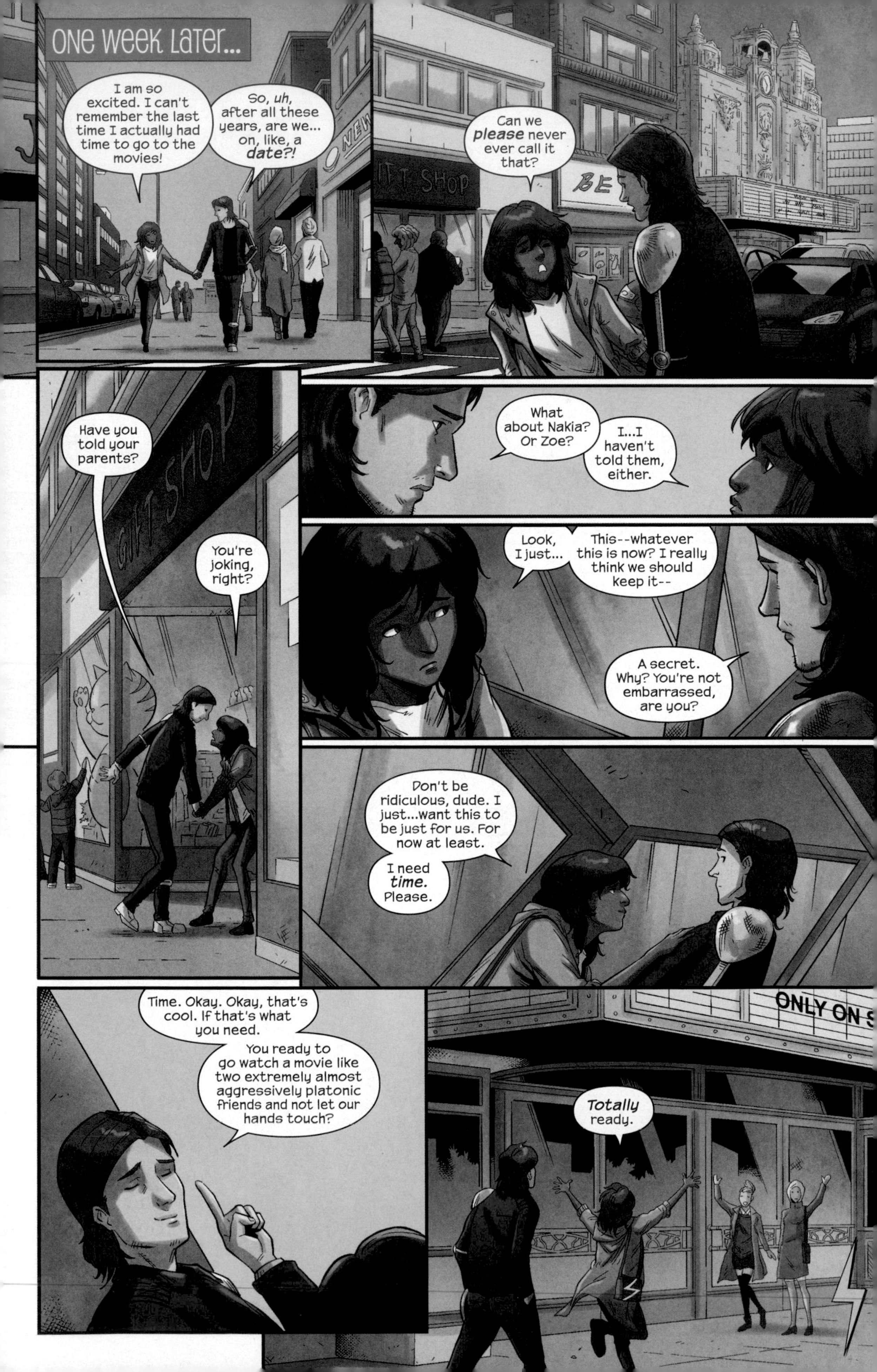
ONE WEEK LATER...
I am so excited. I can't remember the last time I actually had time to go to the movies!
So, *uh*, after all these years, are we... on, like, a *date?!*
GIFT SHOP
Can we *please* never ever call it that?
Have you told your parents?
You're joking, right?
What about Nakia? Or Zoe?
I...I haven't told them, either.
Look, I just...
This--whatever this is now? I really think we should keep it--
A secret. Why? You're not embarrassed, are you?
Don't be ridiculous, dude. I just...want this to be just for us. For now at least.
I need *time.* Please.
Time. Okay. Okay, that's cool. If that's what you need.
You ready to go watch a movie like two extremely almost aggressively platonic friends and not let our hands touch?
ONLY ON
Totally ready.

BRETT MONOPOLY DESIGNS BY
JOEY VAZQUEZ

ALTERNATE STORMRANGER COLORS BY
IAN HERRING

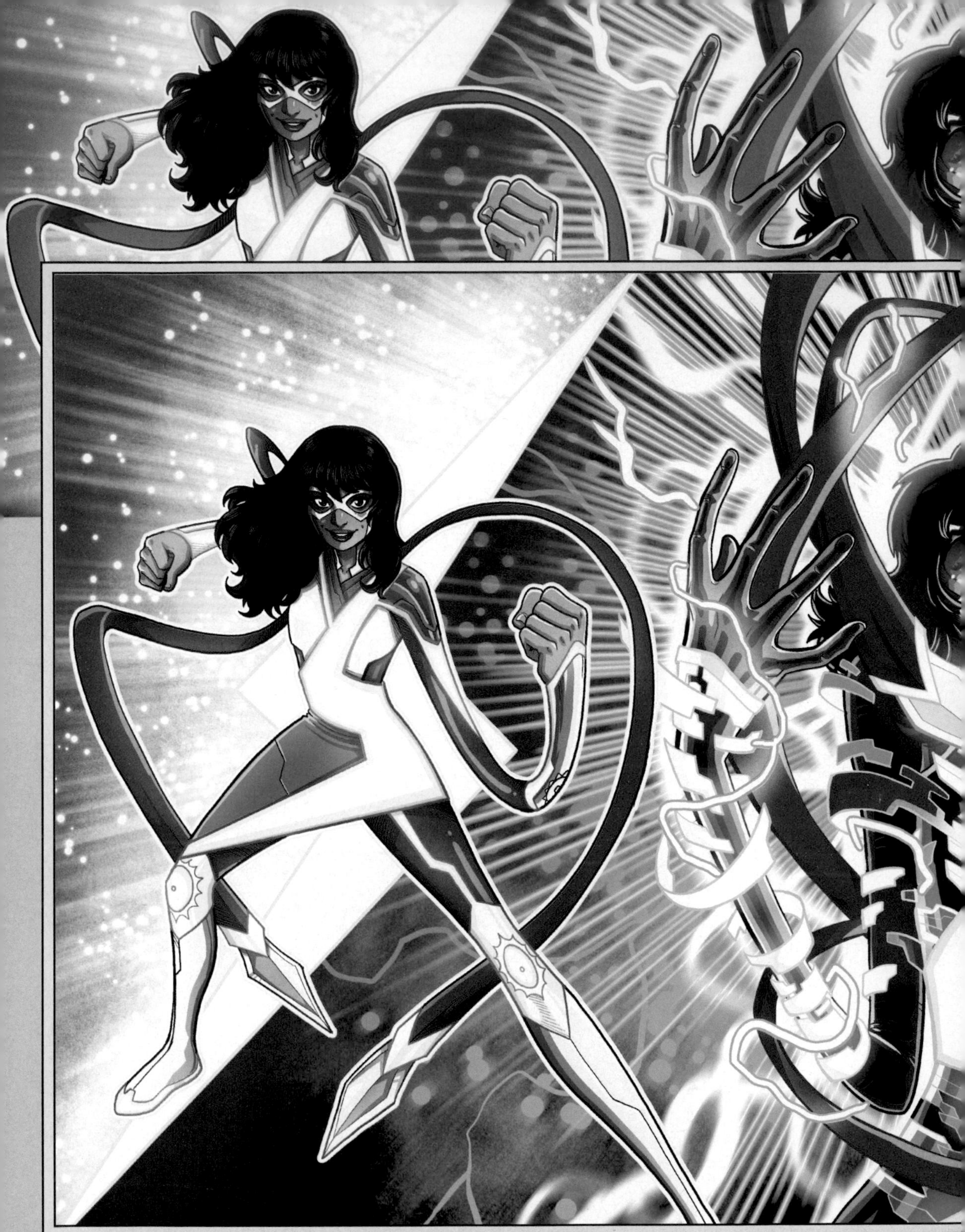